Electronic Communications
for Home and Office

Electronic Communications for Home and Office

Ronald G. Albright

Chilton Book Company   Radnor, Pennsylvania

To the women in my life:
  Louise, who is always the one who understands and loves
    without reservation
  Rhonda, who makes me proud to be a parent every day of
    my life

Copyright © 1989 by Ronald G. Albright
All Rights Reserved
Published in Radnor, Pennsylvania 19089, by Chilton Book Company

Designed by Adrianne Onderdonk Dudden
Manufactured in the United States of America

Library of Congress Cataloging in Publication Data
Albright, Ronald C.
    Electronic communications for home and office / Ron Albright.
      p.   cm.
    ISBN 0-8019-7993-5
    1. Business—Communication systems—Data processing.
  2. Telecommunication systems.   3. Electronic mail systems.
   4. Information storage and retrieval systems—Business.   I. Title.
  HF5541.T4A43   1989
  651.7—dc20   89-42857
                                                  CIP

1 2 3 4 5 6 7 8 9 0   8 7 6 5 4 3 2 1 0 9

Contents

Contents

Contents

Foreword

Communications is the best reason for buying a personal computer.

Fortune placed me in a position to be one of the first people to make that statement nearly a decade ago, and I'm happy to say it still is true today. In fact, as my good friend Ron Albright demonstrates in the pages of this book, it is even more true today than it was back in 1981.

It makes me feel old to say so, but by golly what a time that was. The Apple II had been around for a number of years, but the most advanced model could not yet generate lowercase letters. In the non-Apple world, an operating system called CP/M was king. Exxon made word processors, and 64K was considered an enviable—nay, nearly inconceivable—amount of memory at the time.

Then, in "the Autumn Revolution" of 1981, IBM introduced the first PC, and within a few short months computer frenzy was upon us. Every major, general-interest business and news magazine carried at least one cover story on the personal computer phenomenon. *Time* even made the machine the "Man of the Year."

Everyone wanted to buy one of the new machines. But no one could figure out what they would do with it once it was ensconced on the desktop. Computer salesmen were happy to provide the answer. Why, you could use the machine to balance your checkbook or organize your recipes, they solemnly affirmed. Now, will that be Visa, MasterCharge or American Express?

The fact that these jokers could make such statements with a straight face may be a tribute to their sales training, most of which was acquired selling cars, white goods, and other high ticket/high commission items. Or it may be a tribute to their ignorance.

Most computer salespeople at the time, like most customers, were so eager to jump on the PC bandwagon that no one stopped to think about just how your recipes were supposed to get into the machine in the first place and the hours of data entry that would be required for you to be able to generate a list of every dish calling for celery salt. Or to think about the fact that with a $10 pocket calculator and a pencil you could do a better, faster job of balancing your checkbook than with a $2,000 computer. After all, who wants to boot up and key in data every time they write a check?

Personally, I had been pulled into the computer age a few years earlier, more or less through the back door of word processing. I had written five or six how-to sports books on the same Royal Ultronic electric typewriter that had seen me through many an all-nighter at school. My dream was a correcting IBM Selectric, but I couldn't afford it since, contrary to popular belief, book writing in general is not a highly paid profession.

Then I met a man who introduced me both to word processing and the lucrative world of corporate communications. The first time he told me about his dedicated CPT word processor, I thought it an elaborate toy. I simply could not understand his enthusiasm. Then I tried it for an hour or so and was irretrievably hooked. Within six months, courtesy of this patron and employer, I had my own machine and was busily scrivening away turning out speeches, brochures, video scripts—you name it. This first cousin to a personal computer literally changed my life.

But I had another surprise in store. One day I walked into the office to find my friend "online" with something called The Source. He showed me how he could send and receive "mail," chat with people online, pull down stock quotes and news stories, and even play games, all through this magical online service. I was absolutely spellbound.

This really was something completely different. I devoured The Source manual, a thin, comb-bound, green-covered affair that I've still got somewhere in the attic. I struggled to learn about modems and packet switching and in general to take it all in.

In short order a number of things became clear. First, The Source, CompuServe, Dow Jones News/Retrieval, and bulletin board systems represented incredible life-expanding possibilities. Second, you absolutely had to have a personal computer to tap in and take advantage of this potential. Unlike recipes and checkbooks which could better be handled with 3 x 5 card files and pocket calculators, the computer was an essential component to going online.

Third, search as I might, I could find no single, comprehensive (and comprehensible) source of information on this new field. There was nowhere the average person could turn to find out about the hardware and software required to go online or what they would find once they got there. In short, there was no book on the subject.

I had given up doing books and would have been perfectly content to continue with the daily challenge, variety, and satisfaction of corporate communications. But the idea would not let go. Once more into the breach, dear word processor. One more book proposal and we'll give it up for good.

If *this* book had existed at the time, I would still be doing brochures on commodities trading, single-premium life insurance, and limited partnership real-estate-investment opportunities. For as you will see, it contains everything a new online communicator could want or need.

You'll find enough technical information on how everything works to make you dangerous, but not more than you want to know. You'll find hands-on tips on what to look for in communications software. And you'll find action-provoking information on electronic and voice mail, sending facsimiles without a fax machine, electronic data interchange, and how to quickly get your hands on hard core, industrial strength information through such online services as DIALOG, BRS, Orbit, and The Knowledge Index.

When you finish Dr. Albright's book, you will certainly agree that online communications is *still* the best reason for buying a personal computer. But, as someone once said to me, "it's still something of a black art." The more light that can be shed on the subject, the better. Ron Albright's book is a worthy addition to that select handful of beacons shining through the mist. I guarantee that if you follow his advice, *Electronic Communications for Home and Office* will change your life.

Alfred Glossbrenner
"Kabeyun"
Yardley, Pennsylvania
July 1989

Acknowledgments

As usual, when one puts together a book of this size, there are more people to thank than can possibly appear in this section. Nevertheless, I must name a few. Foremost, I want to thank Alfred Glossbrenner, perhaps the single author who has done more through his writing to advance the consumer interest in computer-mediated communications, for graciously offering the Foreword to this book. Also, to Nick Cvetkovic, John Everett, and Craig Mellor, my thanks for contributing their expert insights to this book. These four authors and I have never met or even spoken on the phone. Yet, through the world of electronic communications, they have contributed to your knowledge.

Others, who have been long-time "digital pen pals," have been supportive and understanding throughout this process. Howie Rosenberg, Paul and Sarah Edwards, Dale Lewallen, Peter Silver, Toby Nixon, Cathryn Conroy, Charles Bowen, Ward Christensen, Jim Horn, Lewis Mann, Dan Johnson, Gary Green, Paul Gilster, Duncan Frisell, Morris Fineberg, Hal Crawford, Dave Brace, Tom Ballard, and dozens more have my appreciation. Many of these helpful people offered advice after I posted a message on CompuServe's "Working At Home" Forum describing my project.

AT&T Mail and Western Union's EasyLink allowed me the opportunity to have practice on their networks, for which I am grateful. Several companies, including U.S. Robotics, Murata Business Systems, Ven-Tel Modems, and Touchbase Systems, graciously allowed me to reproduce product photographs for this book. Natural Microsystems graciously furnished an evaluation version of the Watson Voice Mail System, as did Quadram for their "JT Fax Portable." And, of course, the patience and love shown by my wife, Louise, and children (Rhonda, Ronnie, and Danny) were so evident while I was busy with the book's preparation.

Introduction

The new technologies of communications have the power to change the competitive game for almost all companies of all sizes.

—Eric Clemons and F. Warren McFarlan, "Telecom: Hook Up or Lose Out"

One of the characteristics of human nature is that change is generally not accepted easily, comfortably, or readily. We like familiarity and, as much as possible, eschew the new and the strange. This tendency exists in each of us to varying degrees and, at one time or another in the human past, was probably a protective trait in some way or another. In our daily personal and business lives, the comfort of sameness brings a modicum of serenity to our chaotic world. In a world where technology is advancing by quantum leaps almost daily, it is natural to seek to hold on to the tranquility of the past and what we are familiar with. Who can blame us?

Customers, clients, and associates, that's who. In the world of business, we must adapt and change. We must take hold of the tiger of technology and ride along, or else be eaten alive by the competition. The days of "standing pat" and "let's wait and see" are gone. For those of us with small businesses (those with a home business included), every edge we can find to help our endeavors is important—even more, critical—to getting and staying ahead. Whether we like it or not, we must learn about and put into effect those technological advances that can give us the advantage that is critical to our success.

INTANGIBLE RESOURCES

One of the most important commodities for the small business, *information,* is a prime example of an area in which to go after an advantage. That we need information for success is not debatable. The challenge of the 1990s will be to find ways to acquire and analyze the information flood and pinpoint the subtle trends and shifts that can determine our business survival. It is becoming more apparent, though, in the "information age," that not only do we need precise information but we also need it *fast.* Roger Blackwell, a marketing professor at Ohio State University, has said that a 15-minute advantage over the competition is probably all that can be expected these days, since news and information is delivered so fast.

A small business has little time to make a countermove after an announcement from the competition or a court decision which affects the business. The key is to have the flexibility to direct resources and implement changes quickly, but it is also necessary to have up-to-date information available on which to base such decisions. In the flood of information sources today, we must do a great deal of filtering to find what is important to us and what is not. Further, those of us in a small business must do the sifting with much fewer resources than the conglomerates have available. With rapid change being such a fundamental aspect of business, the business person must have a finger on the pulse in order to keep up. However, our information-collecting habits were formed in decades gone by. We try to read, clip, file, photocopy, and digest the many journals that we subscribe to. We rely on mental recall. And it is impossible to keep up in this manner, as you well know.

A second critical element to success in business in the 1990s is communications. We need to be able to contact who we want when we want. It does no good to have the latest information if we cannot disperse it to the people who need to act on it. We need to be able to direct our employees and contacts to take action on our decisions quickly. Otherwise, our strategic information is yesterday's news.

The good news is that just because a business is small, doesn't mean it has to forgo the latest in high-tech communications. This book will introduce you to the information and communications technologies of the 1990s in a way that will inform, guide, and direct you to make the hard decisions you will need to make. This book will not intimidate; rather, it will intimate. And it will comfort, rather than alarm. The technologies available to you today to move your business and your personal life into the future will be explained in a way that you can understand and reflect on. No decisions will be made for you. The decisions are yours—but you can make them based on sound facts that you understand.

Electronic Communications for Home and Office is not about *computers.* It is about *productivity.* This book will arm you with the information you need to make informed decisions in a tough business world. It will give you the edge you need to compete with big business in its own game—high-tech productivity.

HOW TO USE THIS BOOK

I hope you are convinced that it is time to proceed into the future. Let's think briefly about some of the things that you can do with the technology already available. Of course you will want to consider word processing, mass mailings, keeping records with database software, and other familiar applications you have read about. However, in this book we will concentrate on some other major applications. The topics covered are introduced briefly below, with the four main applications first.

ELECTRONIC MAIL (CHAPTER 4)

Why continue to play telephone tag? Leave messages on a remote computer where your correspondent can access them within seconds when he or she is available and reply just as rapidly. From a simple "Hey! I got the shipment!" to a 20-page proposal can be transferred across the country in seconds.

INFORMATION ACCESS (CHAPTER 5)

Today, there are somewhere around 3000 computerized databases available to your computer. With this wealth of data at your disposal [it is estimated that 90 percent of the information published in the past 15 years is accessible in this fashion (Paul and Sarah Edwards, *Working from Home*)], I can say, with a great deal of confidence, that whatever information needs your business may have can be found somewhere electronically.

VOICE MESSAGING (CHAPTER 6)

Deliver listener-directed telemarketing messages, and receive messages at one phone number and have them automatically forwarded to another. Enter the wave of the 1990s now.

FACSIMILE (FAX) TRANSMISSIONS (CHAPTER 7)

Whereas electronic mail can send messages and documents composed on a computer, fax can transmit replicas of documents—contracts, advertisements, photographs, virtually anything. The image of the original is transmitted in a few seconds to the receiving machine and then printed for viewing there.

RESISTING COMPUTERIZATION (CHAPTER 1)

There are many arguments and excuses for not learning about and implementing computers. This chapter diffuses those arguments and shows why a smart business person should catch up with technology.

HOW IT WORKS—EQUIPMENT AND SOFTWARE (CHAPTERS 2 AND 3)

This book also explains how some of the "magic" works. In "How Computers Communicate" (Chapter 2), we will dwell on the basics of digital communications which underlie much of the technology we cover. This is a sojourn into the technical aspects of computer-to-computer communications. The information will be helpful as you advance into using the technology, but you may want to put it off initially. Chapter 2 addresses the equipment components of a communications system, and Chapter 3 discusses the other half—the software. If you don't have the gusto to attack these topics right off the bat, simply jump ahead to Chapter 4 and Chapter 5, where you will be given quite enough impetus to come back to the nuts and bolts later.

MISCELLANEOUS (CHAPTER 8)

In this chapter, a few shortcuts, insider tips, and miscellaneous bits and pieces of information about computer-assisted communications are offered. This chapter covers where to find help (your local users group), free sources of software and practice (your local "bulletin board system"), and other topics.

WHAT TO LOOK FOR IN THE FUTURE (CHAPTER 9)

Changes are occurring at such a rapid pace in the electronic communications industry that you will need to see some trends now and follow them closely. The two most important are a changeover from the current sound-only phone system to the new Integrated Services Digital Network (ISDN). This fiber-optic network will allow transmission of digital as well as the usual sound communications at extremely rapid speed. Secondly, the X.400 and X.500 communications standards will be adopted worldwide, making communications across the various commercial providers a reality. A single "electronic address" can open you up to transmissions from anywhere in the world.

THINGS TO THINK ABOUT

You have probably heard about these various applications. But have you thought about how they can help you do more business? How they can bring more customers and increase your network of contacts? How they can be used to get advice on tough issues and problems you may face in your business?

How they can make you more effective, more informed, a better networker, more open to national and international markets? How they can enhance your image to your customers, suppliers, and the competition? If you haven't, I invite you to read on and join the world of computer-assisted communications.

1

Jump Right In

Computer literacy will be essential for the next generation of senior
executives—and their employees.

—Clemens P. Work, "The 21st Century Executive"

In this text I will, for the most part, confine our discussions to one aspect of
computer productivity—the computer as an information and communications
tool. You will not learn to use it for word processing, or spreadsheets, or
database (though you should be using it for all these things!). Those subjects
are for other books.

Too many business people, salespeople, and others in small or home
business ventures are hesitant to get into computers. Though they are working
with personnel and resource constraints that their competitors do not have,
they are hesitant to adopt the very technology that can eliminate these barriers. Most of these people realize, on some level, that computers can streamline their operations, but, because they think that learning about and implementing computers in their business will take time and expertise that they just
don't have, they shy away.

EXPOSING THE ARGUMENTS

In my experience, there are several arguments which crop up frequently in my
discussions with business people in all areas as to why they have not become
acquainted with computers. The arguments run, in their various forms, something like these:

    1. *"I am too busy running a business to learn about computers."* My

standard reply to this argument is that "one of the reasons you don't have time to learn about computers is because you don't use them!" In their most rudimentary uses, computers are timesaving devices. They keep track of things for us (schedules, billing) or do our repetitive tasks (dictations, mass mailings) for us much better than we can do them ourselves. Even more, they can keep track of the business world for us and help us stay abreast of what developments are important to our work much more easily than we can do it alone. Computers can, literally, be our window to the world. The application of computer technology gives us more time, not less. By not using them, we use time wastefully and inefficiently.

2. *"I can hire people to use the computers for me."* Perhaps your business is successful enough for you to have salaried help use computers for scheduling and billing your clients and routine correspondence. But what about for the small-business person? Even if you can afford a secretary for filing, correspondence, and record keeping, what about the other tasks computers can be doing for you? Information retrieval, electronic mail, communications, and so on? Unless you are thoroughly familiar with what can be done with computers, how can you be sure your staff—regardless of how large it is—is using your computers to their full capability? How can you expect to make intelligent buying decisions and plan for future growth if you're not involved?

3. *"I am not a programmer!"* Neither am I! Nor do I see a burning need for me to become one. The applications you should be using for your computer do not require any programming experience. The programming instructions have already been done—all you need to do is to have the computer execute them, usually by your typing in a word from the keyboard.

The other arguments against learning how to use computers are equally full of holes. Despite that, the arguments against learning persist. I don't think I have ever seen any device come into common use that has been more able to elicit this reaction, which may have something to do with fear of failure, than the computer. But we all had to learn how to drive a car and to use a calculator, a typewriter, and even more complicated tools, and the computer is just one more (big) move toward efficiency. We should try to be like our children or our neighbor's children, who take to using computers so easily and quickly because they are not afraid to fail—nor do they worry that the learning time could be better spent doing something else.

Once we confront the arguments and apprehensions head on, we can be more realistic about learning to use computers. Accept the computer as another business tool—nothing more, nothing less. As a small-business owner, you must learn how to use every new tool at your disposal. It is your duty—to your business and yourself. Put excuses aside for the benefit of your business, your clients and, if you have them, your investors. Take the time to learn. Once you have, you will never look back, and those depending on you for their livelihoods will thank you for it.

There is one argument against learning to use computers that is not as easy to refute as the others because in many ways the argument is valid. This is the complaint that "Computers are just too difficult to learn." Despite the fact that great advances have been made in "user friendliness," the days of the computer as an appliance are still a long way off. Computers are not easy to learn and use. While advertisements for computers may give you the impression that you just plug them in and get to work, "it just ain't so." Computers are complex, powerful tools that demand training for their optimum use. It may take you hours just to get the system powered, plugged in, and started up.

Even the industry's own gurus seem to agree. Mitch Kapor, founder of Lotus Development (a major software producer), told one audience: "Personal computers are too hard to use and, all things considered, don't offer much to the ordinary person." But, as a business owner, you are not an "ordinary person." Certainly, starting up is difficult. But, once you get over the initial hump, learning accelerates rapidly. It may take several days or even weeks to get up to speed but, once there, you will start reaping the benefits of timesaving information access, enhanced communications, better record keeping, and the other well-publicized improvements in productivity. The question you have to ask yourself is, "Do I want to expend the effort?" It is a difficult question and one only you can answer. Hopefully, after reading this book, you will have a clearer idea of your answer.

AVOIDING THE TRAPS

There are three traps waiting for the small-business person who starts thinking about computerization, each trap fatal in its own way. Business owners may (1) remain interested observers on the fringe of the computer world, starving themselves of all the benefits available to themselves, their businesses, and their clients through informed, active computer usage; (2) leap into the purchase of computer equipment for business or personal use with inadequate information or on the advice of a salesperson or a well-meaning friend who has a computer (in my experience, the advice is seldom better than asking a car owner which brand of automobile to buy; seldom will you get anything other than the name of the car owner's current brand), or (3) buy a computer, based on whatever information they have available, but then confine and limit it to one application (billing, word processing, or spreadsheets) and ignore the computer's full potential as a communications and information access tool.

All three situations can lead to trouble. In the first, the business person falls further behind in knowledge and experience and continues to add to a store of "they sure look complicated to me" observations. The more of these the person accumulates, the harder it will be to finally move forward to start learning how to use the machines. The mystery, if left to time and sporadic encounters, may grow to such immense proportions that the resolution to finally sit down and use a computer will never come, because the experience would be just too overwhelming to consider.

The second trap is even, potentially, more costly. A well-meaning friend or co-worker who owns a computer will extol the virtues of his or her machine as being the ideal. Such friends will elaborate on how they have used their computers to perform wondrous tasks (which will appear to be wondrous to the uninitiated) and each will tell you that his or her machine is all anyone could ever need or want. Seldom is that the absolute truth. While acquaintances who own computers can help you get a feeling for what computers can do and to allow you to learn more about computers by using their machines, seldom should they be relied upon to make decisions on buying specific brands.

Another source of biased, inadequate information is computer salespeople. The uninformed computer buyer is a computer salesperson's dream come true. According to *The Washington Post* (April 1, 1988), ignorance appears to be the biggest problem for small businesses of all types that are trying to automate. Nancy Stephens, executive director of the Washington Independent Computer Consultants Association was quoted as saying, "They can't make decent comparisons unless they are familiar with the buzzwords salesmen use. They don't know anything, and they put themselves face to face with a salesman and they've had it." The real threat of computers to small businesses is the costly inconvenience of a poor investment. Stephens said small-business owners should do their computer homework before making the purchase, but they shouldn't procrastinate. "If they're waiting for the most perfect machine at the lowest price, they'll wait forever. They should go ahead and get something. Then at least they'll be able to make a more intelligent choice the second time around."

All this is not to say that computers are sold by any method worse than those used to sell other merchandise. But, without clear ideas about what you want to do with a computer, you are, generally, going to be sold more than you need (in dollars) and, often, something that does not adequately do what you require. The advice of computer marketers can be tainted by the brands they have available (and often, unfortunately, the brands they have available in the greatest stock). Further, commercial software varies in the amount of margin the dealers have to work with. Salespeople in a given store may make a larger profit on one package than on another; if they make $100 on the sale of one package and $50 on another, which do you think they might push harder? Ever have a Ford salesperson objectively assess your car needs and inform you that a Chevrolet would better fit your needs? So, unless you have a clear understanding of what you need your computer to do, you will most likely be sold what comes closest in any given computer store, whether it is the ideal solution or not.

Finally, the third trap, to buy a computer and then relegate it to the usual, more familiar tasks of word processing, scheduling, billing, spreadsheets, etc., is a waste of immense potential power and benefits. As you read on, this waste will become more apparent.

Computers are as multifaceted as a finished diamond. On one side you have word processing, on another, spreadsheet analysis of budget and fore-casting. On another, billing and scheduling. Turn it over and there is commu-nications, graphics, desktop publishing, and project management. Of course, you will probably buy a computer to attack some well-conceived tasks. However, remain open to all the possibilities a computer offers. The potential is amazing. The key is not to take on too much at once. Start with your most important application and learn it well, then add another and learn it. To buy five different applications at once and sit down to learn them simultaneously is inviting frustration, anxiety, and defeat.

None of these scenarios needs to prevail. With the information provided in this book, you will be able to make informed decisions about what you want to do with a computer in one specific arena—computer-assisted commu-nications—and have a good idea how to go about doing it. You will not emerge from these pages as a programmer or as one ready to lead your next staff meeting in a discussion of the virtues and cost-effectiveness of com-puterizing. You will, however, come away with a clear sense of what com-puters are capable of doing for you and your business in the areas of informa-tion gathering and communications. You will be able to listen to the pitches of computer salespeople and separate truth from hype. You will be able to make informed choices on products and technologies. Most of all, you will under-stand computers for what they are and what they are not. They are ma-chines—tools, if you will—that are able to enhance your capacity to manage information and to assist you in managing your business. They are not devices contrived to confuse, frustrate, or embarrass you. If you accept these facts as you read this book, its purpose will be fulfilled.

LEARNING FROM SUCCESSFUL BUSINESSES

You already know what the giants of business are doing. They are jumping in with both feet when it comes to applying computers. Here's proof. A survey commissioned by Digital Equipment Corporation (and reported by UPI) found that 9 out of 10 senior business executives believe that U.S. companies have successfully made computers a vital part of their business. Based on interviews with 320 chief executive offices (CEOs), chief operating officers, and strategic planners, the survey shows that "computers are now an integral factor in major U.S. corporations," with applications ranging far beyond data processing. The survey also reported that

- An overwhelming 98 percent believe that senior executives must understand computers and "their business impact."
- 81 percent agreed that computer networks are "critical" to doing business abroad.
- 88 percent said they are using computers to increase communications.
- 87 percent said computers already have cut time needed to develop products.

The survey also showed that a majority (53 percent) believe that computers give them an edge in the marketplace, that is, they agreed with the statement "Computer technology provides my company with a strategic competitive edge." At the same time, 78 percent asserted that U.S. companies are even with or leading foreign competitors in acquiring and installing computers.

Still not convinced? A survey of 701 "knowledge workers" (professionals and managers) in *Fortune* 500 companies was made by Honeywell Techanalysis, the research division of Honeywell, Inc. When asked what they would do with $10,000, an overwhelming 68 percent of these knowledge workers answered that they would purchase computer hardware or software. Ninety-four percent agreed that office automation gave them more time for planning and evaluation activities and enabled them to make better and more informed decisions (*Management Review,* May 1985).

That is what big business is doing, thinking, and planning. But you probably already knew that trend. Allow me to throw another log on the fire. According to The Yankee Group's "Small Business Survey" released in 1988 (and reported on in *Inc.* magazine's August 1988 issue), 40 percent of the fast-growing small businesses use computers to access a database inside the office and an additional 20 percent use them for the same purposes inside and outside the office. A whopping 70 percent of the fastest-growing small firms use electronic mail!

2

How Do Computers Communicate?

Every time I start to tell anyone at length about how computers can exchange information with each other, I am reminded of the story about the little boy who had a question. His father was busy at his desk with some work, and the boy bothered his father until he got his father's attention and then asked the question. The father, trying to get some peace, asked, "Son, why don't you go ask your mother?" And the little boy replied, "Because, Dad, I just don't want to know that much about it!"

Maybe you don't "want to know that much" about computer-to-computer communications, but you do need to know the basics. And that is what this chapter covers. We discuss how a modem (the little hardware device that takes a computer's information and sends it across the phone lines) works, why modems are needed, and what to look for in buying one. We omit a lot of "hacker's" trivia because you don't need the minutiae. You do need a rudimentary understanding of what a modem is expected to accomplish so that you may deal with the salespeople who sell modems and also the modem itself. We also cover what your software should be able to do in conjunction with your modem.

One simple point is stressed throughout this chapter and this book. It is simply that one does not in any way have to understand how these electronic communication systems work at the most minute level to put them to use. At the end of this book, you will not be an associate member of the Honored

Guild of Computer Hackers, Anonymous. They would laugh both of our applications right out the window. When I first started using computers in 1981, I had no formal computer training, and I still have never taken a computer course and am just a computer user. I know how to turn a computer on, load my commercial software, and use it to benefit my business. I do not know the architecture of my computer's chips, or how to solder in replacement chips, or anything of that nature. I have learned, through practice, how to operate spreadsheet, database, word-processing, and communications software. And, as far as the "innards" of my computer, that is all I know. More importantly, that is all you will need to know as well. With just the simple explanations in this chapter, you will get along fine as well.

Just because you don't know all the terminology, catchphrases, and jargon bantered about by the "experts," you should not shy away from the technology itself. Computer communications can be used with a modicum of knowledge and with much less than you will know after reading this book. Without donning pompons and a short skirt, I feel the urge to shout, "You can do it!" And you can. It's high time you started.

If you do not want to dive right into this brief foray into technical language, just jump ahead to the next chapter. The basic tenet of this book is that you don't have to know this stuff to be effective in electronic communications. But, if you are curious about how the "magic" takes place, read on.

THE DIGITAL-TO-ANALOG PROBLEM

The first thing you have to realize is that computers and phone lines don't have a lot in common. Computers understand only digital information, the simplest form of information coding you can imagine. There are only two possibilities —"on" (a positive voltage) or "off" (a negative voltage). By stringing a series of voltage changes together, computers can communicate with their own chips as well as those of other computers. The "conversation" on an oscilloscope would look something like the graphic in Figure 2-1.

Computers rely on a special language that is based on digital signals and the computer's limited ability to handle anything other than positive or negative voltages. Because it consists of just two parts, a computer's information coding is said to be *binary* and works on a *binary number system*. As opposed to our decimal numbering system, which uses ten symbols, only two symbols are used for binary numbers, a 0 or a 1. Hot or cold, black or white, Giants or Dodgers. With a series of on and off voltages, with the "on's" representing a 1 and the "off's" representing a 0, computers handle their information needs quite well and, because of the simplicity of the language, quite fast.

This is all well and good when a computer is moving data from chip to

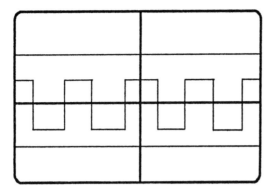

Figure 2-1 Graphic of digital signal.

chip in its own chassis, but what about when it tries to connect to a computer across a phone line? Unfortunately, phone lines can only carry analog information, which does not work on an on/off system. Transmitting the smooth, undulating changes in sound frequencies that characterize the human voice is what Alexander Graham Bell had in mind when he invented the telephone. Analog wave forms on an oscilloscope look like the graphic in Figure 2-2.

The ordinary lines of today's phone systems do not handle the sharp on/off spikes of digital signals very well at all. Problem #1: How do we get the digital signal of computer language (computerese) across a hostile phone line and back?

ENTER THE MODEM

Where there is a need (particularly when there are dollars to be made), there is a solution. Actually, it was AT&T itself who solved the problem. When the government developed the "Distant Early Warning" system (DEWline) in the 1950s, it needed a way to get priority computer data from various installations

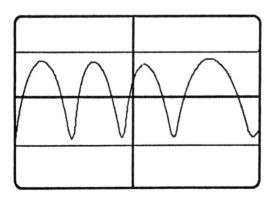

Figure 2-2 Graphic of analog signal.

to processing centers. AT&T invented the modem in response to this need. (These pioneering devices were not called modems, however. AT&T dubbed them "dataphones.")

The problem of digital data being incompatible with analog phone lines was solved by logic much akin to the logic in the old saying "if the mountain will not come to Mohammed, then . . ." Thus, if phone lines cannot carry digital signals, why not make digital signals analog? A miraculous little device called a modem was devised. The name tells what it does: *modem* is an acronym for "*mo*dulator-*dem*odulator." The electronics in the device takes the spiking digital signals and modulates them into smooth analog signals that can be carried across telephone wiring. At the other end, a similar device demodulates the analog signals back into digital forms that the receiving computer can understand. And back and forth the noise goes. AT&T is happy, the personal computer (PC) is happy, and the information flows to and fro.

The modern modem comes in all shapes, sizes, and configurations. There are the old acoustic varieties, which work by placement of the handset of the phone into cups with a speaker at one end and a microphone at the other, and the newer direct-connect varieties, which plug right into the familiar RJ11 modular wall plug. Acoustic modems are still popular among portable or "laptop" computer users, as an effective connection can be made from a phone booth, hotel room, or wherever there may be no way to plug directly into the phone connection. Except under these special situations, probably 99 percent of the modems sold today, however, are of the direct-connect variety. Acoustic modems are limited in that they can only work at the slowest transmission speeds and are susceptible to noise occurring around them when in use.

Today, for the desktop computer, the two most popular constructions for these direct-connect modems are internal cards and stand-alone devices. The internal cards (see Figures 2-3 and 2-4) plug into a computer's expansion slots and draw power from the machine. The external, stand-alone models (see Figure 2-5) have their own power supplies but require a special port in or on your computer to plug into called an RS232 or serial port.

While I swore up front that this was not to be a technical treatise, I do have to mention the RS232 interface you will need to deal with if you go the external modem route. The RS232 link dates back to 1969, when the Electronic Industry Association (EIA) adopted it as the standard for serial communications between terminals and modems. You will also hear the RS232 port referred to as a "serial" or "serial communications" port. The "recommended standard number 232 version C" or ("RS232C") has been adopted by the personal computer industry as well. Again, unfortunately, only "more or less." The convention calls for a 25-pin (some newer machines use 9 pins) connec-

Figure 2-3 Direct-connect modem with internal card.

Figure 2-4 *Direct-connect modem with internal card.*

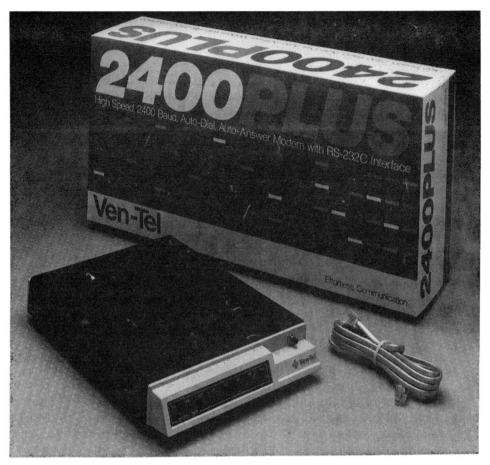

Figure 2-5 *External stand-alone direct-connect modem.*

tion between the computer and the modem and specifies which signal is to be carried by each pin. For example, pin 1 is a ground, pin 2 transmits data, pin 3 receives data, etc. The connector for the RS232 is labeled a "DB-25" connector. Some say the "D" comes from the fact that the connector is shaped like the letter "D" with one side slightly longer than the other. Whatever it looks like to you, it is your outlet to the world.

External modems may also be categorized into full-size units and portable units. The portable units (see Figure 2-6), which weigh about 6 ounces and are often only 4 to 5 inches long and 2 to 3 inches wide, have flourished with the popularity of the laptop (portable) computer. They are usually battery-powered and are perfect for staying connected electronically while traveling on the road. The Novation Parrot 1200 modem runs off the spare power

Figure 2-6 *The Worldport 1200, a portable, battery-powered, direct-connect modem. (Photograph courtesy of Touchbase Systems, Inc.)*

emitted from the computer's RS232 interface and does not need a power supply of its own at all. The Worldport series of modems from Touchbase Systems also has a connector that allows the modem to be used with acoustic cups for times when there is no way to connect the modem to the phone line directly.

There are 300-, 1200-, 2400-, and even 9600-baud modems. A *baud* is defined as "a variable unit of data transmission speed." In simplest terms, baud is merely a "speedometer" scale measuring how fast information is transmitted. As a general rule, the higher the available baud of a modem, the more expensive the modem. The tradeoff, though, is that on most commercial communications networks you are billed for your time on the system. The longer you stay connected, the more your session costs. Though more expensive to buy initially, the faster modems can offer considerable cost savings in the long run.

While some systems may charge twice or even three times their normal fee (set for the old standard, 300-baud access) for using their facilities at 2400 baud, you can accomplish your online tasks in one-eighth the time. If your online time is considerable, the faster modems can pay for themselves in short order. Savings using a 2400-baud modem over a 1200-baud modem can be equally substantial. Some general communications systems (such as CompuServe) now bill 2400-baud access the same as they do 1200-baud usage. Which modem speed to choose really boils down to these two choices —1200 baud or 2400 baud. Most industry experts agree that you cannot go wrong with a 2400-baud, stand-alone modem. Prices of such modems are falling rapidly, and these modems will likely be the standard for the next 2 to 3 years. In fact, 1988 was the first year that 2400-baud modems outsold their 1200-baud counterparts.

THE BASICS OF COMPUTER COMMUNICATION

Fine, now we have the modem as our bridge across the phone lines. What language shall we use? Fortunately for us, computers do not speak in "IBM-ese" or "Apple-ese" but have a standard dialect. Referred to as ASCII (pronounced "as-key"), the *A*merican *S*tandard *C*ode of *I*nformation *I*nterchange is the language adopted across the computer industry for storing and transmitting information. Since computers understand only numbers and, specifically, numbers in a binary form, the ASCII code assigns a unique number to every letter of the alphabet, to each numeral, and to each of the common punctuation marks. Certain combined keystrokes are represented as well and serve special functions. For example, (and don't be concerned if this sounds somewhat foreign), CTRL-A (formed when the Control key and the letter A are pressed simultaneously) is assigned the number 1, CTRL-L is ASCII 12 and represents a form feed for the printer, CTRL-M serves as a carriage return, and CTRL-J is a line feed. Other control codes represent a space, backspace, tab, etc. The first recognizable character is the exclamation point, which appears at ASCII 33. Let's see how this system works.

BINARY AND BITS

In our day-to-day lives we use a base 10, or decimal, number system. Each place in a number stands for a power of 10; ten to the zero power is 1, ten to the first power is 10, ten to the second power is 100, and so on. Starting from the rightmost figure of a given number and working left, the first digit is multiplied by the zero power of ten, the second by the first power of ten, and so on. For example, the number 563 is $(5 \times 10^2) + (6 \times 10^1) + (3 \times 10^0)$

=500 + 60 + 3 = 563. Since decimal is the system you're familiar with, the calculations seem redundant.

However, computers do not use the decimal system. Computers only understand whether a circuit is on or off. This lends itself to the binary, or base two, number system. In binary, "on" is represented by a 1, and "off" is represented by a 0. A 1 or a 0 is called a *bi*nary digi*t*, or *bit* for short. Like decimal numbers, binary digits can be strung together to represent numbers larger than a single digit. The difference is that each position represents a power of two rather than a power of 10. For example, the binary number 10 is really $(1 \times 2^1) + (0 \times 2^0) = 2 + 0 = 2$. The binary number 1001 is equal to $(1 \times 2^3) + (0 \times 2^2) + (0 \times 2^1) + (1 \times 2^0) = 8 + 0 + 0 + 1 = 9$, in decimal.

With one bit, you can code two states or numbers: 0 or 1. If you combine 2 bits, you can code 4 numbers: 0, 1, 2, or 3 (in binary, 00, 01, 10, or 11). With 3 bits, you can code 8 numbers, with 4 bits, 16 numbers, and so on. So, by stringing the bits together to form more logical possibilities, the binary system is able to represent the larger numbers necessary for the ASCII code. For you mathematic types out there (and I am certainly not counted among your group), it becomes clear that the number of possibilities (x) for a binary number increases in the fashion $x = 2$ to the y power, where y = the number of binary digits in the number. For example, with a 4-digit binary number, the possibilities are 2 to the 4th power, or 16 ($2 \times 2 \times 2 \times 2$).

Let's do some more thinking about this. How big a binary number do we need to represent simple English text? There are 26 letters in the alphabet and there are uppercase and lowercase letters, so we have 52 right there. There are the 10 number symbols, so we are up to 62. If that is all we had to worry about, we could get by with a 6-digit binary number (2 to the 6th power covers 64 possible numbers). But there are punctuation marks as well as dollar signs, ampersands, asterisks, etc. Those alone push us above the limits imposed by a 6-bit binary number. What about a 7-bit binary number? That gives us 128 possibilities (0 to 127), and it turns out to be more than enough to cover the usual text-based symbols in the ASCII code. The remainder of the available numbers have been assigned to nonalphabet characters (like spaces and backspaces) and the keystroke combinations CTRL-A through CTRL-Z (which are put to good use in computer communications).

So, we absolutely need, at a minimum, a 7-bit binary number to transmit each letter (and nonletter) of common *alphanumeric* text. With this system, we can easily convert the ASCII code of the word *The* to its binary representation for transmission across a computer connection. To represent the letter *T,* which is ASCII number 84, the binary number would be 1010100. Here is how it is broken down. For each "place" in the 7-bit number, a 1 gives that place a number value dictated by its position and a 0 gives it a value of zero (for example, a 1 in the 64ths place gives a value of 64). Then you just add the number value of each place with a 1 and the sum total is the ASCII number represented. The binary representation for the letter T is

	0 or 64		0 or 32		0 or 16		0 or 8		0 or 4		0 or 2		0 or 1
T =	1		0		1		0		1		0		0
Sum =	64	+	0	+	16	+	0	+	4	+	0	+	0
Total = 64 + 16 + 4 = 84 (ASCII)													

For the full word *The,* the 7-bit numbers for each letter are as follows:

	T	h	e
ASCII	84	104	101
Binary	1010100	1101000	1100101

A quick aside: There are two general types of communications, synchronous and asynchronous. *Synchronous* means that information is sent in a steady stream. There is a timing pattern to the information sent so that the time interval determines where one bit ends and another begins. The synchronization between transmitting and receiving devices is achieved through timing bits or characters at the beginning of the transmission. Once the timing is set, the data stream is marked off into its logical segments by the time interval at which each arrives. It is analogous to a conveyor belt with a long salami going through a cutting device. The cutting of the salami into slices occurs at set time intervals, and as long as the conveyor belt moves at a constant speed, the slices will be more or less uniform in length. This form of communications is more likely to be found in environments where there is little chance of external factors disturbing the timed flow of information. For example, synchronous data transmission is often used with computers wired together in a local network. These systems cannot be affected by long telephone wires and distance.

The second form of data transmission is *asynchronous* (start-and-stop) communications. In this form the pieces of information—the individual bits—

are not marked off by time intervals but by special bits. To continue the analogy of our conveyor belt, the salami would not be sliced on a timed interval, but the knife would be directed to cut along special marks on the salami that section it off in equal parts. Since long-distance computer communications can be affected by all sorts of delays and interruptions along the phone lines to their destinations, synchronous communications is virtually useless. But with asynchronous patterns, it can be accomplished. This form is what is used on the communications systems discussed in the rest of this book.

It is the responsibility of the software we use for communications to tack these additional "sectioning" bits onto the data. Specifically, these are called *start bits* and *stop bits.* A start bit is always a 1, and a stop bit is always a 0. They mark off the beginning and end of each *binary word,* the term applied to the 7-bit binary digit representing an alphanumeric character. They are called, in the pervasive jargon of telecommunications, "framing bits," because they do just that—they frame or mark off the individual binary words and separate them from each other.

A BIT ON PARITY

As it applies to computers, the term *parity* (which actually means "equivalence") refers to a simple form of error checking. With all these 0's and 1's flying across the noisy, static-plagued phone lines, it is quite easy for one or more bits to be changed from a 1 to a 0, or vice versa. You can, with your knowledge of binary digits, see how the change of a single digit can alter the letter or word arriving at the remote computer. How can transmissions avoid this? One way is to use parity bits.

Let's use an example. Suppose we send the letter *T.* Looking at the binary word for *T,* we see 1010100. When you are using parity checking, both computers agree to use it and expect to encounter a parity bit in the data stream. If you have agreed to use even parity, both computers have effectively said, "When I send a word to you, the arithmetic sum of the correct digits in the word plus the parity bit I send should equal an even number; if they do not, let me know and I will send that word again." The transmitting computer (really, the communications software) then totals the digits in every binary word. If the total of 1's and 0's is odd, it adds a 1 as the parity bit to make the total an even number; if the number is already even, it adds a 0 as the parity bit to keep the number even. In the above instance of the letter *T,* the sum total of digits in the binary word is 3. In even parity, the parity bit is, thus, a 1. What about for the binary word for *h,* 1101000? The total is 3, and under even parity, the parity bit would also be 1. For *e* (1100101), the total of the digits is already an even number, 4. The added parity bit is then a 0. When computers agree to use odd parity, the reverse is true. The added parity bit would make the total an odd number. Under odd parity, the parity bit for *T* and *h* would be a 0 (to keep the total odd); for e it would be a 1.

Once both computers have agreed on a method of parity checking (it's done right at the start of the connection), the error checking begins. Suppose even parity is agreed upon. If the receiving computer receives a binary word with the sum of the digits it counts being an even number and it sees a parity bit of 1, it knows something is wrong. It sends a message to the sending computer to resend that binary word. All, of course, in microseconds. Parity is a rudimentary form of checking, but it is fairly effective for text-based information exchange.

Once the parity bits, stop bits, and start bits have been strung together, the whole string of binary information will be sent out to the modem as a stream. The final product for transmission of the word *The* is shown in the chart below. The spacing between binary digits is artificial and is for illustration only. Notice that the word appears to be backwards because of the direction of data flow; the *T* is transmitted first.

Direction of Data Flow Out to Modem ⟶
0	0	1100101	1	0	1	1101000	1	0	1	10101001	1
st	P	e	ST	st	P	h	ST	st	P	T	ST

ST = start bit   P = parity bit   st = Stop Bit

SETTINGS: DUPLEX, ECHOPLEX, AND DATA BIT

Another significant source of needless confusion in computer-to-computer communications are the terms *duplex* and *echoplex*. We hear that some systems use "full-duplex," while others use "half-duplex." "Local echo" and "remote echo" are also bantered about. *Duplex* is derived from the Latin words meaning, roughly, "two surfaces." *Duplex,* from the old days of "duplex telegraphy," simply means a two-way communication. All computer communications that we will deal with in this book are duplex. The question is, which duplex? There is *half-duplex,* which is a two-way communication, but only one way at a time, and *full-duplex,* which is communication that goes both ways at the same time. A common analogy is that voice telephone conversations are like full-duplex because both parties can talk at the same time. Ham radio is like half-duplex—each party politely waits until the other is finished before sending. Most systems you will be communicating with use full-duplex (one exception that comes to mind is GEnie, a major general communications network we will discuss in future chapters).

The second two designations, "local echo" and "remote echo," concern the term *echoplex*. This term refers to the source of the characters that show up on your monitor as you type. There are only two possible sources. The characters you type either show up from your local input as you type them (local echo), or they can be "echoed" back to you from the remote computer as it receives them. Thus, you can have local echo or remote echo for your echoplex setting.

The settings for duplex and echoplex are intimately meshed in almost all communications software. If you think about it for a minute, you can understand why. Suppose, for the sake of discussion, that you set your software settings (duplex, echoplex, as well as the previously discussed parity settings are software-controlled) to half-duplex and remote echo. What do you think might be a problem with that?

If you initiate these settings, you tell the host to send data back to you only when you have stopped your sending but you also tell the host that you will depend on it to echo back your input before your input appears on your screen. If you were a fast typist, you may find yourself merrily typing away with none of your characters showing up on your screen until after a significant lag time. Since you have instructed your software to rely on the remote computer for the characters it is to display as you type, even at fast transmission speeds you may outtype your display's ability to show what you are typing. Or, even worse, the remote system could be at half-duplex and would not even echo your characters back. You would type and nothing would show up as your input. This can happen if you connect to GEnie with these settings.

Another problem may occur. Suppose you set half-duplex and local echo, a more logical choice. You connect to a system and type "What manner of speech is this?" You see this on your screen:

WWhhaatt mmaanneerr ooff ssppeecchh iiss tthhiiss?

What do you think is causing this display? Think for a minute before reading on. This situation can occur when you connect your computer set for local echo to a system set up for remote echo (as are most common systems). Not only do you see characters as you type them from a local display, but you also get a repeat performance from the remote echo of the system you connect to.

As stated, duplex and echoplex are generally associated in most software. In point of fact, with most popular software, all you will ever set is whether or not you want characters echoed locally or remotely. The software will run at full-duplex regardless (unless you change it, which you need not do). You can connect to half-duplex systems (like GEnie) at full-duplex as long as you choose to have a local echo. (Not to confuse the issue, but you can signal GEnie to remotely echo if you like; just send a CTRL-R at the "U#=" prompt when logging on. GEnie will then switch to remote echo).

As a rule, just set things to remote echo. If you connect and what you type is not appearing on your screen, switch to local echo. Don't even fiddle with the duplex setting—keep it at full-duplex. With that simple plan, you will seldom go wrong.

There is one more setting that your software may call for. It may ask for word length or number of data bits. If it does, it will give you a choice of 7 or 8. Why does some software even ask? We learned in the beginning of this chapter that for text all we need is a 7-bit binary number to transmit all we will even need to use in English text. The 7-bit binary number enables us to send 128 different characters, more than enough for plain, ordinary text—right? Right. Seven bits is the most common setting and is generally the correct setup. In fact, virtually all the systems I use connect with 7 bits. What is this 8-bit stuff?

We will not go into much of the why of 8-bit data transmission other than to say that it involves the ability for computers to send other, nontext types of files (like programs and graphics), as well as text. These special files contain characters which are numbered in ASCII code higher than 128. These characters are called the "high-bit" characters and are numbered up to 255 (remember, an 8-bit number can be as large as 2 to the 8th power, or 256, making available 0 to 255) so 8-bit binary numbers (words) are needed. They are sent by a special method called a "protocol transfer." Suffice it to say that 8-bit communications can be done; they are, generally, special cases; and they allow transfer of special, nontext files. One other thing: If you use 8 data bits, you always have to use no parity. Why? Because parity checking, as we discussed previously, uses the eighth bit for the parity bit, either odd or even. In 8-bit transmissions, that bit is used for an extended binary number and is not available for parity checking. So, it's either 7-bits with even or odd parity, or 8-bits with no parity.

With most systems, initially just set up at 7-bit word, 1 stop bit, even parity, remote echo, and full-duplex. You will seldom go wrong. If you see garbage that looks like this on your screen

W# $%∧ he@@!$ tho&*∧ @#$er

specifically, nonsense with interspersed normal-looking characters, you probably have a problem with the data-bit setting and parity. Switching to 8 data bits and no parity will probably correct the problem.

BAUD RATES

One final term. You'll need to know about *baud rates.* As mentioned earlier, you can think of baud as the miles per hour rating for your modem, the speed at which information can be sent from and through it. Common baud rates are 300, 1200, and 2400 (see Figure 2-7). Modems are becoming available that have a rate of 9600 baud, but these are high-budget items. Most modems sold today are in the 1200- or 2400-baud category, but 300-baud modems are still relatively common. The baud rate is often considered to be synonymous with *bits per second* (bps), the true measure of transmission speed. While this is not strictly true, the issue is too complex to examine here. Suffice it to say that both baud rate and bps are measures of transmission speed (*see* Glossary).

All commercial systems and most local "bulletin board systems" (BBSs) will accommodate either 300- or 1200-baud modem connections. You should be aware that 1200-baud modems can run at 300 baud if necessary, but not vice versa. When the communications software you use asks you at which baud to run, just use the fastest your modem offers.

Figure 2-7   *Modems with various baud rates.*

What if you set your modem at 1200 baud, call a local BBS, and then see this:

xxx?@xx@#xxxxx$!!xxxxxx

This "message" means that you have connected to a 300-baud system which cannot accommodate your 1200-baud modem. You will also see this as the initial message when connecting to Tymnet, one of the common carriers for long-distance computer communications. The Tymnet system answers every call initially at 300 baud. On this system, however, when you press "a," Tymnet will sense your modem's speed and move up to 1200 baud. Unfortunately, a local BBS system running at 300 baud probably cannot work at 1200 baud. Just reset your baud rate to 300 baud and you will be able to communicate.

SELECTING A MODEM

Now that you know the terminology, we can discuss actually choosing your modem. While the final decision on the make and model is entirely up to you and your local computer dealer or computer guru, I will offer some suggestions. But remember, setting up a Brand A modem on an Brand Z computer has nuances that cannot be solved in a single book. You will probably need the help of someone locally.

STAND-ALONE VS. INTERNAL

Most experts recommend buying a stand-alone modem with, at the minimum, 1200-baud capabilities. There are some trade-offs with this selection. A stand-alone modem requires a special cable and maybe even a separate card for an RS232 connecter (depending on your computer). It also takes up desk space and requires an electrical plug. But think of this: With computers changing so rapidly, the chances of your moving to a different machine somewhere down the road are good. Your business may expand to the point that you need a computer with more power, speed, and storage capacity. Odds are, then, that you will some day buy a new machine. When you do, if you have an external modem you can simply make another cable, plug the old modem right in, and keep on communicating. Generally speaking, a stand-alone modem is more of a problem to set up initially (with it's cable requirements) and may cost a bit more (mainly because it has a case with LED status lights and its own power supply), but the added flexibility of being able to shift the modem to a replacement or a second machine is worth the hassle. At least think about it. It may make more sense to buy an internal modem, if, on the other hand, (1) you cannot see yourself buying a new computer within the next 18 to 24 months (at which time the modem industry will be completely changed and repriced anyway), and (2) you currently own a machine that readily takes a cheap, internal modem, and (3) your particular computer did not come with a built-in RS232 port and you would have to buy one for an external modem, and (4) you don't have access to a full-service computer store or a local computer user group to help you with putting a modem cable together, and (5) your desk space is already at a premium. All five must apply for an external modem to be the practical choice. The point here is that you need to be aware of the factors involved before you make your choice.

FEATURES

Let's discuss the features you should look for in a standard modem. First of all, the importance of "Hayes-compatibility" should be mentioned early. The Hayes modem command system has assumed a position as the de facto standard in the modem industry. Since Hayes modems have captured an estimated 75 percent of the market, Hayes must be considered the standard. The Hayes command set is used by most terminal emulator software packages (see Chapter 3 under "Communications Software") and the commands are now emulated (more or less) by virtually all popular modems on the market today.

The language of the Hayes command set is based on the "ATx" command sequence, where "AT" tells the modem to jump to *AT*tention, and "x" is the subsequent command. For example "ATDT999-9999" is the command to come to attention (AT), dial (D), and dial in a tone fashion (T) the phone number 999-9999. The command "ATDP" would do the same, except that it would instruct the modem to dial in a pulse or rotary fashion. Other commands are available to have the modem answer an incoming call, to turn the speakers off and on (did you know most modems came with speakers?), and so on. You need not worry about these commands for the most part, as the software you run will control most of them for you.

An important point: Many modems are advertised as being "100 percent Hayes-compatible," but you may be a bit disappointed when you try to figure out exactly which commands the manufacturer means. The manufacturer may define "100 percent compatible" as meaning "yes, when we get an 'ATDT' our modem knows to dial a number using a tone sound." That may be all the manufacturer means by "100 percent Hayes-compatible." When your software tries to use other standard ATx commands, your modem may balk. Even a supposedly Hayes-compatible modem with an identical command language may still prove to be incompatible with some software, due to timing differences and minor changes in the hardware registers and configurations. Fortunately, the problem of incomplete compatibility is easing in the latest modems, but it still exists.

Some modem makers shield the incompatibilities by "bundling" (offering as part of your modem purchase) software that will work nicely with their hardware (the modem). Their chosen terminal emulator may work just fine, but then someone else has chosen your software for you. The program may not be comfortable for you (see Chapter 3), and you might have a rude awakening if you try to run a different software program that demands a more rigid compatibility and use of the Hayes command set. It can be a jungle out there at times.

Of course, one way around the problem is to buy a Hayes modem to begin with. You generally can't go wrong with the choice. Hayes has a superb reputation for customer support and service. Hayes offers a two-year limited warranty on its products, with the option of a four-year extended protection plan. Hayes modems are designed and manufactured in Norcross, Georgia. They are beautifully constructed and built to last. With all this in their favor, why is there even a choice? Because Hayes modems generally cost up to 2 to 3 times what you would pay for one of its competitor's modems. If you can afford a Hayes modem for your system, there is little reason not to buy one.

The bottom line is this: Pick out the software you want to use, and try it with the modem under consideration *before* you buy. Make the dealer set up the modem for use, preferably on your computer brand as well, and then run the software you have chosen. Put the emulator through all of its paces or have the dealer do it for you while you watch. If there are snags that cannot be resolved, don't give the software up in favor of the modem. The software is the most important thing, and you should demand a modem that will run with it. Period.

Once you get past the sticky problem of compatibility, the rest of the features offered by the current crop of modems are pretty much a standard fare, luckily so. Early in the history of modems you had to deal with such things as whether a modem offered full- or half-duplex (or both), whether it provided autoanswer and/or autodial, and whether the modem supported Bell 103 (for 300 baud) or Bell 212A (for 1200 baud) protocols. Now, standardization along these lines is the rule. Virtually all modems in production today offer both autoanswer and autodial (the modem can accept incoming calls as well as make outgoing ones), have the capacity to operate at either full- or half-duplex (and can switch via software control), and work well enough with both Bell protocols.[1]

---

[1] There are new protocols being developed on a global scale that will eventually replace the provincial Bell protocols. The CCITT (see Glossary) has adopted new modem transmision standards: the V.22 for 1200 baud, the V.22 *bis* for 2400 baud, and the V.32 for the cutting edge 9600-baud modems. American modem producers are beginning to adopt these standards, so they should at least be a part of your vocabulary.

MORE ON SPEED (BAUD)

Possibly the only choice you will need to consider in choosing a modem is what speed potential you want to pay for. As noted earlier, modems are now available in everything from 300 baud (generally, modems that are confined to this speed today are the acoustic type) up to 9600 baud (see Figure 2-7). The most common types are still 1200 baud, but modems of the 2400-baud variety are gaining fast and will soon be the standard. More and more databases are offering the 2400-baud speed option, and, although it usually costs more to use the systems at this speed, the cost-effectiveness is still there.

The term *baud* is derived from the name of the French innovator Baudot, who developed a 5-bit code for early teletype machines (see Chapter 8). The term is currently applied to the speed with which binary information is transmitted and processed by the modem. As a general rule, think of baud rate in this simple way: Since each ASCII character requires 10 bits—7-bits for the letter or number itself, a start bit, a stop bit, and a parity bit—the characters a modem can transmit per second is the baud rate divided by 10. Thus, a 300-baud modem can move about 30 ASCII characters per second (which means you can transmit about five words per second if the average word is six characters long). A 1200-baud modem quadruples that to 120 alphanumeric symbols (20 words or so) per second. A 2400-baud modem doubles that again to 240 letters per second.

What does all this mean to you? Time! For example, to transfer a 5000-character file (approximately 700 words) it takes 2 minutes and 45 seconds at 300 baud, but only 20 seconds at 2400 baud. Of course, these speed approximations assume ideal phone line conditions.[2] Those, unfortunately, are rare. The bottom line is that when you are gathering information online, speed is of major importance, and should be considered carefully. If you plan to do any serious work online, buy at least a 1200-baud modem. Get a 2400-baud modem if you can possibly afford it.

There is another reason to consider buying a 2400-baud modem. These modems perform better than their 1200-baud counterparts under most phone line conditions. They handle noise and static better than 1200-baud modems, particularly when you run the 2400 baud at 1200 baud. Data transmissions from a 1200-baud source which can arrive garbled and "trashed up" (contain nonsense characters and unneeded line feeds and screen clears), with a 1200-baud receiving modem can be crystal clear with a 2400-baud receiving modem running at the lower (1200-baud) speed. If you have a phone system that is

---

[2] When the telephone lines are not "clean" and are prone to line surges and other electrical havoc, modems will drop back in speed to accommodate the disrupted transmissions. Think of the baud assigned to a modem as you do the EPA gas mileage rating for your car. Seldom will you be able to get your machine to achieve either ideal.

part of a large, buildingwide network, or if you are in a rural area where the phone lines are not optimal, you may want to consider paying the extra $50 or so for a 2400-baud modem for that simple reason.

While 9600-baud modems are not that common yet, they do deserve a word here. The modem industry has come a long way since the days of the 300-baud modem. The 9600-baud modem (first introduced by Codex in the early 1980s, with a price tag around $10,000) has become a viable, if specialized, communications product (see Figure 2-8). Imagine: A 100-kilobyte file that takes almost an hour at 300 baud, 15 minutes at 1200 baud, and 8 minutes at 2400, can be zipped across conditioned and protected phone lines in about 2 minutes at 9600 baud.

But with the triumph over time came several major snags. With 300-, 1200-, and 2400-baud modems, hardware-to-hardware compatibility is not a concern. Modems in these incarnations use the same patterns of frequency and volume modulation to send data. As long as the modems have the same speed capabilities, a modem from manufacturer X can speak coherently with one from manufacturer Y. The same is not true for 9600-baud modems.

Figure 2-8   *A 9600-baud modem.*

Modem technology has outrun the ability of the Consultative Committee in International Telegraphy and Telephony (CCITT; see Glossary) to get out universally accepted standards for 9600-baud transmissions. Actually, the CCITT has outlined two "recommendations"—V.29 and V.32—but neither has been completely acceptable.

Modem producers have moved ahead with products which follow only the standards they establish for their own products. Schemes to transmit data at 9600 baud require incredibly complex manipulations. As a result, the individual methods, while ingenious, are generally incompatible with modems from another maker. Fortunately, most of these modems will, when encountering a modem from a "foreign" manufacturer, automatically drop down to 2400 baud and use transfer protocols both understand. But to get the data across at the highest speed, you will have to have modems from the same manufacturer at both ends of the line. And speaking of the lines, unless you have the best of connecting phone lines, you will not be able to get the maximum speeds. Just as with their slower kin, these Ferrari's will drop back to low gear to adjust to poor lines. The other major drawback is price. While 2400-baud modems can be had for well under $250, the 9600-baud models range from $750 to over $2000.

FINER POINTS

While most of the complicated choices have been eliminated in choosing a modem, there are still differences among brands of modems. It's just that these differences don't lie so much in features offered as they do in quality of signal throughput. What the heck is that, you ask? Simply this: Some modems work better with phone lines than others do. They produce clearer output from the signals coming in from the lines and are less sensitive to outside disturbances—principally, electrical static. This subtle difference can be important. I, for example, live in a small-to-medium-size community. I do not have direct lines to any of the large information producers (CompuServe, Dialog, etc.). I communicate by way of the various "packet-switching" networks (discussed later in this chapter) that serve these areas. Thus, since my communication connection to the providers may often be routed over some bizarre paths by the Telenet or Tymnet services, my calls are subject to highly variable influences. Though I may be calling a system 500 miles away as the crow flies, my modem transmission may end up going through a Wyoming snowstorm or a thunderstorm in Texas to get to its destination in New York. In addition, I telecommunicate at the office over a multiuser phone system (the kind with five lines and all the blinking push buttons). With folks clicking buttons all over the place, the voltage peaks and valleys are atrocious.

As a result of the aforementioned conditions I live with what the optimist might call "less-than-perfect data lines" (I call them noisy, static-ridden, electrical hotlines). My transmissions are garbled, full of nonsense characters and control codes that I nor anyone else ever typed. They just appear. Since the modem has to, in a sense, interpret the analog message it receives and convert it back to a digital signal, it can be totally confused by electrical static. With a significant power surge on the phone line, your display can suddenly appear to be in direct contact with a Martian intelligence. If you are concurrently sending output to your printer, that device can be sent into a fit, complete with extra form feeds, beeps, and so forth. The nice modular-to-digital conversion can become a nightmare for you and your modem.

I have used several brands of modems, and they vary greatly in their ability to handle this form of interference. The differences can be incredible. To further confuse the issue, performance appears to have no relationship to modem price. I have had an $80 "no name" internal modem card work much better on my lines than a $500 brand-name, stand-alone beauty.

A small detail: You should look for two jacks on the modem. One should exist for plugging the modem into the wall plug, and a second for plugging your phone into the modem. You will probably want to share your phone line with both your modem and a telephone. If your modem has two jacks, you can plug the phone right into the modem. When you are not using your modem, the phone will work normally. If the modem you buy doesn't have two plugs, you will be eternally plugging the modem or the phone into the wall plug, depending on what you need to do at the time. So do yourself a favor—get a modem with two jacks.

One final tip: For your first modem, buy from a local dealer. Mail order can save you money later as you become more experienced in the products. However, for your first modem purchase, bite the bullet. Spend the dollars added by local retailers and buy where you can try the modem out first and have some local support as you learn to use it.

PACKET-SWITCHING

As far as using online information systems goes, you are fortunate if you live in Chicago, New York, Los Angeles, or any of the other larger cities in the United States. If you do live in a large city, most of the connections you make to online information systems will be through a direct connection on a phone system dedicated to serving that particular network. Most of the larger networks have their own connections. CompuServe, GEnie, and Dialog all have their own communication networks in place. You place a local call and are "magically" hooked up to Columbus, Ohio (CompuServe), or Rockville, Maryland (GEnie), or Palo Alto, California (Dialog) in an instant. These links are generally free of excessive line noises and respond with a minimum of delay to your interactions.

However, a large segment of the population does not enjoy the electronic benefits of urban life. In most small towns and even some medium-size cities, direct connections to the major information systems are not available. There are no local numbers to call to access the systems. Are you relegated to placing a long-distance phone call to the nearest city with an access number? To do so would certainly put a damper on your enthusiasm for using electronic libraries and communications systems. The cost of a toll call added to the access charges levied by the systems themselves would strain the budgets of most small businesses. Fortunately, when there is a niche for services in American business, the niche usually gets filled. The problem of achieving a less expensive telephone passageway is no exception.

With the packet-switching or "public data" networks (PDN)—the major ones in the United States are Telenet and Tymnet—virtually all areas of the country are served with a low-cost alternative to long-distance calling. Telenet, alone, offers nearly 17,000 local telephone exchanges for entry. While certainly not every phone exchange in the country is supplied, the areas without either Telenet or Tymnet services are few and far between. With them, telecommunications becomes much more affordable and available than it is if one had to rely on the standard telephone system.

Telenet and Tymnet are, in simplest terms, high-tech versions of the old party-line phone systems. You may or may not be old enough to remember party lines, which were shared phone numbers that served several separate households. When telephone cable was at a premium in the "old days" (the 1950s), the connections were made using a co-op system. That is the principle behind packet-switching. Instead of having a dedicated system serving each individual information system, Telenet and Tymnet allow calls to be shared among all users. The result is that where there is sharing, there is cost reduction.

COMPUTERS TALKING TO COMPUTERS TALKING TO COMPUTERS

When you place a call to a Telenet or Tymnet access number, you are really calling another local computer with a modem. Usually, more than one modem is connected to allow more than one caller to use the local number at the same time. The calls are handled on a rotating basis and each call is accepted and circuited to an open modem. Each local "node" (composed of a computer or computers and their supporting modems) can handle six or more local calls simultaneously. It is possible to get a busy signal (or more commonly, no answer) when the local ports are filled, particularly at peak usage hours, but such an occurrence is rare.

Once your system is connected, some truly innovative electronic sleight of hand is carried out. The node's computer functions as your basic mail clerk. Instead of dealing with ZIP code–tagged paper mail, the node deals with mail of an electronic nature, coded for its destination system. For example, when you connect to a Telenet node and are prompted for which system you want to reach, you enter a "C xxxxxx" sequence. The "C" means Connect to and the "xxxxxx" is a unique system identifier given to each destination served by Telenet. For example, to designate CompuServe, you enter "C 202202." These codes are the ZIP codes for your subsequent transmission.

After that, the "magic" starts. The node acts to collect transmissions seeking a common destination, and collects the bits received into electronic "packets." Each packet is about 128 bytes of data. The systems wait until a packet is full (or until an "idle timer" has expired, after about one-tenth of a second) and then tags the incoming information identifying it as to which is yours and which is another user's. The data is then sent along the lines to another node in the Telenet chain. The packet is then examined with new data from that local node being added or removed), repackaged and retagged, and moved along to another node. The routing instructions issued by the nodes at each step of the way may change for each packet, depending on the least busy route, as determined by the node computer. Through this series of packaging and repackaging, the information is transported through the fastest (if not always the shortest) route to its target.

As you were reading this discussion, you might have been remembering the mail clerk analogy and been assuming that the process is tediously slow. Not at all. Certainly the routes that your data may have to negotiate are not as fast as the direct, dedicated system lines available to those in the larger cities. However, the difference in transmission speeds is hardly noticeable. The information you type in at your keyboard will reach the host system in fractions of a second, even with the packet-switching taking place all along the way. While this is usually true, you should be aware that when peak usage is in effect (generally, from 6:00 P.M. until midnight, your local time) things may slow down a bit. The data returned from your host may not show up for a second or two and then it may race across your screen at breakneck speed. This variation is nothing more than a packet being received back from the host and being separated and dumped to your computer. When you remember that the node modems are transmitting your data not at your modem's speed of 300, 1200, or 2400 baud, but at 9600 baud, you can grasp why things do happen so quickly.

There may be times when there is a noticeable delay in the appearance of what you type in at the keyboard showing up on your screen (remember, it must be echoed back from the remote host). When you consider the meandering path your data takes, the transmission delays are not bad at all.

The cost savings make the minor delays in data exchange even more acceptable. Telenet and Tymnet charges are only $2 per hour between 6:00 P.M. and 6:00 A.M. Monday through Thursday and from 6:00 P.M. Friday to 6:00 A.M. Monday. During the prime usage hours—the hours between 6:00 A.M. and 6:00 P.M. Monday through Thursday—charges are $10 per hour. When compared to long-distance rates, packet-switching is much more cost-effective. The charges are also conveniently billed through the commercial host as well, so you do not get a separate bill from Tymnet or Telenet. Your CompuServe, The Source, or other network account will automatically include these packet-switching charges right along with your access charges.

How busy are these packet-switching systems? Telenet alone is said to handle over 10 million data calls and log over 1 million connect hours per month. They transmit over 1 billion packets of data or the equivalent of 28 million typed pages of information. Now that is a lot of activity.

FREE PRACTICE

If you want to experiment with your modem without charge before you tackle the pay-as-you-go systems, Telenet and Tymnet make it easy. Each runs its own free information system as part of its network. You can access these information system hosts from any Telenet or Tymnet node, and there are no charges for fooling around with them.

Tymnet.　The Tymnet information system is the best for practicing with menus and different modem and software settings. Just call any Tymnet access number. If you are calling at 300 baud, you should receive the following message:

please type your terminal identifier:

If you are using 1200 baud or higher, you will instead see

xxxx@#$xxx#$xxxxx@#$xxx!@ (and so on)

or something similar. Why? Because Tymnet answers every modem call expecting the user's modem to be running at 300 baud. Earlier, we discussed what you see on your screen when there are mismatched baud rates. When you access Tymnet at baud rates above 300, you see the gobbledygook.

As soon as you press "A" (the same as you would to answer the real query about your terminal identifier), Tymnet will recognize that you are using a higher baud rate and switch speeds. Thereafter, the transmission is readable.

After you have your baud rates straightened out, you should see a number which identifies the node you have reached (unique for every local Tymnet number). You will see

-4443-001-
please log in:

At this point you enter the specific code for the system you want to switch to. For CompuServe, for example, the code is "CIS02." Each host served by Tymnet (and Telenet) has a unique identification (ID) number. (By the way, the codes used for a given host are not the same on Telenet and Tymnet.) To connect to the Tymnet Information System, type in "information" at this point. You will then be presented with the following menu:

TYMNET INFORMATION SERVICE

Welcome to TYMNET's Information Service! TYMNET is the world's largest Public Data Network, with local access in over 750 U.S. and Canadian cities and access to and from over 70 foreign countries.

MAIN MENU

1. **Direct Dial & Outdial (R) Access**
2. **Data Base and Timesharing Services**
3. **International Access**
4. **Certified Products**
5. **Computers Interfaced to TYMNET (R)**
6. **Sales Office Directory**
7. **Technical and User Documentation**
8. **Electronic University Network (R)**

If you need assistance, type 'HELP'. When you are finished, type 'QUIT'. Type the number of the desired menu item at the prompt.

YOUR SELECTION:

On this thoughtful service, you can learn how to manipulate your software to scroll information to your printer, capture information to your disk, and move through a menu system. Just choose a number from the menu and follow it with your Enter key or carriage return key, and then you can maneuver about. And remember, it does not cost a cent.

Telenet. Telenet has a smaller information system as well. It can be reached by calling any Telenet number. When you have connected, press your Enter key or carriage return key twice. You will then see

TERMINAL=

Simply press the Enter key here. You are then presented with the character "@" (or "caret"). This is Telenet's request for a system ID code (analogous to Tymnet's "please log in"). To get to Telenet's information system, type in "mail." You are then asked for an ID code. Reply with "phones" and a carriage return. Next, you are asked for a password. Enter "phones" again with a carriage return. From here you should be whisked away to the Telenet menu system. There are few choices other than to get a listing of access numbers, but that is all it was meant to do. You can practice your "software footwork" nevertheless.

INTERNATIONAL NETWORKS

While Telenet and Tymnet dominate in the United States, there are other providers that serve the same purpose for data transfer in their areas. Canada's Datapac and France's Transpac are examples. And interconnectivity, since the networks adhere to CCITT X.25 or X.75 protocols, can be achieved. For example, Tymnet offers international connections to 70 countries, from Antigua to Zimbabwe. Making international connections is still an intricate process, but it can be done and is a way of life in some international companies. For this reason, you should be aware that it exists.

RESOURCE LIST: MODEM MANUFACTURERS

AT&T Information Systems
P.O. Box 19901
Indianapolis, IN 46219
800/432-6600

Hayes
705 Westech Dr.
Norcross, GA 30092
404/449-8791

Cermetek Microelectronics
1308 Borregas Ave.
Sunnyvale, CA 94088-3565
800/862-6271

IBM Corporation
1000 NW 51st Street
Boca Raton, FL 33432
800/447-4700

Commodore
1200 Wilson Dr.
West Chester, PA 19380
215/431-9100

Prentice Corp.
266 Caspian Dr.
Box 3544
Sunnyvale, CA 94088
408/734-9855

Prometheus Products, Inc.
P.O. Box 4156
Fremont, CA 94539
415/490-2370

U.S. Robotics, Inc.
8100 N. McCormick Blvd.
Skokie, IL 60076
312/982-5010

Racal-Vadic
1525 McCarthy Blvd.
Milpitas, CA 95035
408/946-2227

Ven-Tel Inc.
2342 Walsh Avenue
Santa Clara, CA 95051
408/727-5721

The April 26, 1988 issue of *PC Magazine* reviewed 13 modems offering 9600-baud operations. They included Cermetek (9600E), U.S. Robotics (Courier HST), Racal-Vadic (9600VP), and Hayes (Smartmodem 9600). Other companies listed for 9600-baud operation included

Codex Corp.
7 Blue Hill River Road
Canton, MA 02021
617/364-2000

Microcom Inc.
1400A Providence Hwy.
Norwood, MA 02062
617/762-9310

Data Race, Inc.
12758 Cimmaron Path #108
San Antonio, TX 78249
512/692-3909

Telebit Corp.
1345 Shorebird Way
Mountain View, CA 94043
415/969-3800

Fastcomm Communications Corp.
12347 E. Sunrise Valley Dr.
Reston, VA 22091
703/630-3900

Universal Data Systems
5000 Bradford Avenue
Huntsville, AL 35805
205/721-8000

Gandalf Data Inc.
1020 S. Noel Avenue
Wheeling, IL 60090
312/541-6060

Companies that manufacture portable modems include

Novation Inc.
21345 Lassen Street
Chatsworth, CA 91311
818/998-5060

TGI Touchbase Systems Inc.
160 Laurel Avenue
Northport, NY 11768
516/261-0423

3

Buying Software

The most expensive, state-of-the-art, top-of-the-line computers and modems can do very little on their own. In point of fact, they can do absolutely *nothing* on their own. All those expensive silicon chips and shiny, printed circuit boards they plug into will just soak up electricity and emit barely enough warmth to warm a hamster cage without instructions. They need someone to tell them what to do—every step of the way. That someone is the computer programmer. This rare breed of human can sit and write instructions for the computer in a language (usually with mysterious names like C or Prolog or ADA or Fortran) the machine can comprehend. These instructions (usually in the form of software) are read by the computer and then, and only then, can the magic of the computer begin.

In computer communication it is not so much the type of machine that is important, but the quality of the software you use. As discussed in Chapter 2, the brand of computer, itself, has very little to do with the effectiveness and even speed with which you accomplish your communications tasks. That is determined more by the modem you use with the computer. Similarly, it is the software—not the computer—that will determine how successful and easy your online sessions are. How to choose that package is what this chapter is about.

THE GOLDEN RULE OF COMPUTER SUCCESS

Before specifically addressing buying communications software, we need to think about the process of selecting programs in general. There is no more critical rule in buying a computer than to first find software that can provide what you need to accomplish your objectives, then—and only then—choose the hardware you need to run it. This should be called the golden rule of computer success. Far too many new buyers are sold the hardware and then are stuck with the process of fitting the software to this least important part of the success formula. Before you have a computer, buying software—and you can apply this to any software—should be a four-step process: (1) identify your needs, (2) talk to other computer users, (3) choose the software, and (4) choose hardware that will run the software. These steps are discussed below.

IDENTIFY YOUR NEEDS

Sit down and write out what you want to be able to do with your computer. Do you want to do word processing? spreadsheets? accounting and bookkeeping? database management? communications? There are some excellent, general-interest books describing exactly what these and other functions are and how they can be used in your business. Think of the future as well. It is certainly best to make your decisions based on what you want to implement initially, but leave yourself some room to grow.

TALK TO OTHER COMPUTER USERS

Talk to others in your community who are already using computers. Don't be hesitant to let others know you are new to computers and really have a lot to learn. Most of them will enjoy sharing their successes and, perhaps even more valuable, their failures, with you. Another underutilized resource is the local users group. These groups are found in most every community and are made up of people who use computers. The members meet on a regular schedule to discuss their problems and triumphs with computers, demonstrate software, and how they are using it, and generally provide, perhaps, the most unbiased, frank evaluations of what is new in the marketplace that you will find. These are the grassroots users. They are not tied to any commercial gains. They, in the immortal words of Howard Cosell, "tell it like it is." If you want to know what the really useful software is, this is the place to ask. Even if you have not joined their ranks as a computer user, you will be welcomed, and your questions, regardless of how rudimentary, will be answered.

How do you find a users group? If the owners you already know aren't aware of when and where a group meets, call the computer stores. They will usually be able to direct you to a contact person. So ask around. Before you step one foot in a retail computer store, soak up information from your friends, associates, suppliers, and other sources (but remember that people are often biased toward what they own and are using, as discussed in Chapter 1). Once you have gathered some preliminary opinions, it's time to go to the library. Read all you can about computer software—what is on the market, product comparisons, product reviews, and so on. This may seem self-evident, but this step is often overlooked. Verify the "hot tips" you acquired through word of mouth.

There are a number of excellent magazines covering the computer industry that provide some clear, hard-hitting reviews and comparisons of the available software and hardware products. Confirm that the local "intelligence" and impressions are shared by the national experts. Even if there are products rated higher than what your friends are recommending, having someone who is actively using the software locally may be a factor to sway you in the other direction. Having a local "expert" can help you to get up and running more quickly. Use the software yourself. Use any software for an hour or more before you buy. Read at least a chapter or two of the instructions ("documentation") that is provided with the software. Does it make sense to you? Is it written in plain English or jargon? Does it assume you are a inveterate hacker or a novice?

CHOOSE THE SOFTWARE

Pick out the software that will help you accomplish what you need to do in a way that seems most comfortable to you. You can determine this aspect by watching the software being run at a local computer store (or users group) and by using it yourself. While a veteran may be able to make the software sing and dance with amazing speed and dexterity, keep in mind that you are the one who will be using it in your business. While the opinions of the national experts and your local gurus are important to consider, buying software is a very personal thing. Even if you are a novice in using computers, how the software operates—called, in the jargon, the "user interface"—is a variable which can only be dealt with on a very personal, gut level.

The keystrokes used to perform the various software functions on a specific program may be intuitive to one person with one program and totally inane to another person using the same program. When you are first starting with computers it is a minor problem, because prior computer experiences and expectations do not influence your thinking. However, as you use more programs for different purposes, these biases become more apparent. It is this interaction between the software and the user that determines, more than any other factor, how fast the user gets up and running productively. Make sure that the software "feels right" to you. This is where you must break away from the crowd of experts you consulted to start with. Just because Joe next door likes Program X, that doesn't mean you will feel comfortable with it. At this point it is important that you go by your own instincts.

CHOOSE THE HARDWARE

Finally, find out which computer will run the software you have selected and buy it. Pick a system that is adaptable and expandable. Don't box yourself in. You will, as you implement computers in one area of use, quickly become aware of other functions they could be doing for your business. As you can see, the hardware (the computer) purchase is the last in the logical first-purchase sequence. This is as it should be, but often isn't.

WHERE TO FIND SOFTWARE

Software is marketed and distributed through four basic channels. In order of price, but certainly not sophistication or capabilities, kinds of software, based on their distribution channels, are public domain, user-supported, commercial, and customized.

PUBLIC-DOMAIN SOFTWARE

In the early days of computing, most of the programming for computers was done by hobbyists who made their work freely available to anyone who wanted a copy. It was free without strings, to be shared with everyone who wanted to try it out. The only rewards available to these programmers were the accolades they received from those who tried the software and found it useful. But, in a time when computers were used by only a small band of devotees, that was all anyone could really hope for. The potential marketplace was small, and little commercial return was available.

This form of software is alive and strong even today, even with the mass of possible customers. While it lacks the slick documentation and 1-800 help lines typical of the classic commercial packages, there are still innumerable pearls in this universe. Examples of what is available absolutely free is best seen in the program libraries of the local users group. Once you have established an online connection with a modem and communications software, you can download (see below) other programs from electronic libraries maintained on national networks (such as CompuServe, GEnie, and Delphi) or from the local "bulletin board systems" (BBSs) in your area.

USER-SUPPORTED SOFTWARE

When Andrew Fluegelman wrote the communications software PC-Talk, he had neither the funds nor the network to take his package to the buying public with printed ads or a high-priced marketing plan. He chose another route. He called it "Freeware." He trademarked the name, and today the method goes by the names *user-supported software* or *shareware*. It is a simple scheme, regardless of the name applied. You are allowed to freely copy and distribute this kind of software to anyone. New users put the software through its paces, and, if they decide it is something they will use after the trial period, they send payment to the author. The software is still copyrighted, and users have the same legal responsibility for payment as they do for more conventionally marketed software. You cannot sell the software (other than a small fee for reproducing it on diskettes), nor can you modify it, call it your own, and sell it for profit. The concept is a marketing one: Let the users, themselves, distribute, advertise (by word of mouth), and reproduce the software for the author. The instructions for using the program are usually provided as a file that must be printed out from your own computer and printer. Of course, the underlying premise is that when computer owners use the software they will pay for it. When a copy is paid for ("registered"), the buyer sometimes gets a printed and bound copy of the documentation as well as support (a phone number to call to ask questions); also, future improvements ("upgrades") to the software will sometimes be sent free of charge.

The success of the marketing system quite obviously hinges on the honesty of the users. Today, it remains a viable alternative to the programmer who has little funds to mount an advertising campaign but has produced a quality product. For some, it has been quite successful; for others, it has been disappointing. But, the fact remains that the software in this genre is often as good or better than many orthodox commercial packages. These programs are available at users groups and electronic networks as well as through the authors themselves.

What's available? Virtually everything across the spectrum of software products—communications, databases, spreadsheets, taxes and accounting, word processing, etc. The Association of Shareware Professionals (325 118th Avenue SE, Suite #200, Bellevue, WA 98005) was formed in 1987 to provide a validating group for these unique programmers and to provide standards for this type of product. The Association is another contact point if you are interested in this approach to buying or selling software. For sources to write for catalogs of available programs, see Chapter 8.

COMMERCIAL SOFTWARE

While user-supported software is certainly "commercial" in every sense of the word, this category will be used to group that software produced and distributed through more traditional outlets—computer and software stores and mail-order companies. Their products are the glossy, shiny, shrink-wrapped, heavily advertised offerings you see on the shelves of your local stores. They are also the subjects of most of the reviews in computer magazines and books. These are the name brands of software—Microsoft, Ashton-Tate, Borland, Lotus, and others—familiar to you if you have done your homework.

Where to Buy Software.   Where should you buy software? The local store's price for software may seem much higher than some of the prices in the mail-order ads you will invariably run across in computer magazines. Certainly, mail-order prices are much cheaper, sometimes by hundreds of dollars. Why is there such a price difference? Because when you buy software from a store you are paying for "service after the sale." This trite expression means several things in buying software. First, you are buying convenience from your local retailer. You are paying for the chance to try out the software at the store. When you buy mail order, you give up this privilege, because most software is nonreturnable. There is a very simple reason for this. Software, in 99 percent of cases, can be copied. This feature is necessary for the legitimate owners so that they can make backups in case their original disks fail, get lost, or ruined by some natural disaster. But there are some unscrupulous souls (actually, they are plain thieves) that will buy software, copy it, and pass it around or even try to return it to the seller. It is, therefore, an unfortunate fact of life that there is often a "no return" policy for software sales.

Despite the fact that commercial software packages are shrink-wrapped and often carry imposing agreements on the cover, at your local dealer you can usually try before you buy. Your local retail outlet should have a demonstration copy of the program opened and ready to run. Insist on it. After all, you are paying for the privilege. Would you buy a car before you have taken it on a test drive? With the price of some of these software products running up to several hundreds of dollars, it is bad judgment not to give them a test drive as well. Ask the dealer to show you the software package. Have the dealer put the software that interests you through its paces. But don't stop there. Ask to use the package yourself. Seldom will you be able to take the package home or return the package after you have bought it, so set aside a few hours to use the programs in the store.

Software Support from Sales Personnel.   When you pay the higher price for software at a local store you are also buying the local sales personnel's ability to teach you how to use the software and resolve your problems with it after the sale. When you buy via mail order, you will often pay less, but you give up the hand-holding you will probably need to get started.

For the new user, it is generally prudent to gulp down the added costs and buy from someone nearby (depending on the software you are shopping for). If, however, the salesperson does not offer to provide the support you have paid so handsomely for, you give up this advantage. But you should not give up the dollars as well. Make sure your salesperson understands and agrees to this contract. Get it put into writing if you have any doubts. Let the people at the store know that you will probably be back and that you expect to receive some attention after they have your check. Ask questions early on, also, before you buy, to make sure that the retailer is familiar with the software and that the personnel can communicate with you in a way that you can understand and benefit from. Many computer and software dealerships teach regular classes, either at no charge or for nominal cost, for the more popular commercial packages.

CUSTOM SOFTWARE

Some businesses have specific software needs that simply cannot be met by off-the-shelf packages. With the software industry as mature as it is today, this is a rare occurrence, but it does still happen. Since you are probably just starting off with computers, your needs are probably not yet clearly defined. But later they will be, and you should be aware that there are custom software programmers who will, for a hefty fee, write a program that addresses your specific needs. The costs are very high, which should encourage you to exhaust all other possible avenues before you seek custom software development. If you have any doubts about your knowledge of the available software, it is more cost-effective to hire a consultant (who may or may not be a programmer) to assess your needs and make recommendations before you jump to the next step of a custom package. For more about how to find and chose a computer consultant, see "How to Find and Select a Computer Consultant" later in this chapter.

COMMUNICATIONS SOFTWARE

Fortunately, there are dozens of communications programs available today. You will be able to find one just right for your needs and at a price you can afford. But with the riches comes a certain degree of confusion. How can you separate the good from the bad? What features should you look for in software packages of this type? The functions available can be categorized into three groups:

- Essential features
- "Nice to have" features
- Superfluous features

Another brief disgression is appropriate here before we discuss these three categories of features. Why are the software programs used to run a telecommunications session often referred to as *terminal emulator software?* A simple answer which is rooted in the history of pre-PC, pre-modem computer hookups will explain everything. *Terminal emulator* is a term that refers to the way old-fashioned computer mainframes are linked up through direct wiring (other than by modems) to their peripheral work stations. These work stations—each of which consists of little more than a video display and a keyboard—are referred to as *terminals.* These stations are where users in the accounting department or personnel department, for example, access the storage and computing power of the large mainframes and enter or retrieve data (although the PC and modems have begun to change this scenario). The terminals usually have no storage capacity of their own and can only transmit and receive data to and from the larger computers to which they are connected. What comes across the video display is lost forever, unless the terminal is connected to a printer and the output is directed to paper. Such terminals generally cannot run any software, and therefore they rely upon the host mainframe to direct their activities. For this reason they were dubbed "dumb terminals."

These terminals have importance to us as modern telecommunicators because the large computers we wish to connect to are still set up to handle the standard screen displays used by these old-fashioned work stations. (Don't get the idea that the days of the dumb terminal are long-since dead: it was not until around 1986 that the sales of PCs surpassed those of dumb terminals. They are, indeed, still of importance as inexpensive tools to access both in-house and remote mainframes). In fact, these standards are so important to these mainframes that our computers need to be able to emulate or impersonate one of these standard dumb terminals. A PC, with all its "smarts" and storage and speed, must be reduced to the level of a dumb terminal before the mainframes can talk to it and control how the information we receive appears on the monitor's display. For the remote computer to send text to a PC in a format that we can read on the video, we must have software that makes the PC screen display information the way a terminal does. Thus, the software is called terminal emulator software. We will talk more about the different terminal emulation modes later.

Now, what features should you look for in terminal emulator software? Let's talk about the "essential" features first.

ESSENTIAL FEATURES

Compatibility with the Modem.   First and foremost, the software should support your particular modem. That may sound odd to mention, but some packages rely on specific features of a modem for the software to work properly, and it is important to test the package completely with the modem you plan to use before buying the package. Most software today is set up to use the Hayes standard command set, based on the modems produced by the de facto industry standard, the Hayes series of Smartmodems (Hayes Microcomputer Products, Inc., Norcross, GA). While most other brands of modems sold claim to be "100 percent Hayes compatible," the manufacturers neglect, sometimes, to tell you which "100 percent." This varies from manufacturer to manufacturer and can be a problem. Without true duplication of the Hayes commands, the modem may not be able to function to a Hayes modem's full potential or, worse, may be completely useless with a given software package which expects to be working with strict Hayes standards. Choose wisely and try before you buy. Insist, again, on trying out the specific combination of computer-modem-software at a dealer before you buy. It is not by accident that this feature has number one ranking in our "essential" category.

Flexible Communications Settings. The software should have flexible communications settings. You should be able easily to change from 8-bit, no parity, full-duplex to 7 bit, even (or odd) parity, half-duplex (see Chapter 2), both before connecting and after the hookup is made. It is inconvenient to have to disconnect and redial if your first setup is incorrect.

Variable Storage Options for Text-Based Information. You should be able to direct text-based information to be stored in a variety of ways. The whole purpose of using remote computer systems is to exchange information. The data you will most often seek is in simple text or ASCII form (the only real exception is the "protocol transfer," which is discussed below). This is the same form that you see presented on your computer monitor as you maneuver on the networks. When you read your electronic mail (E-mail, see Chapter 4) or look up an important stock quote or journal article (Chapter 5), you need to have some way to capture the words and sentences as they scroll across your screen so that you can read or manipulate the information after you have disconnected from the provider. There are three ways available to you with most software.

The first, and most useful way, is to direct everything that comes across your connection to be stored automatically to a disk. As the data flies across your screen, periodically it is "written" to your disk as a file. This file can then be loaded into a word processor and read, leisurely, after you have hung up on the host. Even more, the text that you have captured can be manipulated—

you can add comments or additional facts to it, and then you print it out for others to read as well. The second way to archive (store) the characters received is by directing them straight to a printer. This option has its obvious drawbacks, though. If the printed copy is all that you have, someone would have to retype the information on a word processor or typewriter if you wanted to add anything to it. Unless you need an immediate printed copy, it is better to preserve the text flow to disk and then print it out later in the format you desire and with the corrections or additions you need to make. The third method is the use of a "screen buffer," discussed more fully below under "Nonessential Features." In essence, this method makes use of the computer's own memory chips to store the information in temporary hold so that you can move the product elsewhere after hanging up. This is the fastest method of storing data, but it depends entirely on your remembering to save it to disk or print it out before you exit the program. This method is also contingent on your having a computer with a robust memory excess. One caveat: If, by some accident, you suddenly lose power to your computer, everything stored in the screen buffer is lost as well. Your emulator software should, ideally, offer all three modes as each may be needed under certain circumstances.

Ability to Emulate Several Terminal Protocols. Finally, the software should be able to emulate several of the standard dumb terminal protocols mentioned earlier. The most common protocols you will run into are (in no particular order) the Wyse 100, the IBM 3101, the VT-52 and VT-100, the Lier-Siegler (LS) ADM5, and the TVI 920 and 950. If your software can mimic at least three of these terminals, you should have no trouble with any system you are likely to connect with.

Since we will be dealing, primarily, with text-based information, these are the main features you absolutely, positively need in a software package. Other computer users may (and probably do) disagree. But if you can set up flexible communications parameters, connect to a remote system simply and efficiently, and capture the information you are after, additional features are just icing on the cake.

THE "NICE TO HAVE'S"

Online Help. Online help is nice. This feature allows you to press a specified key (often F1, "?," CTRL-H, or some other combined key press) and get a "help screen" of instructions for whatever you are doing at the time you request help ("context-sensitive help"). When you are learning how to use a package, online help could almost qualify as an essential feature.

Ability to Exit to DOS While Maintaining Connection.   Exit to DOS (*Disk-Operating System*) without breaking connection is another feature on the fence between "essential" and "nice to have." This feature allows you to leave the communication mode at any time, exit the program, and then perform any number of functions of your particular DOS. You could, depending on your DOS, delete files on your disk to make room for saving more data there, find the name of a file you need to send to your host computer, or even format a disk to make room for an unexpectedly large download. This can be a lifesaver during those rare but unpredictable occurrences that make up "the perils of online communications."

Script Language.   A script language in the program is a "nice to have," because it certainly can make some repetitive communications tasks easy. With some software programs, there is a built-in programming language of sorts. The language, like any other computer language, has specific commands and actions. And, like any other computer language, learning the syntax can be challenging. But once you have learned it, you will be able to run scripts to automate virtually your entire communications session. You can have the software dial a remote computer, enter your identification and password, access a specific area of its files, select information or program files, capture them in the manner you specify, and then log you off the system. All without your ever touching the keyboard. If you plan on doing a lot of online work (and you should!), this capability moves very close to the "essential" category. For the infrequent user, it is a nice feature to have available.

Macro Capability.   Macros are single or combined keystrokes that can be set up to send a much longer phrase to a remote system. Let's use an example here to clarify. Suppose you wanted to enter the phrase "GO EXCALIBUR" at some point in your communications session. With macro capability in your software you could set up a specific key combination (such as ALT-F1 or just F1) to represent that 12-keystroke phrase. An even nicer feature is the ability of your software to access multiple macro files—one file for each system you use, with each file containing its own set of macro command phrases. Again, nice to have, certainly.

Dialing Directory.   The emulator should have a dialing directory for your frequently called phone numbers, and it should be able to save the numbers and their communication settings so that, once you set them up, you do not need to enter or change them each time you want to dial a system. The size of the dialing directory is frequently flaunted by some software ads;

however, most people seldom need more than a few dozen. A 100-number dialing directory is hardly something you will crave.

NONESSENTIAL FEATURES

Memory-Resident Mode.   Some emulators have been designed to fit in with the current software craze and can operate in a "memory-resident mode" [or "terminate and stay resident," (TSR)]. The program loads and stores itself in a segment of the computer's memory where it lies dormant and out of sight. You can call the program into action by pressing a special key, which can be done, generally, at any time, even while you are using another program. You could, for example, be operating a spreadsheet program or your word processor and, having the sudden urge to go online, press the designated key and have the emulator jump right out of its idle state to allow you to go online. Then, when you were finished online, you would be returned right to the place in the spreadsheet or word processor where you left it. You would not have to exit the program you were working in to use the emulator. Examples of software having this ability are SideTalk (Lattice, Inc., P.O. Box 3072, Glen Ellyn, IL 60138) and BackComm (LaSalle Micro, Inc., 1254 Devonshire Rd., Buffalo Grove, IL 60089). Both programs are for the MS-DOS market.

Background Operation Mode.   Once you get online and start doing some program downloads from a system to your computer, you will sometimes be frustrated at the length of time your computer is tied up with the task. Some longer programs can take over an hour to download. Some emulators can operate in a "background" mode, which means they can start a download and continue it while returning your computer control back to you. You can then move on to some other task while the downloading continues. You no longer have a lot of dead time while you computer is tied up with an online task. This feature is very useful if your computer sports a fast enough microprocessor (the control unit of the machine). Otherwise, you will notice some real delays in how your other programs function while a download is taking place.

Learn Protocol.   When you are first starting out, particularly if you do not have the time to master writing script files to direct your online actions, you might want to look for a "learn" feature in your emulator. With a good learn protocol, the software "watches" you sign onto a system the first time, noting how the remote system prompts you for your password and what you enter, how the remote asks you for what you would like to look at next and what you enter, etc. The software then will write its own script file for that system. The next time you log on to the remote computer, you can run the script file that the software, itself, wrote, and save yourself those extra keystrokes. It is just as if you wrote the action file yourself. For those who plan to do a lot of online work and have no desire to work through writing their own scripts, the learn feature can be quite useful. Unfortunately, it is still a rare bird among currently offered software packages and is usually found only in the more expensive programs. (This will undoubtedly change, though).

Word Processing Capabilities.   Some terminal emulators come with their own word processors. These are usually relatively limited in capabilities and will not replace your full-featured editor, but they can be convenient to have available with your emulator. When you telecommunicate, your goal is to communicate with others. Composing and sending messages to online contacts is part of the technology's attractiveness. The process of writing messages should *always* be done while you are disconnected from the host. No human can type error-free at 120 letters per second, so composing messages online is costly and counterproductive. Get offline, compose what you want to say with an editor, reconnect, and upload your message. Having the editor built right into the emulator makes the process quick and easy. But you do, then, have to learn how to use another program (the emulator's editor). Some packages go one step further and allow you to use your own favorite word processor from within the emulator. This is much easier, as you do not have to assimilate another program. You tell the communications software what program you want to use for a word processor, where and how to load it, and then, when you press the key to call up the editor, your old standby editor is loaded. No new learning required.

Screen Buffer.   Screen buffers of various sizes are offered by many software packages. A *screen buffer* is simply a part of memory that is blocked off (designated) to keep the words and sentences in as they scroll by on your screen. Then, at any time, you can press a key and scroll back through whatever has already passed off your screen. It is not lost forever with a screen buffer. [A buffer can be likened to a water hose. The size (in kilobytes) determines the length of the hose. As water (data) is poured in one end, the buffer fills up until it is full and then the "oldest" water (data) spills out the other end as it is replaced by fresh water (new screen characters)]. If you wanted to reply to a long message that has been pushed off your screen by more information, you could, with a screen buffer, go back and review the message before or while you compose a reply. Some software, notably Crosstalk XVI (DCA, Inc., 1000 Holcomb Woods Pkwy., Roswell, GA 30076), has the ability to search selectively through a buffer for words and phrases. Screen buffers are nice, but hardly essential.

Screen Dump. Another screen feature offered by some emulators is a "screen dump." This feature enables you to take quick "snapshots" of your screen's display and have the screen in its entirety saved to disk. Suppose there is an important message on your screen and you neglected to have it printed to disk. Press the "hot" screen dump key and Voila! the screen is saved to your disk (usually as a plain ASCII or text file) and can be loaded into your word processor offline for review.

Character Filter. One feature that is often useful (but cannot be moved up in rank since it is not ordinarily needed) is a character filter. In many areas, phone lines are terribly noisy with electrical static. Those who have to use Telenet and Tymnet for communicatons may find that these lines are not as "clean" as a direct network connection. If they are not ideal, you may get a lot of "garbage" on your screen due to these electrical gremlins. The screen clears inadvertently, line feeds come out of the blue, and bizarre high-bit characters (characters in ASCII codes above 128 that show up on the screen as peculiar shapes) appear at random, unbidden. If your program has a character filter, you can instruct your software to screen the character codes coming through the phone line and remove, selectively, any particular characters or sets of characters that have no place in text information. This feature can be a lifesaver for those of us with less-than-ideal phone lines. Fortunately, most of you will not be so cursed.

Menu Mode. A menu mode of operation can help the novice ease into a program. With all the options presented on a menu, from which the users can pick and choose what they want to execute, program operation can be simplified and the learning curve for the package can be improved. The problem with menus is that, after you have learned a program, menus start to slow you down and get in the way. After awhile you know what you want to do, and going through three layers of menu choices to do it can be frustrating. The ideal software allows for both a menu mode for the greenhorn and a command mode—no menus—for the expert. Make sure when you buy a package with a nice menu interface that there is a way to turn it off when you want to start using the faster command mode. You will get to that stage quickly as you use the software and will curse the program that forces you to stay a beginner.

Remote Computer Operation. Some programs allow for "remote operations." This capability allows a user to call a computer that is running software of this type and, once a modem-to-modem connection is established, actually operate the host computer. By operate, we mean access files and actually run other computer programs on the host machine. For example, you could call into your home computer from another machine at work or elsewhere and run WordPerfect or Lotus 1-2-3 right on your home machine. Your activities within the program would show up on your computer and would appear just as if you were running WordPerfect or Lotus right from home. If you are out of the office and have a laptop portable computer with a modem handy, you can call into your office machine and retrieve any files you may have forgotten. It should be noted, though, that you must have a high-speed modem to run the software (but not, necessarily, to retrieve the files) off the remote machine effectively. At least a 2400-baud modem and preferably a 9600-baud transmission speed are required to make this tolerable. While not, in the strict sense, terminal emulator software, this class of package is noteworthy. One example of software that has this facility is Carbon Copy Plus (Meridian Technology, Inc.).

TRANSFER PROTOCOLS

We have saved for last the communications software feature called "transfer protocols," which most software packages have in some form. This was done because it requires a prolonged discussion. As stated, the main purpose of information access online is text retrieval: finding pure English text online, capturing it to your disk or printer, and exiting the remote system, stage left. You may (and probably will) eventually be enticed to obtain more from the host system. When you get online with CompuServe, GEnie, or your local BBS, you will find a wealth of public-domain (i.e., free) and shareware software programs available for you to download to your machine and subsequently run. These programs will execute just like a package from the local computer store (albeit, probably with less frills and features and with a manual you print out yourself). But transferring these special files to your machine involves more than just capturing text. The files are not text at all, but instead are a combination of special ASCII characters which, if you attempt to read them, will wreak havoc on your computer screen.

So, how do you get the files from Point A (a host computer) to Point B (your computer)? Virtually all communications programs have some kind of transfer mechanism to do this magic. In the jargon such a mechanism is called a *transfer protocol*, and it is nothing more than a standard set of rules that both computers "agree" upon so they know what to expect from each other when the transfer of information takes place. Since the transfer involves very specific information, very stringent error-checking routines must be followed by both machines. In text, an occasional character out of place is not a big deal. You can usually tell what the botched character was and replace it in the document by using a word processor. However, in a program transfer, one wrong bit of information is disastrous if you try to run the program. Furthermore, in most cases you don't know which bit is wrong and thus are unlikely to be able to fix it. With protocol transfers, errors are checked for at the receiving end, and, if an error is received, the receiver can tell the remote to resend the previous information (and to keep resending until the information is transmitted error-free). The information is sent in blocks of varying sizes, depending on the protocol being used. Each block is tested for accuracy as it is received, and even one bit out of sync can be detected. The process is quite accurate, as it must be.

Legend has it that the first error-checking protocol was developed by Ward Christenson for use on his and Randy Seuss's Chicago CBBS. From those simple origins, a new era was initiated. The ability to move programs effectively from one computer to another has, almost single-handedly, spawned "the BBS age." The phenomenon of the public BBS is still growing today. The software Christensen developed in the late 1970s for the first BBS included the XMODEM transfer protocol. For the first time, at least on a broad scale, remote users of a central computer could download more than just text files. The XMODEM protocol soon became the de facto standard of the file transfer protocols and is probably offered by every software package available today as well as every remote system, at least in one form or another.

Today, there are many other transfer protocols available. It is difficult to keep up with all that are available. Though XMODEM remains the standard, there are now such protocols as Kermit (yes, named after Jim Henson's famous frog) and a newer Super Kermit, Ymodem, Modem7, X.PC, and MNP, among others. Some emulator programs have their own protocols to allow computers running the same program to transfer files particularly fast; Crosstalk XVI is a prime example. Some remote systems, such as CompuServe, have also developed their own proprietary transfer protocols (as well as their own terminal emulator software to run on your machine). It can become somewhat confusing as you look at which emulators offer what protocols.

Don't get bogged down. If a software package has a good method of capturing text to disk or printer and has a solid Xmodem file transfer protocol, it probably has all that you will need. Don't be inordinately impressed with the packages that offer "13 file transfer protocols." You will not need them.

NETWORK-SPECIFIC COMMUNICATIONS SOFTWARE

Several of the larger general communications and information systems now make available software specifically designed for use on their networks (see Chapter 4). They may be produced by the system themselves, such as AT&T's Mail Access PLUS or CompuServe's Professional Connection. Furthermore, there are communications packages that have been developed by other manufacturers for use on specific systems. A couple of examples are Lotus's Express, designed for the MCI Mail system, and "TAPCIS," designed for use with CompuServe. Instead of having to "roll your own" script files and learn the commands to maneuver on these networks, you can use these packages to make your use of these systems almost automatic.

The key benefit of these packages is, simply, to make using the specific networks as "transparent" to the user as possible, which in communications software lingo means that rather than learning the specific system's commands, you learn just the software and it does all the maneuvering for you. Once you have set up the software (typically, with your identifying codes and passwords, the phone number to dial, and what you want to do on the system once connected), it links up with the specific network and does your bidding for you—transmitting all the commands for you, automatically—while you simply sit back and watch.

Advantages of Network-Specific Software. The advantages of using these packages are clear. They include:

1 *Simplification.* Learning how to use new software is easier than learning about an entire communications network. It's just a fact of life online. Though things are improving rapidly, you still have to wade through some awfully thick manuals and stumble around for hours learning how to navigate a new system's command structure to gain the proficiency you need to get your activities online up to optimum efficiency. With software expressly designed for a single system, you can get up and running much more quickly.

2 *Cost savings.* As a new user, you often have a mental clock running in your head every time you connect to a system; you see dollars rolling by as you painstakingly enter commands and fumble with the manuals. The initial slow-going is part of a natural learning process that can be worked through, but the fact that the meter is running can make the pressure at the start intense. The software allows you to get everything ready offline, and then it translates your commands into a language the communications provider can understand and enters the commands with maximum speed; hence, the pressure on you is lessened. The software can type faster than you and does not make typos. It knows what and how to enter commands. It does not have to consult a manual when it is confronted with a new prompt or enters unfamiliar turf. So the cost savings come into play at the start—by removing the initial time-consuming learning phase—but the savings can continue every time you have a communications session.

3 *Enhancement of the system.* Often specially designed software can enable you to do things on a network that you could not do using an ordinary terminal emulator. Lotus's Express for MCI Mail is a good exam-

ple. It offers two major enhancements. First, it can operate in a fully automated background mode (discussed previously in this chapter, under "Nonessential Features"). Once loaded into your computer's memory, Express can, at any time interval you set up, "poll" MCI for any mail you have waiting and retrieve it, all while you are either away from your machine or doing some other work with it. Second, you can transmit files other than simple ASCII messages to other MCI users who connect with Express (or even the Macintosh version, Desktop Express). These files can be, generally, anything—formatted word processor files, spreadsheets, or databases. As long as both you and your correspondent have Express, you can attach virtually anything a computer can store on it to message and send it across MCI.

Disadvantages of Network-Specific Software. The disadvantages of network-specific software are confined mainly to expense. Since the software is designed for use by a relatively narrow market (compared to more generic communications software which can be used on any system), they are often quite expensive. A cost of $100 to $150 is typical. That may, at first glance, seem outrageous for a program so limited in use. But, as suggested above, look again. If your communications are frequent and confined to a single network, a devoted terminal emulator can end up saving you money over the long term. The seconds saved with automation add up to serious money over weeks and months of frequent use.

HOW TO FIND AND SELECT A COMPUTER CONSULTANT
by Nick Cvetkovic

■■ Small businesses can benefit from the services of a computer consultant at the right time just as larger businesses can. Computer consultants can help bring the power of the computer to bear on solving business problems.

There are many reasons why a small business might want to avail itself of a computer consultant's services, but the reasons usually fall into one of three broad categories: system selection, system application, and training. Detailed treatment of these items is beyond the scope of this article, but a brief description of each will give more meaning to the task of finding and selecting a computer consultant.

Nick Cvetkovic is president of N.B.C. Associates, Inc., a Cherry Hill, New Jersey-based computer consulting firm. The firm is now in its tenth year of operation. It specializes in large-scale DBMS design and implementation but also helps small businesses implement microcomputer-based systems. Nick Cvetkovic, N.B.C. Associates, Inc., 808 Richard Road, Cherry Hill, New Jersey 08034-1838; 609-779-0202 (office) 609-779-8941 (home).

System selection involves helping a client decide on the right combination of hardware and software for the client's particular business needs. A consultant's experienced approach to system selection helps ensure that the system selected will be adequate for the client now and in the future and is not just the current special at the local computer store. Deciding which functions can best be computerized first is also a factor in system selection.

System applications means putting the computer to work where and when it makes the most sense to do so. It involves deciding whether an available commercial package can do the job. If not, a moderate amount of custom programming may be required. An experienced consultant will help a business avoid two of the most common mistakes: computerizing functions which are best done manually and failing to computerize those which are done best by the computer.

A computer consultant is in a good position to provide highly focused and effective training for a business that is just starting out with computers. Bringing specific industry and in-depth software package experience to bear on the training means that a business can get up to speed very efficiently. Most standard training classes are geared to a very generic, lowest-common-denominator class, which means that any introductory training will not have much specific content for any one person's needs. Using a consultant means that a business can schedule training at its convenience and for whatever time interval it has available.

Recognizing how and why a computer consultant can help a business in a cost-effective manner brings the business to the next hurdle of finding and selecting a qualified computer consultant. Since computer consultants charge from $25 to $75, and more, per hour, it's easy to see how their charges could very quickly amount to much more than the cost of the base hardware and software. Yet, utilizing a computer consultant where appropriate can result in advantages to the business that more than offset the fees. A consultant's understanding the major factors involved in the total evaluation process can prevent costly mistakes.

Computer consulting for small businesses is a new and very rapidly changing field. While the overwhelming majority of computer consultants are reputable, as well as highly capable, the potential problems of a mismatch are so large that the selection process must be undertaken with great care. Let's first look at how to find a computer consultant, and then look at what should go into the selection process and ways to avoid problems. We'll finish up by discussing the actual consulting services agreement between the computer consultant and the small business.

Finding a computer consultant is really very much like finding any other service specialist for your business. Personal referrals from other satisfied users is, by far, the best way to pre-qualify a potential candidate. A word-of-mouth recommendation from someone in a similar small business can be a powerful persuader that the computer consultant will be of help. Letting others know your business is seeking the help of a qualified computer consultant should result in some recommendations.

Other sources of possible computer consultants include the trade association of your particular industry, your local chamber of commerce, and any of the many associations of computer consultants. The Independent Computer Consultants Association, headquartered in St. Louis, Missouri, has chapters in many large cities. These chapters all offer some form of consultant referral service. The number 1-800-GET-ICCA will put you in touch with the nearest chapter. Many larger cities have personal-computer users groups. These user groups sometimes have consultant special interest subgroups which are another source of potential computer consultants. Attending a couple of meetings should turn up some people who have successfully used computer consultants. Choosing names from the Yellow Pages is the least-recommended method for finding a consultant.

Once a business has a small list of possible candidates, the selection process can begin in earnest. The first step is arranging for a brief interview. This session, which should always be provided at no charge to the small business, is very important and serves a number of purposes for both sides. This meeting helps to determine whether the chemistry is right, to make sure that the consultant is qualified for the job the business wants to have done, and to make sure that the consultant understands the needs of the business. This set of requirements is not as daunting as it may seem to a small business with no experience with either computers or computer consultants. The process is similar to qualifying any other professional service provider. You don't need a medical degree to understand whether a doctor will be helpful or not. On the other hand, there is no certification for a computer consultant that is equivalent to a medical degree, so the potential buyer must take some extra steps they might not take with a more established profession.

While many small businesses are familiar with selecting a service provider, it's helpful to discuss some points that are important to examine while talking with a potential consultant. Since the consultant is there to determine what your needs are, he or she needs to address your specific business needs. That means he or she should spend the majority of the time at the initial meeting either asking specific questions about your business or listening to your answers. As stated earlier, this session is provided free of charge, so the small business should take advantage of it.

Taking advantage means taking the steps to ensure that the consultant is suitable, but not trying to get the consultant to give away his or her solution.

This questioning and listening give-and-take should enable the small business to determine whether the consultant possesses the necessary expertise and good interpersonal skills, as well as a good reputation and ready references. While specific expertise and experience is important, an exposure to a broad set of problems and solutions makes for a more well-rounded consultant.

The small business should also take the initial and, if required, subsequent interview sessions to look for some "red flags." A red flag isn't an automatic reason for disqualifying a particular consultant, but, rather, is a warning to get further explanation. One red flag is that the consultant can begin at once. While, on rare occasions, a consultant may be between assignments, the good ones are busy at least 75 percent of the time. On the other hand, if a consultant looks harried, haggard, distracted, or tired it may be a danger sign that you are dealing with someone who is already overworked. This may or may not be a problem, depending on the nature of the problem you need to have solved. As indicated earlier, the consultant should spend most of the time either asking questions or listening to responses. The idea is that the consultant is there to absorb information about your business. People who talk too much may not be listening. Also, it's possible that consultants who are extremely quick to offer their own opinions may then go to great lengths to justify their own pre-conceived notions rather than producing insightful solutions after further study.

If it is successful, the interview process should establish a degree of rapport between the interviewer and the computer consultant that leaves the interviewer feeling comfortable. The potential client should now feel that the consultant is someone with whom the small business wants to working closely. All reputable computer consultants should be willing to provide a potential client with one, and preferably two or three, recent client references. It is extremely important that these references be checked. The only exception would be if the computer consultant had been referred to a business by someone who gave the detailed reference at the time of the original referral. Failure to check references is a common factor in most cases involving computer consultant–client dissatisfaction.

Computer consultants can be found in a large assortment of specialities and usually have very diverse backgrounds. However, the good ones tend to share some common qualities that can be checked for during the interview process. Some positive and negative signs were discussed earlier. Since a computer consultant can play such an important role in the small business's computer success or failure, after the interview you should ask yourself some of the following questions to assure a proper fit:

1 Does the consultant project an air of professionalism by appearing to be articulate and objective?

2 Does the consultant project an air of competence?

3 Does the consultant project an understanding or, at least, a real concern for your business's problems?

4 Does the consultant project a broad perspective rather than seeming to push a particular solution?

The proper answers to these questions can help to build your faith in the consultant's ability to perform well for your small business.

Even after you have checked the computer consultant's references to your satisfaction, come to believe in the consultant's ability to perform, and become comfortable dealing with the consultant face-to-face, there are still some other tasks you need to take care of prior to contractually engaging the consultant to do work for your small business. It is extremely important that the two parties define the scope of services to be performed and also a timetable and terms for payment.

Scope of services refers to what exactly the business is engaging the consultant to do for it. If the business doesn't know what its computer needs are then the scope of services might be for the consultant to define those needs in a specific way. Terms for the contract can be either time-and-materials or fixed price. Time-and-materials refers to a fixed rate per hour, whereas under a fixed price arrangement the full cost is stated up front as a specific dollar amount. Time-and-materials contracts are usually reserved for larger contracts and often have a "not to exceed" amount associated with them. It is usually to the small business's advantage to begin a relationship with a computer consultant who is confident enough to quote a fixed price for the proposed work; however, this will not be possible in all cases.

Now, having gone through the whole selection process and having agreed on the important details, the small business wants to get started right away. The consultant is eager to pencil this new business into his or her engagement calendar, now that he or she has passed a thorough and professional screening process. One more step is needed. The parties have to put their agreement into the form of a written, legally binding contract. While all consulting engagements should be defined and protective of both parties' rights via a written contract, the larger the contract is, the more important it is that the contract be correct for both parties.

Most local bookstores carry a book of business forms, and the consultant has a form for consulting services agreement, but it's extremely important that the small business have the agreement reviewed by its own attorney. Insisting on a written, attorney-blessed contract is a proper business practice and not a sign of doubt or mistrust. The written contract will help to protect both parties against unforeseen circumstances. It should also leave no open questions that can cause problems later. An example of the kinds of far-sighted questions the contract should answer is defining who owns the rights to the source code for a custom-developed program for the small business. The contract should spell out the previously discussed scope of services, and it should also define the terms of payment in specific dollar terms and specify dates or number of days. For example, will the invoice be paid upon receipt or in 30 days?

Once a contract has been agreed upon, the consulting engagement can begin in earnest. Computer consultants are usually highly motivated professionals in a rapidly changing and exciting profession. Making judicious use of their expertise can leverage your own special business expertise by combining it with the appropriate technology to increase your productivity and efficiency. ■■

THE VIRUS PROBLEM

As you have probably read in the general press, there is a problem lurking out there with some free software. The programs you retrieve from BBSs and commercial systems may be "infected" with so-called viruses. The sensationalism applied to this topic reached its peak with the incident in November 1988, when a student (the son of a major governmental computer security expert) was accused of implanting a virus in a national network of computers. The virus led to some serious problems, and the press made it a major story for weeks. (You can tell that a problem has reached significant public awareness when a prime-time soap opera weaves it into its continuing plot, as "Knot's Landing" (CBS) did in April 1989.) The problem has also become international in scope as viruses have been reported on computer systems in Russia as well. It should also be pointed out that commercial programs are not immune to virus infections either. It doesn't seem to matter where you get your software; any software can be susceptible to "attack." To begin to understand the problem and view it in a proper perspective (and it is not the perspective you might get from the news reports), you must know exactly what you might be dealing with.

Rob Rosenberger[1] and Ross Greenberg wrote a superb discussion of the problem of faulty programs and placed it on several systems to educate the computer user about the problem without adding to the rampant media hype. They define their terms first, some of which are already familiar to you:

BBS. Bulletin board system. If you have a modem, you can call a BBS and

[1] Rob Rosenberger has been working professionally as an IBM PC consultant since 1984. He is the author of Qanalyst, a shareware program that can accurately calculate the telephone costs of using a modem. Rosenberger is a member of the Association of Shareware Professionals (ASP) and is the official ASP product catalog editor. He is versed in information systems security and has experience in military computer security software. He is currently working as a systems programmer for a major defense contractor. You can write to him at Ansoft, 25 Neuner Drive, Fairview Heights, IL 62208.

leave messages, transfer computer files back and forth, and learn a lot about computers.

Bug. An accidental flaw in the logic of a computer program that makes it do things it shouldn't really be doing. Programmers don't mean to put bugs in their program, but they always seem to creep in. (The first bug was discovered by pioneer Grace Hopper when she found a dead moth shorting out a circuit in the early days of computers.) Programmers tend to spend more time debugging their programs than they do writing them in the first place.

Hacker. Someone who really loves computers and who wants to push them to the limit. Hackers don't release **Trojan horses** onto the world, it's the **wormers** who do that. Hackers have a healthy sense of curiosity: they try doorknobs just to see if they're locked, and they tinker with a piece of equipment until it's "just right."

Trojan horse. A set of computer instructions purposely hidden inside a program. A Trojan horse tells a program to do things you don't expect it to do. The term comes from a historic battle in which the ancient city of Troy was offered the "gift" of a large wooden horse that secretly held soldiers in its belly. The Trojans rolled the horse into their fortified city and the soldiers jumped out, ready for battle.

Virus. A term for a very specialized **Trojan horse** that can spread to other computers by secretly "infecting" programs with a copy of itself. A virus is the only type of **Trojan horse** which is contagious, like the common cold. If it doesn't meet this definition, then it isn't a virus.

Worm. A set of hidden computer instructions that is similar to a **Trojan horse** but with no "gift" involved. Worms do not get past the gate imbedded in a "gift," but they can bypass your defenses. An example of a worm is an unauthorized program designed to spread itself by exploiting a bug in a network software package. (Such a program could possibly also contain a **virus** that activates when it reaches the computer.) Worms are usually released by someone who has normal access to the computer or network.

Wormers. People who unleash destructive **Trojan horses.** These people aren't angels. What they do hurts us, and they deserve our disrespect.

Viruses, like all Trojan horses, are purposely designed to make a program do things you don't expect it to do. Some viruses are just an annoyance; for example, one displayed a "Peace on Earth" mesage. The viruses we're worried about are the ones designed to destroy your files and waste the valuable time you'll spend to repair the damage.

According to Rosenberger and Greenberg, "Trojan horses have been around since the first days of the computer. Hackers toyed with viruses in the early 1960s as a form of amusement. Many different Trojan horse techniques were developed over the years to embezzle money, destroy data, etc. The general public wasn't aware of this problem until the IBM PC revolution brought it into the spotlight."

Rosenberger and Greenberg deny that computer viruses are widespread. There are only about 50 or so known viruses "strains" at this time, and a few of them have been completely eliminated. Your chances of being infected are slim if you take proper precautions.

One of the most interesting observations Rosenberger makes is this:

> I can't identify a single virus that made its way around the country by infecting a shareware program. I *can* name four highly publicized viruses spread by commercial packages. One of the viruses was sold to American tourists in Pakistan who wanted cheap software. Another virus was sold here in America at computer stores across the nation. Still another was passed around in commercial software you could check out from a college computer center. I agree that BBSs and shareware can spread viruses, but commercial software has been the culprit so far. I strongly believe that downloading a piece of software from a *reputable* BBS is as safe as buying software from a local computer store.

Many reputable "sysops" (*system operators*) check all new files for Trojan horses; nationwide sysop networks help spread the word about dangerous files. You should be careful about software that comes from friends and BBSs, that's definitely true, but you must also be careful with the software you buy at computer stores.

What can you do to protect yourself? Rosenberger and Greenberg offer this advice:

1 Download files only from reputable BBSs where sysops check every program for Trojan horses. If you're still afraid, consider getting your programs from a BBS or "disk vendor" company which gets its programs directly from the author.

2 Let a newly uploaded file "mature" on a BBS for one or two weeks before you download it (others will put it through its paces).

3 Set up a procedure to regularly back up your files, and follow it religiously. Consider purchasing a user-friendly backup program that takes the drudgery out of backing up your files.

4 Rotate between two sets of backups for better security (use set #1, then set #2, then set #1, and so on).

5 Consider using a program which will create a unique "signature" of all the programs on your computer. Once in a while, you can run this program to determine if any of your applications have been modified— either by a virus or by a "stray gamma ray."

6 If your computer starts acting weird, don't panic. It may be a virus, but then again it may not. Immediately reboot from a legitimate copy of your master DOS disk. Put a write-protect tab on that disk, just to be safe. Do not run any programs on your regular disks (you might activate a Trojan horse). If you don't have adequate backups, try to bring them up to date. You might be backing up a virus as well, but it can't hurt you as long as you don't run any of your normal programs. Set your backups off to the side. Only then can you safely hunt for the problem.

7 If you can't figure out what's wrong with your computer and you aren't sure of yourself, just turn it off and call for help. Consider calling a local computer group before you hire an expert to fix your problem. If you need a professional, consider hiring a regular computer consultant before you call on a "virus expert."

8 If you can't figure out what's wrong with your computer and you are sure of yourself, execute a low-level format on all of your regular disks (you can learn how to do it from almost any BBS), then do a high-level format on each one of them. Next, carefully reinstall your software from legitimate copies of the master disks, not from the backups. Then, carefully restore only the data files (not the executable program files!) from your backup disks.

There is another solution spawned by the panic of the moment. Several software programs are on the market that will check your computer's files for any evidence of virus.

FINAL POINTS

I want to make a couple of points about software in closing. First, don't judge communications software by price alone. There is a segment of the society—which includes a large sprinkling of computer consumers—that are convinced that the way to get the best possible quality in any item is to buy the most expensive one available. This philosophy carries over for those people when they shop for software. Please put aside that mind-set right now! Price alone has very little to do with the capabilities of a software package. There are terminal emulator packages on the market that sell for $500 (or more). Are they the best? Possibly not. They certainly may come with a beautiful manual (at least the covers are beautiful—the content is highly variable), keyboard overlays, colored disks, and dozens of other frills. But, when "the rubber meets the road" and you start to run the software, you may find that it is not all you expected, or, equally wasteful, it is more than you wanted or needed. Don't be overly impressed with price. I began communicating with my IBM clone by buying one of the most expensive software packages on the market. I never liked it. I never felt comfortable with it. It was all wrong for me. I now use and am highly satisfied with a $69.95 program that is on the market as shareware.

Second, don't let someone else make your software decisions for you.

Too many times I have seen new computer users choose their software be-cause "Sam Ramchip, the local user group communications guru, swears by SideTalk. He said if I bought anything else I was crazy." Certainly, solicit and listen to the advice of the ace. But, remember: the ace is likely using the most full-featured and complex software available. As a beginner, you are unlikely to need all those features and should not have to go through trying to learn them. (Or wandering through 300 pages of documentation trying to find the features you do need). Look at other software as well. Personal preferences vary as widely as the features and prices of the software packages being offered. Find one that performs comfortably for you. Even though Sam's "Super-Charged Turbo Hyper-Transfer" software works for him, it may not necessarily be the best package for you.

RESOURCE LIST: TERMINAL EMULATOR SOFTWARE

The March 1988 issue of *Family and Home Office Computing* presented its editors' choices of terminal emulators for several brands of machines. Here are their choices:

DIGA! (Amiga)
Aegis Development
213/392-9972

Flash (Atari ST)
Antic Software
415/957-0886

MicroPhone (MacIntosh)
Software Ventures Corp.
415/644-3232

Point-to-Point (Apple II)
Pinpoint Publishing
415/654-3050

ProComm Version 2.4.2 (MS-DOS)
DataStorm Technologies
314/474-8461

Other popular communications software includes:

ASCII Pro (ProDOS, MS-DOS)
United Software Industries
8399 Topanga Canyon Blvd.
Canoga Park, CA 91304
818/887-5800

Crosstalk XVI and Mark 4
(MS-DOS)
Crosstalk Communications

1000 Holcomb Woods Pkwy.
Roswell, GA 30076
404/998-3998

Freeway Advanced (MS-DOS)
Kortek, Inc.
505 Hamilton Ave.
Palo Alto, CA 94301
415/327-4555

HyperACCESS (MS-DOS)
Hilgraeve, Inc.
P.O. Box 941
Monroe, MI 48161
313/243-0576

Microsoft Access (MS-DOS)
Microsoft Corporation
16011 Northeast 36th Way
Redmond, WA 98073
800/426-9400

Red Ryder (Macintosh)
The Freesoft Co.
10828 Lacklink
St. Louis, MO 63114
314/423-2190

Relay Gold (MS-DOS)
VM Personal Computing, Inc.
41 Kenosia Ave.
Danbury, CT 06810
203/798-3800

Smartcom II (MS-DOS, Macintosh)
Hayes Microcomputer
P.O. Box 105203
Atlanta, GA 30348
404/449-8791

Windows InTalk (MS-DOS)
Palantir
12777 Jones Rd., Suite 100
Houston, TX 77070
713/955-8880

4

Electronic Mail

TIME IS MONEY

"Telephone tag" is one of the great American pastimes. The "game" begins when you call someone and are told the person is "not in" (or you get no answer). So you leave a message. Then the person you called calls back and *you* are not in and *they* leave a message. And on and on. According to a study published in *Entrepreneur* magazine in October 1988, conducted by Priority Management Systems (a time-management firm), during your lifetime, you will spend an average of two years playing telephone tag. Admittedly, this includes time spent in this onerous activity in our personal lives as well as in our business activities, but you can appreciate that it is a time-consuming task.

To assume that someone we need to talk with will be (1) in the office and (2) free to talk with us is to make two very large assumptions. These conditions are rarely both concurrently true. In fact, it has been estimated by Leslie Epstein and Associates (a marketing consulting firm based in Bedminster, Massachusetts), reporting in the August 1988 issue of *Venture* magazine, that 75 percent of all business calls fail to reach the person they are directed to on the first try. Also, as reported in the April 1987 *Teleconnect,* two-thirds of all business calls were rated by the recipients as being less important than the work they interrupt. But, when we need to deliver or get information, it is imperative that communication take place, usually in some expeditious manner.

In the past, a letter has been the surest way to make contact, and the mail is generally reliable. However, there are a few problems with "paper mail." First, the time from transmission (when you mail the letter) to reception (when it is read) can be from one to five days, depending on the distance it must travel. If the information is not time-sensitive—a rare occurrence in today's business world—the delay is not a major problem. But, more commonly, we need to exchange information quickly and effectively. One of the main tenets of this book is that the "winners" in competitive businesses communicate rapidly and efficiently. We can always send by courier (hours) or Express Mail (overnight). However, the costs of these premium services are very restrictive to all but the most critical correspondence. Fax transmission (see Chapter 6) obviates the speed and cost, but the recipient has to have a facsimile machine to complete the circuit.

Second, while the postal service does a yeoman job with its tasks, we get so much mail that important documents, at least the ones we are not expecting, may get lost in the pile. For those sending critical materials, an overriding source of anxiety is the lack of a "trail." Once you drop your mail in the chute, you surrender control of its movement. You have no knowledge of its whereabouts until it is received. Mail does get lost in the system, and, if that happens, there is no way to trace it.

Finally, one of the largest underestimated expenses in the office environment is the cost of a single business letter. In terms of composing, typing, editing, retyping, and mailing, the cost of a single business letter has been estimated to be between $7 and $10 ("How To Choose an Electronic Mail Service," *Personal Computing,* September 1986; pp. 60–67). Not a cheap item at all. If you want a written reply from the recipient, you impose the same costs to them to reply in kind. It can, quite quickly, get expensive. The average electronic message costs $3. Even if you still equate a postal letter with the 25-cent price tag, the accompanying savings—in time, production, and worries that the message will be delivered promptly—with electronic mail (E-mail) are enough to justify the extra costs of this perception.

THE E-MAIL ALTERNATIVE

With E-mail, an alternative "postal system" is in effect. Here is how the system can work:

1 To send a letter, you or your secretary can first type in the message on your computer using a word processor and save the message to a disk.

2 Using a modem and special software, you call up and connect to a national communications service.

3 You "address" your previously composed message to your correspondent and send it to his or her electronic mailbox (actually, merely a section of memory on a giant mainframe computer somewhere).

4 At the recipient's convenience, the next time he or she connects to the same service, a message that a letter is waiting appears. The recipient can read it immediately and respond.

5 You pick up your correspondent's response when you reconnect to the service at some time that is convenient for you.

All this can take place over a period of minutes. The only limiting factor, really, is how frequently you and your correspondents connect to the service in a given day. With this routine, you can collapse the "communications float"—with apologies to John Naisbitt (see Resources). The "communications float" is the time delay between the time you send a letter and the time it is received and read. It is comparable to floating a check, where there is a delay between when you write and cash a check and when the money is actually removed from your account. The communications float, once a hindrance to business transactions, can be reduced using E-mail to minutes and hours instead of days or weeks. By the time your paper letter is typed, proofed, signed, folded, stuffed, addressed, stamped, and mailed, an electronic letter would have already arrived at its destination—and possibly already have been read.

E-mail also allows you to transcend distance and time zones. Electronic messages can be retrieved from any locale with phone service and at any time. If you are trying to communicate with an associate in Hong Kong, you don't need to be concerned with coming into work early or late to call the associate during Hong Kong business hours. You post your message, and whenever (and wherever) the recipient begins the business day and calls up his or her electronic mailbox, the letter will be waiting.

Further, correspondence is received at your computer in a form that can be saved to your disk and then printed out on your printer for distribution. This is often referred to as "recordability." Since it is collected electronically, you can load the text into your word processor, add your own comments, and then print out additional copies for your associates. It also provides a better record of correspondence. A "paper trail," if you will.

A frequently observed benefit of electronic communications is brevity. As users become more familiar with using E-mail and become cognizant of its costs, they almost invariably become more concise and effective in their exchanges. They cut through the fluff and get to the point. They begin to save even more money by transmitting more words per dollar than the typical long-distance telephone call.

Finally, E-mail can be sent to multiple recipients at once, all from the same letter. With the cost of producing and mailing a business letter estimated at about $7, you can see where E-mail can even be more cost-effective for large-scale business correspondence. There will be a time when the U.S. Postal Service will be like United Parcel Service (UPS) is today—a package delivery service. Rather than having to make a dozen calls to alert your sales offices or regional managers of a hot development, simply post one E-mail message and direct it to all of them.

MORE FACTS AND FIGURES

In case there remains a question as to whether E-mail may be of use to your business, here are a few facts and figures to persuade you. E-mail is big business. Its popularity is growing rapidly because of the advantages just discussed. The next few paragraphs present some predictions about the future growth of the industry.

A study from Market Intelligence Research Co. of Palo Alto, California (reported on in the "Viewtext" newsletter) says that, because of the number of personal computers now in use, the E-mail industry is headed for a period of strong growth. The industry, which has more than a million electronic mailboxes in use, became a billion-dollar business in 1985. By 1992, it will become a multibillion-dollar industry, according to the study from the Palo Alto firm. Reporting on the study, the *Viewtext* newsletter commented: "Growth is also expected for the electronic messaging services industry, from estimated revenues of $326 million in 1982 to $1.9 billion by 1992. Those figures represent 395 million messages in 1982, 2.23 billion in 1990, and around 3 billion in 1992."

Meanwhile, also reporting on the E-mail industry, William J. Donovan of *The Providence Journal* noted that one company's system alone—Western Union's EasyLink—has about 170,000 subscribers, sending more than 7.5 million messages per month. In fact, "it would be impossible to find a *Fortune* 1000 company that doesn't have a user community," Donovan was told by Michael Cavanagh of the Electronic Mail Association. "The usage of computer-based messaging is growing dramatically."

Another prediction: E-mail services will triple by 1992 and replace 25 percent of the current courier overnight delivery services. That's the estimate of New York's Frost & Sullivan researchers, who say in a new two-thousand-dollar, 238-page report that those figures actually "are considered conservative predictions for a market which, developing slowly up to now, seems at last ready to make the most of its potential." The Frost & Sullivan study, which projects the E-mail market will "surge" from $415 million to $1.2 billion by 1992, cites vendor acceptance of the CCITT X.400 (see Glossary) interface standard as the key factor which will boost usage (see Chapter 9):

Each vendor up to now has been more concerned with locking users into its particular system than with the free flow of messages between different systems. The resulting incompatibility is the primary reason electronic mail has grown more slowly than expected.

But with general acceptance of X.400, as well as moves toward compatibility between private networks and between private networks and public access electronic mail systems, an international network of interconnected systems is in the making.

COMPONENTS OF A COMMUNICATIONS SETUP

There are three components of a communication setup:

1 *A computer.*   As discussed in Chapter 2, one of the nice things about computers is that they do not discriminate against whom they talk with. A top-of-the-line DEC or IBM mainframe computer will talk just as easily with a $200 Commodore or Coleco Adam as it will with one of the state-of-the-art PCs. It just doesn't matter. So, if you have a computer—at home, at work, or elsewhere—you are halfway to having what you need to start using E-mail effectively. There are a couple of things that you should make sure your computer has available. Your computer should have at least one disk drive. It will need the storage of the disk drive in order to keep your messages saved prior to sending them. You should also have a printer connected to the computer. Any old printer will do nicely. Dot-matrix, daisy-wheel, or laser. You will need the printer to make a *hard copy* (printed) record of your correspondence.

2 *Modem.*   Also as discussed in Chapter 2, a modem is the mysterious link in the chain between your personal computer and world of telecommunications. It is, in its simplest terms, an electronic device that takes the digital signal of your computer and translates it into an analog signal that can be carried across phone lines. When it is receiving a signal from the remote computer, it converts the analog signal coming in to digital information the computer can use. Modems today come in a variety of configurations, but generally there are only two major buying choices to make. First, do you want an external or an internal modem card? Second, what modem speed do you want or can you afford? Choices are 1200, 2400, or 9600 baud. Make sure that whatever modem brand you buy strictly follows the Hayes standard command set and works with your software. The only way to make sure is to test them together before you buy (see Chapter 2 for more detail).

3 *Communications software.*   The software you choose can make your experience with E-mail and computer communications either highly productive or a nightmare. Evaluate your software thoroughly, as discussed in Chapter 3. Find something easy to work with and try it out with your modem and your computer before you buy. Minimum necessary features include a smart dialing directory (so that once you have input a phone number and a particular system's communications parameters you can pick the system from a menu of numbers in the future), the ability to capture ASCII files to printer or disk, and at least the XMODEM file transfer protocol. Don't be overly concerned with the other features. They generally will not be necessary for using E-mail.

DEDICATED E-MAIL SERVICES

Picking a system is not a quick and easy decision, because there are nearly 20 services currently available which provide E-mail services of varying sophistication. They fall into two categories, dedicated E-mail services and information services that provide E-mail and many other services. Dedicated E-mail services do E-mail and, usually, only E-mail. Since that is all they provide, they are generally full-featured but are not necessarily the easiest to use. Examples include:

AT&T Mail, P.O. Box 3505, New Brunswick, NJ 08903; 800/367-7225

MCI Mail, 2000 M Street NW, Suite 300, Washington, DC 20036; 800/ 624-2255

EasyLink, One Lake Street, Upper Saddle River, NJ 07458; 800/336-3797

GTE Telemail, 12490 Sunrise Valley Drive, Reston, VA 22096; 703/689-6000

RCA Mail, 201 Centennial Avenue, Piscataway, NJ 08854; 800/526-3969

McDonnell Douglas OnTyme, 20705 Valley Green Drive, Cupertino, CA 95014; 800/435-8880

ITT Dialcom, 1109 Spring Street, Silver Springs, MD 20910; 800/435-7342

SYSTEM SNAPSHOT: MCI MAIL

MCI Mail is one of the largest and most popular of the dedicated E-mail systems. What began as an alternative long-distance telephone service in 1975 expanded to include E-mail capabilities in 1983. MCI Mail now serves well over 200,000 subscribers. It's popularity can be attributed to its comparatively simple user-interface, its relatively inexpensive costs, and its range of delivery options.

You should know one thing up front. If you plan to use any system with regularity and with anything more than a few messages each week, you should buy the dedicated software designed for a particular system to facilitate your messaging activity. While you can maneuver on the networks using any communications software after a little study, dedicated software will save you money (in connect time) and time (in learning the commands) and thus is well worth the added expense. In both the short and the long term you will avoid a great deal of frustration if you use these right at the start.

In early 1989, MCI Mail underwent a major revision of both pricing and available options. Prior to the modifications, there were two separate interfaces for users. The "Basic Service" was a menu-driven connection that was suitable for the novice user. Every prompt featured a list and brief explanation of the commands available. Basic Service carried no monthly minimum charges and the only fees involved were the annual subscription renewal and whatever usage charges the user actually incurred. The "Advanced Service" was for the more experienced user and those with more demanding E-mail activities. The menus were eliminated, and a $10-per-month mandatory fee was imposed. Along with it came several additional services. They included the following:

- *Longer message storage.* While both services kept unread messages indefinitely, read or created mail was deleted with Basic Service in just 24 hours; Advanced Service kept messages for 5 days.
- *Enhanced command structure.* Advanced Service allowed you to string commands together (rather than entering them one at a time) in an abbreviated format. Suppose you wanted to view a list of the messages you had sent since March 10. With Advanced Service, you could enter the following at a "Command:" prompt:

SCAN OUTBOX SINCE 3/10

or, even more tersely,

SC OU SI 3/10

The Basic Service would have required you to enter the commands one at a time: "SCAN," which would elicit a secondary menu, followed by "OUTBOX," and then another menu, etc. For those well-versed in MCI etiquette, this enhanced command structure sped up activities immensely.
- *Enhanced message handling.* With Advanced Service you could forward mail to other users and add your comments to the original text; or you could include the text of one message into another.
- *Expanded graphics storage.* With Basic Service, you could store only a single graphic—either a letterhead or a signature—to be used with MCI's paper mail option. Advanced Service allowed up to 15 graphics, and these could be combined in any manner.
- *Extended paper mail formats.* With Basic Service, when you chose to send a paper letter to someone, you had only one available format for the

printout—the "letter." Advanced Service users had two additional options—the "memo" and the "document."

With the new MCI, all users were automatically upgraded to Advanced Service. The $10 monthly charge was eliminated and the prices for several message services were reduced substantially. Users could now access MCI by a 1-800 number anywhere in the United States at no extra charge. Previously, access by 1-800 exchanges was billed at an additional 10 cents per minute. Further, as a pricing alternative for the moderate user, a "Preferred Pricing Option" was offered. For the same $10 per month minimum plus a one-time $25 subscription fee, users would be allowed up to 40 messages per month at no additional charge. The messages could be delivered by standard MCI Mail electronically or to a fax machine remote to MCI. Thus, messages could cost as low as 25 cents per message. MCI Mail, already a leader in electronic messaging, was even more attractive.

MCI Mail's organization makes sense. You basically work with four areas where messages can exist. There is an "inbox" for mail addressed to you and currently unread, an "outbox" for mail you have sent to others, a "desk" for mail you have received and read, and a "draft" area where you have created a message but have not yet sent it.

Sending a Message—Step by Step.   Let's look at the anatomy of sending a message on MCI Mail. We will connect to MCI via one of their 1-800 numbers, look up my address, and send a simple test message.

Please enter your user name: ralbright
Password: [the password is entered here]
Connection initiated . . . Opened.

Welcome to MCI Mail!

Attention all Advanced Service Users:
FORWARD your message to other MCI Mail
users with just a few key strokes!

Type HELP FORWARD for details.

MCI Mail Version 4.0

There are no messages waiting in your INBOX.

Command: Create

Sending an MCI Mail message is a four-step process. First, you must signal MCI that you want to start a message. You do so with the "Create" command. Then you must address the electronic envelope for the message. This can include several addresses plus a "CC:" (carbon copy) to any additional parties.

Once the envelope is addressed, you enter the text of your message. Finally, you tell MCI to send the message. At this point, we have completed the first step.

TO: albright

At the "TO:" prompt for the first address, you have a great deal of leeway as to what will work. The only sure way that there will be no ambiguity as far as MCI is concerned is to use the numeric, individual MCI account ID. If you do not know that, you can enter a last name, a first and last name, a first initial and last name, a name and a location, a name and a company, etc. The more specific you can be, the more likely MCI is to find a unique match. Once you have entered as much as you know, MCI checks its directory. If there is only one address that matches what you have entered, you will be shown the full MCI listing for the party that matches. If no matches are found, you will be asked, through a menu, whether you would like to send your message through a postal address, a telex address, or another E-mail system (EMS)—for example, CompuServe which can exchange messages with MCI—or simply delete the name altogether. If there is more than one match for your entry, you will be given a menu of those parties that match, from which you can choose the final address. For illustration, suppose you would like to send me a message. At the first "TO:" prompt, simply enter "Albright." Here is (some of the addresses being pure fantasy) what you might see from MCI.

There is more than one:

No.	MCI ID Name	Organization	Location
0	NOT LISTED BELOW. DELETE.		
1	NOT LISTED BELOW. ENTER AN ADDRESS.		
2	Unlisted user matched		
3	222-2222 Sam Albright		New Orleans, LA
4	333-3333 Marsha Albright		Denver, CO
5	444-4444 Rob Albright		Venice, CA
6	370-7474 Ron Albright		Columbus, GA

Please enter the number: 6 [we entered 6]
370-7474 Ron Albright   Columbus, GA
TO: [we pressed the Enter Key]

MCI always assumes you are sending a message to multiple addresses and will continue to prompt you for addresses until you press the Enter Key alone. Next, you are prompted for the carbon copy address. Press the Enter key here if you don't want a copy of the message to go to anyone else.

CC: [we pressed the Enter key]

After all the addresses are typed in, you are asked for a subject for the message. You don't have to type in anything here and can move on by just pressing the Enter key. However, it is a good idea to use something here to help identify the message's content for the recipient. When they scan their mailboxes or when you scan your "outbox," the subject of the message is always shown. If it tells what the message is about, you and your readers have a better idea of what it contains.

Subject: Test Message

Text: (Enter text or transmit file. Type / on a line by itself to end.)

You now get to the third step, entering the text of the message. When you have finished, you press the Enter key to get a new blank line and then a slash ("/") followed by the Enter key again.

This is a test message on the MCI Mail system.

Regards, Ron Albright

/

Handling:

MCI prompts you for the way you want it to "handle" the message, that is, the way you want your message delivered. The default is an instant electronic message posted to the recipient's MCI mailbox. Additional options include paper mail, telex, etc. This is where those options would be entered if they were desired.

Send? Y

The final step, actually "postmarking" the message and sending it, must be confirmed to MCI. If you are happy with the content, simply type a "Y" (for yes) here. If you want to edit the message, enter "N" (for no). Remember: Unless MCI receives explicit instructions from you to send the message, it will remain in your "draft" box for 5 days and then be erased.

One moment please; your message is being posted.

Your message was posted: Sat Mar 11, 1989 4:05 pm GMT.
There is a copy in your OUTBOX.

MCI politely acknowledges that your message is on its way and that there is a copy in your "outbox." (By the way, the weird "GMT" as a time zone stands for Greenwich mean time.) See how it works? Just to check, let's see if MCI was telling the truth in our example by taking a peek in the "outbox."

Command: scan outbox

The command to peek (take a look) in the "outbox" on MCI is "scan." You must specify "outbox" when it is the area you want to peek into. More on this below.

1 message in OUTBOX

No.	Posted	From	Subject	Size
1	Mar 11 16:05	To: Ron Albright	Test Message	36

Sure enough, there is the test message. Note how helpful a cogent subject line is. It becomes even more useful when your mail areas start to accumulate messages from several parties. Now, suppose we want to check to see if the message from our example has arrived in my "inbox." After all, this is electronic, right? We use the same command, "scan," but there is no need to enter a specific area. The "inbox" is the default area for scanning. You need only enter "scan" without a qualifier to peek in on new mail.

Command: scan

1 message in INBOX

No.	Posted	From	Subject	Size
1	Mar 11 16:05	Ron Albright	Test Message	36

As expected, the new mail area contains the message we sent just seconds earlier.

A Complete System. MCI offers a complete system for your needs. Specifically, in the area of delivery options, MCI can send your messages to MCI Mail addresses, to a remote fax or telex machine, or to a postal address (with overnight or regular delivery). With paper mail, you can register your own letterhead, logo, and/or signature with MCI. MCI will scan what you send to it and then, when you wish, print out your messages with your own graphics. The paper is then delivered just as if you generated it from your office typewriter on your own stationery. There are interconnections with CompuServe as well as France's MISSIVE E-mail network so that subscribers of these systems can send and receive electronic messages from your MCI account.

Additional bells and whistles include the ability to handle mailing lists, support for setting up your own "bulletin board system" (BBS), and receipts for messages when delivery is confirmed. If you would like, when you send an electronic message you can have MCI Mail phone your electronic correspondents to inform them that they have mail waiting (for a $1.00 surcharge). MCI also handles "forms," which are electronic "sheets" which can be "filled out" by your recipients as surveys, order forms, etc.

MCI Mail does not charge anything for reading a message. The only one who pays is the sender. Charges for E-mail range from about 45 cents to $1, depending on message length. As an option, you can send your messages "COD" and have the recipient pay the "postage."

MCI does not produce its own dedicated software for facilitating usage of the MCI Mail system. However, as befits its popularity, a third party has filled the gap. Lotus, the same folks who created the ever-popular 1-2-3 spreadsheet, markets Express (for IBM systems and compatibles) and Desktop Express (for Apple's Macintosh). Both are superb. In point of fact, to eliminate perhaps the biggest shortcoming of MCI Mail, you must use these packages. MCI Mail cannot handle any sort of file other than simple ASCII text. You cannot transmit spreadsheet, database, or formatted word processing files on the standard MCI system. If the problem were insurmountable, it could, conceivably, be a fatal flaw according to some users. With Express or Desktop Express, however, you can send these types of files just as easily as you would plain text. The drawback that remains? Both users must have these communications packages, to send as well as receive. Admittedly, it's a "finger in the dike" approach, but it has kept most critics appeased.

Summary. MCI Mail consistently comes up as a number one pick in most head-to-head comparisons of E-mail networks. The combination of a solid user interface, a large subscriber base (even larger if one considers the interplay with CompuServe's huge collection of users), a full range of reliable delivery options, and very reasonable pricing of services have made it a winner time and time again. With the latest pricing and free 1-800 access, MCI Mail should continue to be a leader in electronic messaging.

SYSTEM SNAPSHOT: AT&T MAIL

One of the newest entries in the E-mail marketplace comes from AT&T, itself. AT&T Mail is one of the smoothest networks available. It is as full-featured as you can find, offering most of the traditional services and, in many usage areas, major enhancements over what other networks provide. Many of AT&T Mail's features are discussed below.

User Interfaces.   Most E-mail networks have two interfaces for their users. You can work with a full menu of available choices or else use a command mode, wherein nothing is shown except a prompt for the next action. AT&T offers *three* means of interaction—menu mode, brief mode, and command mode. The menu or "full" mode is perfect for the new user. Each command is presented along with a one-line description of what the command accomplishes. Here is what it looks like on the opening menu:

CREATE a message.
DELETE one or more messages into the WASTEBASKET.
GET a message from the WASTEBASKET.
HELP - display all commands.
PROFILE - display or modify user profile.
QUIT - leave AT&T Mail, emptying the WASTEBASKET.
READ one or more messages.
SHOW what messages are in a folder.
Command: .   [Command prompts are preceded by a
                  period on AT&T Mail.]

The brief mode presents all the commands on a single line without a description. It looks like this:

create, delete, get, help, profile, quit, read, show
Command: .

Finally, the command mode, for the experienced user, simply prompts you to enter a command without any additional fanfare or explanations.

Autoanswer and Autoresponse.   "Autoanswer" and "autoresponse" are two features not found on any other system.
    The autoanswer function allows each message sent to you to receive a standard reply without your having to connect to the system. For example, suppose you are going out of town on a business trip and will not be able to connect to your AT&T mailbox. You can set up your system to send a reply you have composed and stored on the system. Thereafter (until you turn the autoanswer option off), anytime someone sends a message your way it will get the stored reply from you—explaining, perhaps, that you are out of touch but will reply individually on such and such a date. The message sent to you will remain in your "in" folder and will remain there until you reconnect to the

system. Autoanswer will not send more than one reply to the same person within the same week. Unfortunately, it will not answer telex messages.

Autoresponse is another unique feature. It is available only to subscribers with the advanced "Forms/Files" option, which is a premium service. Suppose you have a catalog of products or services. You can set up a system with autoresponse whereby a customer can send a message requesting information on a specific item by entering a "request" for the item at the "Subject:" prompt for sending a message. Alerted to the request, AT&T Mail will look in the folder you have created for a matching message. When found, the appropriate message is automatically sent to the inquiring user. If no match is found, you can even have a default message in the folder sent for these requests. The default message could inform the sender that the requested information is not available and could give a list of the available requests. No other service supports this form of automation as well as AT&T Mail.

Online Editors. AT&T Mail features one of the best online editors available. It sports super search ("locate") and replace ("change") functions; other editing functions are the best available. For example, you can press the "Delete" key to erase an entire line, rather than backspacing over the entire line. You can also "undo" the last edit command or simply "cancel" the entire editing session.

MailTALK. Suppose you are on the road and your constant companion, your portable computer, goes on the fritz and you are not able to connect to the AT&T Mail system. You are not out of touch. With one of the most innovative features available on any E-mail network, if you can get to a touch-tone phone you can retrieve your messages with AT&T MailTALK. To use MailTALK, you call a 1-800 number and are answered by a female-sounding voice which prompts you for your next actions. You are asked to enter your AT&T Mail user name with the touch-tone phone keyboard and end it with the "#" key. Then the pleasant voice asks for your password which you enter, again terminating your input with the "#" key. Now you are in control of several read functions which you can select from the phone keyboard. Pressing "1" will have the first message in your "in" folder read to you, this time in a rather stacatto but easily understandable male voice. You can reread the message by pressing "5," or you can delete the message by pressing "3." You can stop and restart a message being read by pressing "7" to stop and then pressing it again to start. To read the next message you press the "#" key. You can enter a help mode by pressing "4." You are never completely out of touch with MailTALK; however, you cannot send messages with the voice system, and it is expensive to use (50 cents per minute).

Subscriber Directory. As with MCI Mail, if you do not know your correspondent's electronic mailbox address, you do not have a problem. The AT&T Mail online subscriber directory is accessible from the command prompt. You simply enter the name you know the person by, and AT&T presents you with the possibilities. For example, for my account, after electing to create a message you are prompted for the "To:" address. If you just enter "Albright," you will be shown a list of all the mailbox addresses which might be appropriate. You then enter the number of the address you want and it is plugged into the addressee field. Here is how it looks on the system:

Command: .create

To: Albright

0: Enter Name and Postal address.
1: Barbara A Albright <!albright> Bedminster, NJ AT&T - STAFF SUPERVISOR
2: David Albright <!pfdalbright> Norwalk, CT Corporate
3: David A Albright <!dalbright> Basking Ridge, NJ AT&T
4: R E Albright <!albrightr> Berkeley Heights, NJ AT&T
5: Ronald G Albright, Jr. <!ralbright> Columbus, GA

** Enter a number for a choice, a '-' if you don't wish to choose any of these names.

: 5   [We enter "5" for the address we want.]

5: Ronald G Albright, Jr. <!ralbright> Columbus, GA

If the party you want is not listed, you can still send that party a message via the available hard-copy options by choosing option "0" and then entering the postal address.

Reversed Charges. Like MCI Mail, AT&T Mail does not charge you for reading messages sent to you by another user. Charges apply only for the mail you send. If you are doing work for other subscribers or providing them with information that they request, you may want to use the "COD" option. Just like a collect phone call, you reverse the charges. Instead of your paying for sending the message, the recipient is billed for reading it ($1.25 per message). However, if the recipient does not read it, you are billed. Suppose, for example, you are producing a newsletter which contains time-sensitive information. As a service to your subscribers you offer electronic delivery via AT&T Mail. However, since this is an extra service, you cannot absorb the extra costs of sending the newsletter text through E-mail. You could inform subscribers that they can receive the newsletter electronically if they pay the "postage" for each issue, and then send the newsletter to interested subscribers using the COD option. It will cost you nothing.

Protocol File Transfers.   Other features of AT&T Mail place it squarely in the mainstream of the E-mail universe. It supports XMODEM protocol file transfers, which enables you to send (upload) and receive (download) both simple ASCII text messages of other file types using error checking (see Chapter 3). You can send any type of computer-based file to anyone you choose. With the "Forms/Files" option ($10.00 service charge per month) you can store messages indefinitely and have other interesting possibilities.

Shared Folder.   Let's get back to the newsletter publisher. Let's assume that as the publisher you want to make back issues of the newsletter available to subscribers in an electronic form or you want to have an errata or update sheet for other issues. If you are using AT&T Mail you can establish a special area in your account called a "shared folder." In the folder you can store a past newsletter issue, updates, errata sheets, renewal forms—whatever you like. Then, using a variety of options, you can open the folder to other AT&T Mail users.
Once the folder is opened, or "shared," your subscribers can use the folder just as if it were part of their own AT&T account and read the information stored there. If you like, you can even open up a folder for "Letters to the Editor" and allow those with permission to use the folder to send you messages that other subscribers can read as well. You have the ability to open up the folder to all AT&T subscribers, an individual, or to a special list (suitable for your subscriber list, for example). You can make access to the folder free (you pay access charges) or have the readers pay. You can also set a limit for the time files will remain in the folder and then have them deleted automatically, or you can choose to delete them manually yourself. With the ability to both read and send information to a shared folder, it takes on, for all practical purposes, the personality of a "bulletin board." AT&T Mail makes use of shared folders and provides information about new services or changes in services for subscribers to read.

Delivery Options.   Delivery options on AT&T Mail are complete. You can have messages delivered electronically or through the U.S. Postal Service ($2.00 per letter), overnight ($7.50), or same-day ("urgent") delivery ($27.50). Telex messages and facsimile transmissions are also supported. Domestic fax delivery of your electronic messages costs 55 cents for the first half page and 40 cents for each subsequent half page. Delivery outside the continental

United States varies from country to country (a price list is available online). You can register your logo or signature to be used in delivering your messages with these hard-copy options. You can also have AT&T notify you when an electronic message is read, a recipient signs for an urgent or overnight letter, or when a U.S. Mail letter is printed or a telex is transmitted.

Forms. Forms, which are specially formatted documents with blank spaces provided for you or a recipient to fill in, can be easily created and stored for repeated use. These can be anything from order forms to surveys. They are no different from the printed variety. When someone receives a form from you, AT&T will prompt the recipient to give a response to each field of information you have set up the form to contain.

Mailing Lists. AT&T Mail also supports mailing lists. The list can be sprinkled with electronic addresses as well as any of the available hard-copy delivery options. For example, you can deliver a single message to one subscriber electronically, another by regular U.S. Mail, and another by overnight courier. You can even share mailing lists with other subscribers.

Dedicated Software. The software available from AT&T for using AT&T Mail is superb. In fact, it may be the simplest to use of all dedicated software packages. Access PLUS for the IBM-compatibles, Access III for the Macintosh, and PMX for AT&T's own 3B computers and UNIX systems allows for you to fully automate your mail sessions and enhances your activities.

Summary. AT&T mail is a new entry, and as such its subscriber base may be smaller than MCI or EasyLink and its costs may be pennies over some of the other networks. However, when compared feature for feature, and particularly the quality of its support software, it is quite possibly the best system available. It is hard to imagine a function you might need in communications that AT&T Mail does not provide.

SYSTEM SNAPSHOT: WESTERN UNION EASYLINK

A Tough Start. EasyLink is like a blind date that flowers into an intimate relationship. While it may begin as a series of frustrating encounters, EasyLink is worth the time it takes to struggle through its complexities to gain mastery. With that experience, EasyLink reveals such a full array of features that it may be the only electronic system you may ever need.

The frustration begins early. Instead of offering the traditional user name and password, Western Union requires an initial sign-on code that would tax the most gifted memories. You have to remember a complex series of letters

85

and numbers that signal to the system which terminal type you are using, your ID code (three letters followed by six numbers, e.g., EIC031355), a user name (hopefully, your last name), and your password. The multiple codes are separated by either a space or a period. Of course, with the appropriate communications software you can set all that up as a macro. Better yet, with Western Union's own software, the sign on can be automated.

It doesn't get much better for the beginner. Once you have signed on to EasyLink, you are dropped immediately into the stark confines of its command mode of operation. What you see (and all you see to begin with) is a rather alien prompt, "PTS." If you read the manual, you will see that PTS means "Proceed to select." It would seem that things might be presented so as to make things a little easier, but Western Union appears to believe that all of its users will be accessing the system with its proprietary software. It "ain't necessarily so," but it would sure be easier for those uninitiated in electronic communications to use the software, given the austere greeting you will get as a first-time user.

Using the System.   Once you reach the "PTS" prompt, using EasyLink is not really much different from using any other system. As a novice, you may choose to drop out of the command mode as your first step and work with the prompts available. To do so, you key in "Prompt mode" at the "PTS" cue. Thereafter, things are a little clearer. The menu you receive should seem familiar at this point. The interaction looks like this:

PTS
Prompt mode   **[user input]**
MODE CHANGE ACCEPTED

All typed-in commands, responses, and message text lines must be confirmed by hitting <return> (the return key). You may type "HELP" or "HELP OPTION" as the only input on a line at any time for more information. To discard the current message and return to the "Command:" prompt type "EEEE".

Please use one of the following commands:

ANSWER, FWD, SEND
CRT, EXIT, MBX, MODE, READ, QUIT, SCAN, STATUS
Enter "HELP" or "HELP COMMAND" for more information.

Command: Help   **[user input]**

ANS	-	**Answer a message that you have read.**
FWD	-	**Forward the text of a message sent or received.**
SEND	-	**Originate messages.**

CRT	-	**Modify "screen" length and width.**
MBX	-	**Dump all messages in your mailbox.**
MODE	-	**Change IMS operating mode.**
READ	-	**View messages in any of your files.**
SCAN	-	**List messages in any of your files.**
STATUS	-	**Monitor progress of messages sent.**

EXIT	-	**Return to main EasyLink menu.**
QUIT	-	**Disconnect from EasyLink.**

For more information about a particular command, enter "HELP" followed by the command of interest.

Command:

So, we reach familiar ground. As far as structure is concerned, each EasyLink account has several file areas where your messages are stored. They include a "Mailbox" area where new, unread messages are held. You do not risk losing a message if you go offline for an extended period. Messages are held in the "Mailbox" area (abbreviated MBX on EasyLink) for 10 days and, then, if unread, are mailed out to you through the conventional U.S. Postal Service as a mailgram.

Once a message is read, it is moved to two separate areas. The "Hold" file is specifically for read messages. Your processed mail is kept here for three days and then deleted. You can reread mail here as often as you like. To view messages held here, you simply type "Hold" at any "PTS" prompt. To see what the file contains without reading any messages, you enter "Scan hold." The second area where processed mail is kept is the "Chron" file. Here, all the mail you have either sent or read is stored, again for three days. Again, you can scan or reread the contents at any time.

The final message area is the "Sent" file. It contains just what you would imagine—messages you have composed and sent to other EasyLink subscribers. The standard three-day storage is in effect and you can scan, read, or forward any of the specific letters.

To send mail, you begin by entering the EasyLink mailbox address of the intended recipient. If you do not know the 8-digit code of the addressee, you may be out of luck. The user directory service of EasyLink is one of the weaker facilities on the system. To access it, you must exit the mail area (by typing "Exit") and then select "Directory Information Service" from the resultant main services menu. You are not home free even at that point. To find a company you must know one of three things: the company's name, its telex or EasyLink mailbox address (if you already knew that, why would you be here?), or its telex answerback code. If you are looking for an individual, you may be completely shut out. The directory will not search for an individual name. If you somehow come up with what you are looking for in the directory, you better write it down. There is no other way to use the data found in the directory in the address. You have to exit the main system menu, reenter the mail area, and enter the address to subsequently send a message.

If you already know the EasyLink address, things are much easier. You merely enter the code and terminate it with a plus ("+") sign. The plus sign signals to EasyLink that this is the last address. This is necessary to distinguish instances in which you may want to address a message to more than one recipient (see below). Once the address is entered and identified, you are prompted by EasyLink with "GA" ("go ahead"). You then enter your message. Like other systems we have discussed, it's almost an inflexible rule that you must compose your messages offline and then upload them to the system. If you depend on editing a message on EasyLink, you may be in for hard times. The ability to modify a message is so limited (you can backspace over mistakes or delete an entire line—that's it) that it is covered on only one page of the system manual. Once you have completed a message, you send either "LLLL" to send the message and receive another "PTS" prompt or "MMMM" to send the message and log off the system.

Connectivity. Enough about austerity. What about the niceties? You can send messages from EasyLink to virtually anywhere and anyone in the world. Domestic and worldwide telex, facsimile, telegram (delivered by phone anywhere in the United States or Canada), cablegram (similar to a telegram but for worldwide delivery), mailgram (overnight delivery in the usual mail), or "priority letter" (delivered within two days anywhere in the United States or its possessions). You can mix various forms of delivery while addressing any message. For example, suppose you want to send the same message to one person in electronic form on EasyLink itself, to a second person as an overnight letter, and to a third person as a telegram. Here is how you would enter all these addresses for a single message (the blank extra lines are not entered during an actual session):

PTS	**[The EasyLink prompt.]**
62912846,	**[The first recipient's EasyLink address; the comma indicates that more addresses follow.]**

ZIP	[We cue EasyLink that the next address is to recieve an overnight letter.]
John Doe **123 Main Street** **Anywhere, NY 10000,**	[A standard postal address followed by a comma to continue.]
PMS	[The signal that the following address is to get a telegram.]
Jane Doe **205-945-9414**	[Since telegrams are delivered by phone, a phone number is important; if the phone number is not known, EasyLink will try and locate it itself.]
321 2nd Street **Birmingham, AL 35209+**	[The end of the addresses, signaled by a plus sign.]
GA	[We are prompted by EasyLink to begin entering the text of the message.]
This is the text of our message.	[Our message.]
LLLL	[We type this to end our message.]
ACCEPTED 9876543 **3 ADDRESSES** **EASYLINK**	[EasyLink confirms the process.]

A number of options are available for delivery as well. You can be notified of receipt of delivery (for E-mail, fax, and telex). You can use alternate addresses (useful for telex—if the telex cannot be delivered, you can specify a postal address for delivery). For extremely urgent transmissions to a telex address, EasyLink allows you to connect in "real time" (actual, current time) with the telex. Once you are connected, whatever you type in on EasyLink is transmitted immediately to the host telex. If someone is attending the telex at the remote location, they can even answer you back directly.

For electronic messages, you can check on the status of any message sent in any period up to the previous 72 hours. When asked for, the system will tell you if the message is still in transit or exactly when it was read. You can store mailing lists (called "RediLists") for mass mailings. The lists can contain up to 990 addresses each and can mix all available delivery options. Once stored on EasyLink with a name you chose, you can use the list's name followed by a plus sign as the address for any message.

Beyond E-mail.   An added feature on EasyLink lies outside the realm of electronic messaging. Provided with your subscription to EasyLink is access to two very useful information systems, InfoMaster and FYI News. InfoMaster, produced by Telebase Systems Inc., is the same as the EasyNet service described in Chapter 5. It is the simplest interface available to a wealth of online information resources. InfoMaster opens up a single door to virtually the entire universe of electronic data resources. Providing a single system (and a single set of commands) for tapping into over 800 databases on several complex systems, InfoMaster makes the complex task of searching and retrieving about as simple as it can get.

The second information service provided with EasyLink is unique to Western Union. Called FYI News (presumably, *"For Your Information"*), this service offers daily reports on numerous business topics, including a series of 18 daily newsletters (compiled by Gannett National Information Network) on such varied topics as telecommunications, advertising, real estate, energy, and trends and marketing. Additionally, FYI News is a constantly updated source for reports on domestic (from UPI) and international (from UPI and Kyodo English News Service) news, the stock and commodities market, weather, travel, sports, consumer information, and entertainment. Unlike other databases mentioned throughout this book, FYI News is strictly current. There is no way to access reports older than the current day's stories. Because of this feature, you are assured that the information you receive is the most timely available. Most of the reports are updated daily, and some, hourly.

Besides the quality content and sheer variety of the reports, there are a couple of other niceties about FYI News. You can set up a subscription to any of the reports you choose. If, for example, you want the daily Gannett narrative on telecommunications, you can ask Western Union to have the reports sent to your EasyLink mailbox as they become available. If you have a telex, you can have the reports sent to that terminal as well. You pay nothing for the subscription. The only costs incurred are your usual access rates for EasyLink.

The bulletin board service is a feature that allows companies or individuals to store information in the FYI database for subsequent retrieval via EasyLink or Telex I/II, worldwide by common user groups (e.g., association members, customers, sales personnel, distributors/dealers, or suppliers).

E-MAIL OFFERED AS PART OF AN INFORMATION SERVICE

Now that we have examined several dedicated E-mail systems, we will discuss information services that offer E-mail as one of a plethora of other features. The four major information systems, which all provide E-mail services to their subscribers, are:

CompuServe, 5000 Arlington Center Boulevard, Columbus, OH 43220; 800/848-8199

Summitt Telecommunications, 5707 Corsa Avenue, Westlake Village, CA 91362; 818/707-9991

GEnie, 401 N. Washington Street, Rockville, MD 20850; 800/638-9636

Delphi, 3 Blackstone Street, Cambridge, MA; 617/419-3393

The E-mail services are no extra charge over the system's usual news, software downloading, stock prices, weather, and other services. A comparison chart for these four major providers is shown in Table 4-1.

TABLE 4-1
Comparison Chart of Commercial Network Systems

Feature	CompuServe	GEnie	Summit	Delphi
Access method	Direct, Telenet/Tymnet	Direct	Tymnet, Direct	Telenet/Tymnet
EMAIL	Yes	Yes	Yes	Yes
NewsWire	AP	NewsGrid	UPI, USA Today	AP
Airlines	Yes	Yes	No	Yes
Telex	Yes	No	No	No
MCI Mail Gateway	Yes	No	No	No
SIGs	Yes	Yes	Yes	Yes
Electronic conferencing	Yes	Yes	Yes	Yes
Shopping	Electronic Mall	Comp-U-Store	None	Merchant's Row; Comp-U-Store
Fax/telex	Yes/Yes	No/No	No	No/No
Research	IQuest	Dow-Jones News Service	No	DIALOG Gateway
Reference	Grolier's Encyclopedia	Grolier's Encyclopedia	Grolier's Encyclopedia	Kussmaul Encyclopedia
Money matters	Micro-Quote; online stock buy & sell	Quotes; online buy & sell; access to Dow-Jones News Service	None	Dow-Jones News Service Ticker; online stock buy & sell
Games	Yes	Yes	No	Yes
Subscription	$39.95	$29.95	$24.95	$19.95
Billing	Credit card	Credit card	Credit card	Credit card
Monthly minimum	None	None	None	None
Dedicated software available	Yes	Yes	Yes	No
Cost per hour (non-prime)				
1200 baud	$12.50	$5.00	$6.00	$7.20
2400 baud	$12.50	$12.50	$6.00	$7.20

SYSTEM SNAPSHOT: COMPUSERVE

Background.   CompuServe has been in operation since 1969. It began as a time-sharing service to allow small-to-medium-size companies to have the storage and power of mainframe computers without having to make the capital outlay for their own systems. The businesses could call in and tap the mainframes of CompuServe to handle their accounting, payroll, and other chores handled by computers in those early years.

In 1979, CompuServe established itself in an entirely new market—the hobbyist computer user. As CompuServe mainframes were expanded, this massive computing power was used less and less to its maximum. Most noticeably, at night (the computers were in operation 24 hours a day) when the usual business users were closed, the huge machines were dormant—and wasted. To maximize the potential of their computers, they threw the doors open to individual subscribers in these "off-peak" hours.

The first ones through the doors were the home-computer owners, whose ranks had grown quickly with the sales of the Apple, Commodore, Atari, and Texas Instruments computers. CompuServe called their nighttime system MicroNet. Dialing up to MicroNet, the hobbyists could use the mainframes to program and store their work and, later, to communicate with other users through a rudimentary form of E-mail.

MicroNet was a quick success. In short order, stock quotes, news services, weather data, and other varities of information were added on. The way of displaying the information on the screens of the home computers was called *videotex* (without a final *t*). MicroNet changed its name in early 1980 to CompuServe Information Services, and in May of that year CompuServe became a subsidiary of H&R Block. The subscriber base continued to increase in parallel with the explosive growth in the home-computer market. The users sought and received 24-hour access to the system in late 1980.

CompuServe itself is difficult to categorize or explain because there are so many services offered. The facilities provided by CompuServe and the other commercial networks can be segmented into three major areas:

- Communications
- Information
- Software downloading

Certainly, the first two are the most important. As discussed in Chapter 3, the local bulletin board systems (BBSs) or users groups will provide access to most of the software you will ever need. It is in the realm of communications and information access that the commercial networks offer such enormous promise. Information access will be covered in a later chapter.

E-mail (EasyPlex).   CompuServe's EasyPlex system is very simple to use. It has three levels of menus. You can choose the novice, or full-menus, mode ("menu" mode) to get started. The menus are just what you would expect to see: a list of numbered choices, with a brief explanation of each choice. You choose which activity you want to do—read a message, compose a message, send a message, etc.—by entering its number in the menu. An intermediate mode ("prompt" mode) is useful when you have an understanding of what the commands are but still want to see what is available, in an abbreviated form. The expert mode ("brief" mode) operates the fastest, as nothing must be displayed at your terminal. No matter where you are in the commercial information world, the less that has to be displayed, the faster things move along and the less they cost. Obviously you have to learn the commands to use the command mode at all, but it will become your mode of choice after you have used the system for a while and at frequent intervals. For this examination of CompuServe, let's examine how menus work and how to change some important options.

When you first log on to the system,[1] you will be using all of the systems defaults. These are the settings for how CompuServe will display information on your system and how you will interact with it. It is assumed that you will want to use the full menus to begin. You can change this at any time. One way of setting your operating mode is to use the "PROFILE" section. It is here that your preferences for CompuServe are stored and can be modified. When you have received your new account and password and initially sign onto the CompuServe system, you check into the system as outlined in the manual and receive your first prompt. On CompuServe, the prompt character is an "!" (an exclamation point). The first housekeeping chore you should do is go to the "PROFILE" section of the system to set up how you want CompuServe to present information to your computer or terminal. At the "!" prompt, simply type "GO PROFILE."[2] You will be taken to that page of videotex and this menu will be presented:

---

[1] Starter subscriber kits for CompuServe are sold widely in bookstores and computer stores. They retail for $39.95 and include a manual, an account number and temporary password, and a credit for $25 worth of free access. When you first sign onto the system, you will be asked electronically for billing information for future charges. Once verified, you have the run of the place.

[2] CompuServe displays its information in sections and numbered videotex "pages" in the sections. You maneuver about the massive system using the "GO" directive to specific sections ("GO OPTIONS" or "GO SPORTS") or, as you become more familiar with your destinations, you can pinpoint pages with the sections (for example, "GO OLT-90"—"page" 90 of the *Online Today* electronic magazine). All these steps are clearly outlined in the CompuServe manual.

CompuServe   **PROFILE**

CHANGE YOUR USER PROFILE

1 **Terminal Settings**
2 **Change Your Password**
3 **Password Security Guidelines**
4 **Change Your Billing Options**
    or Credit Card Information
5 **Change Your Billing Address**

!1

By selecting any of the menu items, you will see the connecting screens and additional menus and prompts that will direct you through each of the functions listed. Right now we are only interested in the terminal settings. We select that menu item by entering a "1" followed by a carriage return or Enter at our keyboards. This follows on the screen:

TERMINAL SETTINGS/SERVICE OPTIONS

Use this area to change your terminal type/parameters and/or service options.

Note: Your permanent and session settings match.

1 Instructions
2 Change permanent settings

3 Explanation of session vs. permanent
4 Show session vs. permanent
5 Change current session settings

Enter choice!2

CompuServe makes a distinction between your "permanent"settings (those that will apply every time you sign onto the system) and "session" settings (those options in effect for the current session on CompuServe only). If you want to change your permanent settings (which we do), select item 2.

PERMANENT SETTINGS

1 Explanation
2 Logon/Service options
3 Display options
4 Terminal type/parameters
5 Transfer protocol/graphic support
6 Make session settings permanent

Type EXIT when done

Enter choice! 3

There are several options available here. They are explained in the CompuServe system manual. Most apply to the nuances of the communications software you are using and how CompuServe will interact with it. Right now we are only concerned with the "Display Options" section, since it deals with how CompuServe will ask us for our choices. We pick item 3.

PERMANENT DISPLAY OPTIONS

1 PAGED display	[NO]
2 BRIEF prompts	[NO]
3 CLEAR screen between pages	[NO]
4 BLANK lines sent	[YES]
5 Line feeds sent	[YES]

Enter choice!

At this point, to change your permanent (default) settings to have CompuServe use "brief" or command prompts instead of the full menus, you simply select item 2 from the above menu, and you will be allowed to change to the new format. As you become more familiar with using the E-mail facility, you will certainly want to move as quickly as possible. Command mode will allow you to do that. With the other options available, you can further customize your displays.

You should have a feel, now, for how menus work on CompuServe. These are the simplest ways of manipulating the system. Another way to set up how EasyPlex responds to you is directly through commands. You can set several of the options just by entering the appropriate command at any EasyPlex prompt. This is accomplished by using a "set" command. CompuServe allows you to avoid the above menus and make changes with direct commands. The "set" command can control your displays. The command you type in at a prompt would be "set mode xxxxx." The "xxxxx" can be one of three alternatives: "menu" would instruct the system to present its choices at each stage as full menus—complete with short explanations of each available choice; "prompt" would show only the commands available in a single line; and "command," the third option, would give you only a bare "!" prompt without a clue as to what the available options are.

To illustrate, we will examine how the various commands would work at one particular point on CompuServe, specifically, the entry point into the EasyPlex area. Since you begin on CompuServe with full menus active, here is what you would see entering EasyPlex for the first time:

EasyPlex Main Menu

  *** No mail waiting ***

2 COMPOSE a new message
3 UPLOAD a message
4 USE a file from PER area
5 ADDRESS Book
6 SET options

9 Send a CONGRESSgram ($)

  !

You are told you have no mail pending. Note that the menu, oddly, does not have a menu choice 1. If you had received mail and it was waiting to be read, there would be an item 1: "Read your mail." You would choose item 2 to start typing in a message or item 3 to upload a message you had composed offline and saved as an ASCII file on disk. Item 4 relates to your personal file storage area on CompuServe. This choice enables you to type or upload files and save them to your file section. The items are stored for 30 days. Suppose you have a letter that you send often, to different people. Rather than typing it in or uploading it each time you want to send it, you can place it on the system once and store it. CompuServe will ask that you give the file a unique name and save it with that file name. Then every time you want to send it, you choose item 4. CompuServe will ask you for the file's name and retrieve the document. Then you would enter an address and the document would be sent off to that mailbox. Item 5, the address book, allows you to type in and store (in the same personal file area in which your other documents lie) a list of 50 of your most frequent CompuServe contacts. You will be asked for their names and user numbers. Once this information has been stored, when you are asked for an address for your message you can simply type in the recipient's name and CompuServe will check your address book for a match.

    With this feature, you don't have to remember all your contacts' unique IDs; just their names. Item 6 allows you to set the same three options we are setting manually but this time with menus. Item 9 allows you to send a letter to a representative to the House of Representatives or the Senate. You can even look up the member with an online directory. The electronic message is sent to the representative as traditional U.S. Mail. The dollar sign in parenthesis is used by CompuServe to indicate services that carry a surcharge over and above the usual connect charges. In this case, it costs $1 to send a letter to a member of Congress. Note, also, that a few menu items are missing. These are filled in at various times to offer special E-mail services. For example, during the Christmas season, item 8 becomes "Send a SANTAgram." You can send letters (mailed through the U.S. Mail in envelopes from "The North Pole") to anyone and have them signed by "Santa." Finally, observe how the first word of each menu item is capitalized. This shows you what the appropriate command word would be if you were operating without menus, in the "prompt" or "command" modes.

To switch to "prompt" mode you would type in "set mode prompt" at the exclamation point prompt. The resultant command prompt would then look like this:

SCAn, REAd, COMpose, ADDress or HELp!

Observe that not all the choices found in the menu mode are given here. You could, however, use any of them by simply typing in the command word at this prompt. Even though "CONGRESSgram" is not presented as an option here, simply typing "CONGRESS" will get you into that process. In the prompt mode, commands are presented in an even shorter format. You don't even need to type in the complete command word; just use the part of the word that is shown as capitalized—e.g., "ADD" for the address book, or "COM" to start composing a message. Help is available at any time by typing a "?" or "HEL."

The final, ultimate level of control is the "command" mode. Entering "set mode command" brings this simple prompt:

EasyPlex!

Not much to go on here. When you really get a handle on CompuServe's commands, this mode will really speed you along. But it is only for the experienced user.

The other two options available with the "set" command are (1) the method you want to use to edit your messages (either with or without line numbers) and (2) "page" options. There are two online editors on CompuServe, both of which offer full editing functions, including search, search and replace, and cutting and pasting. If you choose to have the paging on ("set page on"), Compuserve will display 24 lines (the standard that computer monitors can handle as a full screen) of a message at a time and pause. You must press the Enter key on your computer for the next page of text to be displayed. With paging off, the whole message will scroll across the screen nonstop.

CompuServe's EasyPlex network offers many of the features found in a commercial E-mail system. You can send messages worldwide to telex addresses and fax machines. You can send a message to any MCI Mail subscriber, and that network's users can send to your EasyPlex address. CompuServe has liberal online file storage, can send a single message to multiple addresses, has an address book ("mailing list") for frequently contacted correspondents, and supports uploading and downloading of binary files of any type. Since it is the largest single commercial network in existence, based on number of subscribers, you have available the greatest number of potential contacts. EasyPlex delivery options do not include standard mail or Express Mail service to non-subscribers, and it does not support multiple address lists or a list of more than 50 names. But it does offer services beyond E-mail which, if they appeal to your individual business needs, can tip the scales in its favor as one, if not your only, E-mail service.

PUBLIC COMMUNICATIONS

While E-mail is a secure, private form of exchange, CompuServe and other commercial systems also provide for group interaction. Subscribers can leave messages in a common message collection, and all other subscribers can read the messages and respond. This provides a way to get several minds working on a specific problem—be it a computer question or a more ethereal concern. All the systems offer what are called "special interest groups" or SIGs. There are SIGs concerned with specific computer brands—IBM and clones, Apple and Macintosh, Commodore and Amiga, Tandy, Texas Instruments, and dozens more. Other SIGs have members that are interested in a specific application or software for a computer. There are desktop-publishing SIGs, WordPerfect SIGs, Lotus SIGs, Microsoft SIGs, Borland SIGs, and more. There are SIGs directed at members of specific professional groups—entrepreneurs, public relations people, lawyers, military veterans, photographers, race car enthusiasts, yachtsmen, work-at-homers, consultants, and writers are just a few of the examples. (And remember, SIG members are among the very brightest and talented in each field; after all, they are enlightened enough to use this new communications technology, aren't they?) With SIGs you can ask questions and get answers publicly for all to learn from. The support you can find on a SIG for commercial computer software and hardware can rival and often surpass that available from the manufacturers themselves. It is an enormously rich resource.

What kind of discussions go on in a SIG? In computer-specific SIGs, discussions go on about such (hypothetical) things as:

- What is the best terminal emulator, or word processor, or database for the XYZ computer?

- How do you get the ABC printer to interface (hookup) to the XYZ computer?
- What do users think of the new ALPHAWORD word processor software from Dirt Cheap Software?

Through these kinds of questions and thousands of other examples, the experience of others flows down to the novice. Just as the local users group (see Chapter 3) provides a source of firsthand experience, so does the SIG, which is really just an electronic version of a users group. But this group is attended around the clock, seven days a week. There is usually someone who has had experience with the same problem you are confronted with or some-one who has an opinion on your request for a recommendation. The users freely share their evaluations and expertise with you. You are almost as likely to get a message concerning your computer problem from a software developer or professional programmer as from someone with just a passing interest in your request. The SIG is the ultimate problem-solving resource for any computer owner.

A SIG can be devoted to noncomputer interests as well. When a physician in Arkansas experienced a slump in his new-patient appointments and referrals from other physicians, he left a message on the Public Relations SIG on CompuServe. He asked: "How does one go about effectively marketing a professional practice?" A useful and informative "thread" (a series of messages directed at the same original question or topic) resulted that spanned several days. The message thread featured replies from several public relations professionals, each with effective ideas about how to increase the doctor's practice. Some of those answering and volunteering their expertise would charge a "regular" client $100 per hour for similar advice. The physician had several ideas to implement into his practice.

The networking didn't stop there. As a result of the thread, a dentist in New Jersey and a public relations professional in California made contact. The two have agreed to pool their expertise and write a book together on marketing for health professionals. There are SIGs for many specific business areas. On CompuServe, alone, there are groups interested in public relations, working at home, entrepreneurship, consulting, and investing.

In a nutshell, the nature of the SIG concept is people with common interests making contact and sharing their experiences and know-how for their mutual benefit. Like the "old boy" networks in business, where those who attended the same university help their fellow alumni to find business opportunities, SIGs are supportive networks that provide contacts and allow for interactions that probably would never take place if it weren't for the SIG system. They allow worldwide networking, electronically. The result is the generation of countless projects—from books to businesses—that would otherwise never have been.

CONFERENCING

SIG areas also provide a third mode of communication called "conferencing." In the conference areas of a SIG, users can meet electronically and carry on an electronic conversation in "real time" (current time, that is, as if on a massive conference call). What you type in at your keyboard immediately appears on the monitor of the others in attendance. The collection of users can be dozens at once. Special topics can be discussed, ideas presented, and problems solved by experts right from the convenience of your own keyboard. An example of this simultaneous group communication is a special conference that was scheduled one evening on CompuServe's Public Relations SIG to discuss the doctor's marketing problem mentioned earlier. The hour-long brainstorming session was attended by both health and public relations professionals. It allowed all who attended to clarify and expand on the messages they had left in the SIG's message base. Conferences of this sort can be scheduled at a regular time each week, or they can be called at any time (announced with a message from the SIG's system operator, or "sysop") to address a current hot topic in the SIG's message base. Of course, you don't have to attend. But if the topic is of interest, you can connect to the host system and move to the conference area at the appointed time, and join in. If you are unable to make it at the scheduled hour, a transcript of the dialogue is usually made available for reading electronically soon after the session is over. Any question or problem you can think of can generally be discussed if not definitively solved in these digital clubhouses.

The "conference halls" are also available to you and your business associates at virtually any time. You could arrange beforehand to "meet" with your customer or client across the country at a specified hour. You could then both connect to the host service and move to the conference area. There, you could electronically converse and "move information instead of people." If your customer is in Seattle, you are based in Atlanta, and you have an advisor or consultant in New York, you could all meet, exchange information, and disperse. This kind of conferencing is better than a conference call, because you can have a written record of the discourse if you have your communications software capture all the conversation to your printer. Better still, have it saved to disk, edit it, and then send each party a copy of the transcript.

CHOOSING AN E-MAIL SYSTEM

Which E-mail system to use is a difficult choice at best. With the lack of integration currently available,[3] you have little choice but to find out which systems your clients use and subscribe to them. If you are setting up a network for your company, use one of the dedicated E-mail systems. Cost is certainly a consideration, but the systems are close on that front. One point to consider in price is this: MCI and AT&T charge for number of characters sent in your messages—the "electronic ounce." Easylink charges for access time only, with no regard for length of messages. As a result, sending longer reports may be cheaper using EasyLink. If most of your message traffic consists of more than brief memos, you should consider this point. Unfortunately, until the solution of system integration is resolved, you may have to use more than one system. A comparison chart is presented in Table 4-2.

TEN KEYS TO E-MAIL PRODUCTIVITY

Once you begin to use E-mail, you will quickly wonder how you survived without it. However, there are several key points to remember in using the systems that will enhance your activities even more.

KEY #1

Use E-mail regularly and frequently.

For you and your correspondents to experience the benefits of the speed of E-mail, the system must be used frequently and at regular intervals. It does no good to send an E-mail message to someone who checks for messages only once a week. You might as well send a letter. Make it a habit to check your E-mail address(es) on a daily basis at the minimum. Preferably, check twice daily—morning and evening. And respond promptly. If you receive a message and take a week to reply, why bother with E-mail?

KEY #2

Be concise and to the point. Fortunately, E-mail encourages brevity and precision in its communications. Host systems have limits on the length of mes-

---

[3] There is generally no easy way to contact other E-mail users across systems. It is impossible for a CompuServe user to send a message to a subscriber on The Source or Delphi. It is not possible for an MCI Mail user to contact an EasyLink user. System integration and open access is coming with adoption of the standard CCITT (see Glossary) X.400 protocol, but it is not here yet.

TABLE 4-2
Comparison Chart of Four Prominent E-Mail Systems

	MCI Mail	AT&T	EasyLink	CompuServe
Subscribers (approx.)	150,000	40,000	175,000	500,000
Access:				
Local numbers	X		X	X
Toll-free 1-800	X		X	
Packet-switching		X	X	X
Basic Features:				
Permanent Storage		X		
User Interface				
menu	X	X	X	X
command	X	X	X	X
online help	X	X	X	X
Online Editing	X	X	X	X
search & replace		X		X
Delivery Options:				
Electronic mail	X	X	X	X
TELEX	X	X	X	X
Facsimile	X	X	X	X
Telegram			X	
Collect delivery	X	X		
Receipt returned		X	X	X
Gateway— other systems	X[1]	X	X[2]	X[1]
Mailing list management	X	X		X[3]
Forms	X	X		
Attach and send binary files	X	X		X
Voice mail delivery		X		
Logo/ letterhead	X	X		

TABLE 4-2 (*continued*)

	MCI Mail	AT&T	EasyLink	CompuServe
Notified of mail wating	X	X		X
Mail addressed by name	X	X		
Mail requires ID number			X	X
Ancillary Services:				
Database access	X[4]		X[5]	X[5]
Bulletin board messaging	X	X		X
File storage				
Dedicated software	X[6]	X[7]	X[8]	X[9]
Costs:				
Sign-up fee	$25.00/yr	$30.00/yr	None	$39.95 (once)
Monthly fee	None	None	$25/month	None
Access charge	No	Yes	Yes	Yes
Prime time access	N/A	N/A[10]	$30.00/hr	$12.50/hr
Charge per message	Yes	Yes	No	No

[1]MCI and CompuServe users may exchange E-mail across systems for a surcharge.

[2]EasyLink features international electronic mail exchange with MercuryLink in England and France's Cables et Radio "Missive."

[3]Limited to a single list of 50 names.

[4]Dow-Jones News Retrieval.

[5]Both EasyLink and CompuServe offer versions of Telebase System EasyNet service, called InfoMaster on EasyLink and IQuest on CompuServe. EasyLink also offers a daily "FYI" highlight system for news in specific areas.

[6]Lotus "EXPRESS" for the MS-DOS family.

[7]AT&T Mail Access PLUS for the MS-DOS family.

[8]Instant Mail Manager and Instant Forms Plus.

[9]CompuServe Navigator for the Macintosh and TAPCIS for the MS-DOS family.

[10]AT&T does not charge for access time for messages created offline and uploaded to the system. However, if you connect to AT&T and use its system editor to compose or edit a message while you are connected, you are charged 20¢ for up to 400 characters and 45¢ for 401-7500 characters. There is no charge for reading messages.

sages allowed, but these limits are not terribly confining (several pages of text are usually accommodated per message). But remember, you are paying for the transmission time and, sometimes, the number of words or characters in your message. Rambling prose is best suited for letters. Be to the point—and save dollars.

KEY #3

Put your E-mail address(es) on *all* business communication.

Make it known to your business associates that you are available online. Those enlightened enough to use E-mail will appreciate your insight. Place your E-mail addresses on your business cards, letterheads, and brochures.

KEY #4

Solicit E-mail address(es) from your business correspondents.

You will probably be surprised by the number of your associates that are already online with E-mail. Let them know you will be contacting them via E-mail and that you can be contacted in the same way.

KEY #5

Compose messages offline.

One of the biggest errors novice E-mail users make is to compose long replies while they are still connected to an E-mail system. Most systems have connect-time charges based on the minutes on the system (there are exceptions). If you are jotting off a quick "Message received; more to follow," online is no problem. But if you find yourself spending several minutes pensively seeking for just the right word to get your point across, you are wasting money. Collect your E-mail and disconnect from the system. Sit down with your favorite word processor and compose your replies. Remember these rules:

- Don't use tabs, underlining, bold characters, etc. These will not come through on the document transmitted or, worse, will show up as "garbage" characters on the recipient's screen. If you need to convey emphasis for a word, bracket it with asterisks ("*Today*"). For underlining, enclose the word with an underline symbol at both ends ("__IF__").
- Use single spacing for all your documents.
- Turn off your word processor's automatic hyphenation and automatic pagination (which is the program's ability to place a page-break character in the document, usually after every 54 lines of text).
- Set "smart" margins. A line length of 65 is standard for written business communications and should be supported electronically, as well. Of equal importance, messages with shorter lines are more easily read on computer monitors than ones that stretch the full length of the screen. Use a left margin of 0 and a right margin of 60 or 65 (indented from the right by 10 or 15 spaces). If the recipient needs to reformat the document, he or she will have less work to do in removing or adding extra spaces if you stick to a convention.

After you compose your reply, use the word processor's "save ASCII" or "print to disk" or "save generic or DOS text format" command and write the file to disk. If you simply save the message in the usual word processor format it will contain special formatting codes unique to each word processor that will often cause problems with the remote E-mail systems. Check your word processor's manual. Virtually all current programs have the ability to save in this "plain vanilla" format. If you need to maintain special formatting for whatever reason, look for a system that allows you to send a file in a binary format, as formatting can be maintained with this facility. Then, if your recipient has the same word processor that you use, he or she can load the file directly into his or her program and retain the file's formatted features.

Once your message has been composed and saved appropriately, reconnect with the E-mail system. With your communications software you can then transfer your prewritten message to the host system (a process called *uploading*) and mail it off. The systems allow for uploading messages just as easily as they allow for typing them in while connected. Read the E-mail host's manual to find out how. Since you cannot type at 120 (1200 baud) or 240 (2400 baud) characters per second, uploading makes cost-effective sense.

KEY #6

Take advantage of "receipts" when available.

Just as you can send a registered letter through the U.S. Postal Service (for a high fee), you can also ask most of the E-mail systems to send you can electronic confirmation that your message has been read by the addressee. This way you can tell if your E-mail is being read in a timely fashion. There is usually some small surcharge (25 cents or so) for this service. It is available on most E-mail services.

KEY #7

Know the system's file-size limits.

E-mail providers vary greatly on how long letters can be. For example, MCI Mail has a limit of 200,000 characters, while Western Union's EasyLink, on the other hand, allows up to 3 million characters per message. Usually, these limits are not prohibitive and are seldom exceeded in usual business correspondence. Check the system manual for details.

KEY #8

Upload using error-checking if it's available.

If you are like many users of electronic communications, your telephone lines are multiuser systems—the kind with the lighted buttons with several lines active at once. These can play havoc with the precise and delicate functions of modems. The information transferred can contain lots of "garbage" characters (nonsense, bizarre codes generated by slight voltage spikes on the phone lines). A minority of systems allow you to upload a message using a special error-checking transfer protocol (the protocol is usually called XMODEM or some variant of it). With this method, the systems check each other with a standard system and can prompt each other to resend information that has been cluttered up with characters that do not belong. AT&T Mail and CompuServe are examples of systems which accept these forms of uploads. Check the system manual for details.

KEY #9

Be aware of "cross-sending" (integration of services).

As discussed, while very little exists in the way of ability to send E-mail from one system to another, one notable exception is CompuServe and MCI Mail. These two systems allow users to send mail from system to system quite easily.[4]

KEY #10

Study the individual system manuals. Additional capabilities may be available to store your received mail online at the remote host, to forward mail to another user once read, and to generate a letter and store it online for future use in a repeat mailing. Most systems also allow for composing and storing large mailing lists for mass mailings to up to hundreds of recipients. Some of these unique capabilities can be real gold mines to productivity. You will have to dig them out to find them and use your imagination for the ways they can be applied to your particular situation.

STEADY IMPROVEMENTS

In historical perspective, E-mail is still in its infancy. It took years for the world to adopt the telephone, the radio, and television as universally accepted mediums for communications. The advances made in the first decade of E-mail clearly show that it is surpassing those timetables. Systems are becoming simpler to use and are offering more options of services and delivery methods all the time. The exciting developments just over the horizon (see Chapter 9) with improved integration and flexibility will make the popularity of electronic messaging a way of life before the twenty-first century.

---

[4] An interesting answer to sending across E-mail systems is offered by DASnet (DA Systems, 1503 E. Campbell Ave., Campbell, CA 95008; 408/559-7434). For a monthly fee and a charge per message, DASnet will forward your E-mail across systems—including AT&T Mail, Dialcom, MCI Mail, The Source, EasyLink, and others. For more information about DASnet, see Chapter 9.

5

Getting Information from Electronic Databases

The secret of business is to know something that nobody else knows.

—Aristotle Onassis

In business, information is available to you in two forms. Internal information consists of the numbers, trends, and figures you develop as a result of your own business activities. This kind of data is relatively inexpensive and comes from a careful analysis of your own record keeping. How reliable, timely, and accurate your internal intelligence is depends on you and the compulsiveness with which you approach your journals.

The second category of information is external data, which are derived from the developments in your field of business (to include your competitors and *their* internal information) that affect your planning. Dealing with— locating, digesting, and storing—the myriad bits and pieces of external information that potentially and actually affect your business is an immense burden. Our methods for doing this are deeply seated in the past, when things were much simpler, and moved much more slowly.

Our major intelligence-gathering approach is the "keeping an ear to the ground" method (also known as the "grapevine" approach). Using this approach, business people subscribe to a few journals—a few general ones and, perhaps, one or two for their specific areas of work—and attend a conference, convention, or seminar each year. They gather what they can from others writing and working in their fields. They chat with their suppliers, bankers, accountants, and lawyers, picking up a tip or two as they do. The "grapevine theory of information" goes on the assumption that if something important is developing in a person's area of endeavor, sooner or later it will show up in print or in a conversation.

There are a few problems with this approach. In many industries today, there are dozens of journals and newsletters to read. Conferences and conventions are expensive to attend and take time away from actual management. And, since things move so quickly in business and producers are faced with ever-shortening product lives, relying on word of mouth is risky and unreliable, as is the grapevine.

A BETTER WAY

Once you have become comfortable with the techniques of general telecommunications—and you should practice, first on the local BBS and then on the general commercial networks—you may want to tackle the next level of information access, specifically, the "hard-core" electronic databases. You should at least have a familiarity with what is available to you and your business from these high-powered electronic libraries.

You should be aware at the start that these mammoth systems are not for the novice or even the experienced telecommunicator without a true need for the resources available. The electronic database is an expensive, sophisticated, and complex facility that requires extensive preparation and study to use efficiently. However, if you are in a business or profession that demands that you stay abreast of all the developments in a rapidly changing field, these systems can be time-savers and, occasionally, "business-savers."

A database begins when someone perceives a business opportunity to supply information. The producer of the database is an "information provider," sometimes called an "IP." The specific information may already exist in a printed form such as a magazine, newsletter, or periodical, or it may be produced as a value-added service. Since most publications today are put together using computer technology (at least, electronic word processing), putting the already-digitized information into a computer database is a minor gyration. For the second form of data, the value-added or enhanced information, there is a little more work involved. An example of this format would be abstracting or providing commentary or interpretation of existing information. In both instances, making the information available in an electronic form adds certain enhancements to the data that are not found in its original format.

First, there is improved accessibility. You may not have the need or the money to subscribe every month to a particular magazine or periodical. Still, there are occasions when you need a particular article or issue. The traditional alternative has been a trip to the public library to read or photocopy an article there. Of course, there are some problems with that route. You may not have the time to trek across town or even across the street to get to the library, and, even if you do, the library may not have a subscription to the particular magazine you need. Even if they do receive the journal, it may be at the bindery, lost, or otherwise not available. By producing a collection of the material which can be conveniently accessed from your home or office by a modem, the information provider is betting that you will choose to use their service rather than go through the drudgery of a library visit.

Second, there is the ability to search information that spans a period of time. Using a collection of magazine or newsletter articles or abstracts in a digital form, you can search through previous editions for references indexed under a single topic. You may need to find papers that deal with a specific topic. By your entering the appropriate search commands into the system, the citations—current and past—can be found and displayed on your computer screen. You usually can enter the time frame you want the system to search as well. For example, you may want to search through only the past year's articles. If you have ever spent some time with the *Reader's Guide to Periodical Literature,* you know how tedious that process can be when done manually. With electronic databases, the searching is done quickly and the results are available immediately.

There is also the capability to do extensive cross-searching. For example, suppose you wanted to find all the articles written by Jeane Kirkpatrick within the past 18 months that deal with her views on U.S. trade with Russia. Can you imagine how difficult that might be using the library's resources? With the digital library a search like this can be performed (with the appropriate hard-earned expertise) in a few minutes.

Finally, there is the added benefit that the information retrieved can be captured to disk, loaded into your word processor, and modified with your comments or other additions. There is no need to retype the facts as you would need to do with a printed source.

THE NEGATIVES

While there is great potential for using these electronic marvels, there are some drawbacks to consider as well. These services are expensive. There is no disputing that. They are not for the faint of heart or shallow of pocket. Charges levied for using them vary greatly, but costs range from a few pennies a minute up to $2 or $3 per minute. An online search can resemble a frantic quest to find your car in a huge parking lot in the dark while spending $150 per hour for the privilege. There may be additional charges depending on the number of references your searching retrieves. Additional subscription costs and monthly minimum surcharges can be prohibitive. Even deciphering the pricing structure, itself, can boggle the mind. Again, it all goes back to the question of how much is your time worth? If you perceive the expense of using these services as worth the time you can save compared to a lengthy library search, you are a potential database customer.

Not only are they expensive, but the electronic databases can be complicated beasts to use. Most of the systems were initially developed for use by librarians, who are highly trained specialists. Unlike the relatively friendly menus of the general communication networks, the commercial pure-information databases do not invite browsing. There is a whole new dialogue and logic that is applied to online searching. It involves a major expenditure of time and effort to reach the level of expertise needed to use databases effectively. They are so complex that an entirely new profession has sprung up around the enlarging sphere of electronic information sources. The database professionals are called "information brokers." Just as stock brokers can do your bidding on Wall Street and carry out the complexities of buying and selling stocks and bonds, information brokers can carry out your "information transactions" for you. They will help you define what it really is you are looking for and then, with their skill and experience, find it in the most cost-effective, efficient manner possible. They will charge a fee for their services as well as bill you for the database charges. For the infrequent database user or those not able or willing to study the complex database commands, though, going through an information broker can save money over the wasted time and charges you would run up by fumbling about online on your own. One of the pioneers and experts in the field, John Everett, provides a more thorough look at the profession—including how to find and work with an information broker—later in this chapter.

Finally, most of the databases out there are abstract-only or, worse, reference-only (so-called bibcit, or "*bib*liographic *cit*ation") systems. Rather than providing the full text of an article (which in most cases requires too much storage space for the host computers to bear), the vast majority of offerings are in a capsule form. Someone has read the article and has provided a few hundred words as a summary of the contents. While this summary is often all you really need, there are times when you need the exact details available only in the entire item. Solution: a trip to the library anyway.

The complexities, if not the pricing, of database usage are gradually being addressed by the database systems. The trend is to move toward more friendly menus and simple English commands, all in an effort to expand system usage beyond the information specialist to the general public. The databases offer subscribers seminars across the country that cover how to use their facilities. They are producing instructional videotapes and software tutorials to ease the amateurs into using the databases efficiently. Some information systems are even offering dedicated terminal emulator software programs that allow you to build your search commands offline and then have the software automatically connect to the host, enter your commands, save the data to disk, and then disconnect, all in the most expeditious manner possible. The cost savings can be substantial.

WHAT CAN YOU FIND?

After all this doom and gloom, even if sprinkled with a ray of sunshine, you may be wondering why these monsters are even discussed at all. What follows is the reason why. Once you get even a glimpse of what can be found online, you will feel the power offered. Perhaps, once your interest has been piqued, you will want to undertake the study necessary to use them or choose to use an information broker to tap the wealth of information they can provide. All that can be incorporated in a book not specifically covering the subject is a brief cataloging of a few of the databases offered. More complete discussions can be found in the books listed under "Suggested Reading" at the end of this book. In particular, Alfred Glossbrenner's *How To Look It Up Online* (St. Martin's Press, New York) is highly recommended. Most of the information providers discussed in this chapter provide detailed brochures of their database contents. If you are interested, write to them for further details.

A SAMPLING OF DATABASES

ABI/Inform.   This database provides abstracts of business magazines. More than 350,000 abstracts are available from nearly 700 international business journals, some going as far back as the early 1970s.
UMI/Data Courier
620 S. 5th Street
Louisville, KY 40202
800/626-2823

Electronic Yellow Pages (EYP).   Need to do a mass mailing to all the widget manufacturers in Texas? Check into the EYP database. With its 10 million records of American companies compiled from nearly 5000 telephone books, you can find virtually any company in any industry anywhere. You can even have the information produced in a mailing label format to make the mailout a snap.
Dun & Bradstreet
99 Church Street
New York, NY 10007
212/285-7669

111

Magazine Index.   What ABI/Inform is to business magazines, the Magazine Index is to general-interest periodicals. A million and a half citations covering more than 400 magazines, some extending back to 1959, are online. Eighty-five magazines have the full text of the articles available.
Information Access Company
11 Davis Drive
Belmont, Ca 94002
800/227-8431

Investext.   Investext provides informed analysis by financial experts of 1500 of the largest publicly owned U.S. firms, 1000 emerging companies, and 1500 or so foreign firms. The reports are frequently revised and can be searched by company name, industry, or product.
Business Research Corporation
12 Farnsworth St.
Boston, MA 02210
800/662-7878

Who Owns Whom.   This interesting database provides just what the name suggests: which parent company owns which subsidiary. The 25,000 parent conglomerates are delineated as to their other holdings. Also, historical records (at least back to 1985) can show who bought what from whom.
Dun & Bradstreet
99 Church Street
New York, NY 10007
212/285-7669

Trademarkscan.   Thought of a neat new trademark for your startup firm? Check Trademarkscan to see if it is among the 800,000 or so active or pending trademarks in the U.S. Patent and Trademark Office.
Thomson & Thomson
1 Monarch Drive
North Quincy, MA 02171
800/692-8833

World Patents Index.   Find out what hot new products are being patented in this database of over 3 million patents from 24 major industrial countries. You can search inventor's name, company, subject, or title.
Derwent Inc.
6845 Elm Street
McClean, VA 22101
703/790-0400

PR Newswire.   Want to find out what's new in the world? Check out the press releases from over 10,000 news sources from business to science, sports to medicine.
PR Newswire Association, Inc.
150 E. 58th Street
New York, NY 10155
212/832-9400

Marquis' Who's Who.   Did Bill Cosby get a doctorate and, if so, from where? What was the topic of his dissertation? Search through over 100,000 biographies of people from all walks of life—business, the arts, science, etc.
Marquis Who's Who, Inc.
200 East Ohio Street
Chicago, IL 60611
800/621-9669

Congressional Information Service (CIS).   Need to know what your representatives have been up to in Washington? Search CIS for the abstracts of sessions of the full Senate or House and nearly 300 committees and subcommittees.
Congressional Information Services, Inc.
4520 East-West Highway
Bethesda, MD 20814
800/639-8380

If this book had a few thousand more pages, it could probably come close to having a complete listing. Maybe. According to Cuadra Associates, a firm that keeps track of these things and publishes a directory of electronic services, there are well over 3500 databases online worldwide, produced by over 1500 information providers and found on over 500 database services. The majority are in the business sector, as you can tell by this glimpse, but scope certainly is not limited to business. From medicine to sports, from census data to books in print, essentially everything you can imagine needing in the form of information or research is available online. The depth and breadth of the offerings can, even for the experienced researcher, hardly be fathomed. It is an awesome array.

RESEARCH

Depending on how you approach it, business research or intelligence can be fun or it can be drudgery. It depends on how you go about it and what tools you use. Regardless of what your mental attitude toward research may be, it is a big part of putting together almost anything related to communication. You may live in a small town that has limited library resources. Fortunately, in the "information age" that is not a major hindrance. Through electronic databases, you are no longer limited in your ability to access the entire universe of resources. Whatever you need is only a modem, a good terminal emulator program, and a phone call away. Even if you live in a large city, the time you may save by doing digital research may make it cost-effective and more thorough.

There are hundreds of information providers out there, producing digital equivalents of almost anything you can imagine. Their information is often sold to larger collections of these various databases. These commercial database systems then, for a fee, allow you to hook into them by computer, search the various files, and extract the pinpoint information you need. Fees for this service vary greatly and can run as much as $300 an hour or more on some systems.

Searching is done through the database's own command language, and therein lies the biggest hindrance to their use. The way you must enter statements to carry out a search and extract the required information shows no sign of being standardized among the various databases. This said, the systems can still be used effectively with good study and experience.

DATABASE LANGUAGE: LOGICAL ROOTS

While these databases do not have a stock language that runs across systems and, once learned, would stand you in good stead on any system you needed to use, the underlying "logic" behind forming search commands for various databases gives their languages a common parentage. George Boole was a British mathematician who developed a series of mathematical formulas and presented them in his 1854 book, *The Laws of Thought.* Boole presented a symbolic notation for logical relationships which form the foundations of Boolean algebra. Little did he know that these relationships would be a major part of today's computer systems and how they retrieve data. Boolean logic is particularly useful on computer systems. Computer hardware "gates" (or "switches") use logical tests on circuit conditions using AND and OR relationships. Database software, also, uses Boolean logic to manipulate data.

By using the Boolean operators AND, OR, and NOT, you can construct razor-sharp searches which will produce exact search scenarios. Suppose, for example, that you are looking for general information about modems. If the database uses a "find" command (this will vary from system to system) to initiate such a search, a very broad search statement might take the form:

FIND modems

If you want to restrict your search to using modems for purposes of sending electronic mail (E-mail), you could use the AND operator:

FIND modems AND electronic mail

If the search was too small, and you wanted to include not only articles on "electronic mail" but also those that index it as its abbreviation "E-mail," you might want to expand the search to

FIND electronic mail OR E-mail

The OR operator in this example means that any record that contains the string "electronic mail" will be selected; also, any record that is indexed with the string "E-mail" will be selected. Some records may, in fact, contain both strings, but having *either* string is sufficient for a record to be selected.

If the database is very large, the number of "hits" (found records) that contain either of these strings is quite likely to be very large. You could narrow the search by including additional logical conditions:

FIND modems AND (electronic mail OR E-mail)

Now only records that contain the word "modems" *and* that *also* mention either "electronic mail" or "E-mail" will be selected. The AND logical operator means that both terms must be found for a record to be selected.

By grouping parentheses around terms and operators in this fashion, you can specify in what order the system reads the operators. The laws of Boolean algebra dictate that operators contained within parentheses are to be executed first. Without the parentheses, the AND function is always executed before the OR. Using the above example, if the statement read "modems AND electronic mail OR E-mail," the database would first find the articles containing the terms "modems AND electronic mail" and then all the documents with "E-mail" (including those *without* "modems" in them). You must be careful about how you group the terms in this fashion, but the logic can be most useful.

What if you retrieved a number of papers that were concerned with the nonbusiness "bulletin board system" (BBS) uses of electronic mail. Since you are not interested in these, you could lock out "BBS" from the search with the NOT operator:

FIND (electronic mail OR E-mail) NOT BBS

Depending on the database you are using and how that system has programmed its search logic (there is no standard, really), you may have to use both AND and NOT for a valid search:

FIND (electronic mail OR E-mail) AND NOT BBS

There are a couple of other manipulations available on some systems. The first is the "wildcard." The database software is so good that even minor deviations from the phrase you input will not be retrieved; for example, if you use "investment" as your search phrase, the database will not turn up any references with "invest" or "investor." If you want to include these references, you can use a "wildcard" or truncation like this:

FIND invest?

The question mark will tell the system to find every term that has "invest" as the first six letters, regardless of how the word ends. This would find the words *investors, investment, investments,* and *investing.* (It will also turn up words you are probably not interested in, such as *investigate* and *investiture.*)

Second, you should know how to join search words with the "adjacent" function available on some systems. While some systems allow you to input two words as a single search term (for example, the Knowledge Index system allows this; see below), other systems require you to tell the system that you want the words to be searched for together, and only instances where they are together are to be taken as hits. Using our example term *electronic mail,* some systems will require some binding symbol between "electronic" and "mail" in order to have the combination searched for as a unit. DIALOG requires the terms to be joined as "electronic(W)mail." BRS requires "electronic$mail."

GETTING YOUR FEET WET

One of the simplest and least expensive database systems is Knowledge Index (3460 Hillview Avenue, Palo Alto, CA 94304; 800/334-2564). Produced by Knight-Ridder's DIALOG and actually a small subset of that massive database, KI charges only $24 per hour to use any of its over 50 databases. How can it be so cheap? KI, unlike its parent DIALOG, is available only in the evening hours and for specified hours on weekends. Unlike other systems which tack extra charges on for everything (including the number of citations you view online, the number of search statements you enter, etc.), KI's rate is a flat fee. No minimum monthly usage, nothing.

The databases offered by KI are complete. Sections cover everything from agriculture to social sciences, from arts to mathematics to medicine. The search language is simple. There are only, for all practical purposes, 8 commands you will need to be familiar with. For example, let's suppose that you want to check the *Magazine Index* database (which covers nearly 400 popular general consumer magazines) for recent information on facsimile machines and their impact on home business. The key to efficient database use is to do what you can offline. Don't think about what you want to search for after you connect and the meter is running. Think it out and write it down offline. Construct your search statement first. Use these steps:

1 Decide the basic topics you want to search for. Your topics in the example are facsimile machines and business.

2 Think about other words that may be more general or may be synonyms or common abbreviations. How about *fax* as well as *facsimile?* If you really want only references to *home* business, use the term *home business* for your search.

3 Put together what you have. So far, the terms are *facsimile, fax,* and *home business.*

4 Connect the terms with logical operators. In Boolean logic, AND means that a document must have all terms in it to be found. A search statement of "fax and facsimile" will pick out only those references that contain both of the words *fax* and *facsimile.* On the other hand, OR will find citations that have either word in them (one of the words would be enough to make a reference a hit). So you probably want to put the terms together as

(fax or facsimile) AND home business

Note the parentheses. They group the terms together so that if either term appears in an article title along with *home business,* the article's citation will be found. There is much more to explain, but you get the idea (see the "Suggested Reading" list at the end of this book for the best reference on the subject of database use).

5 Once you have put together your statement, write it down.

After you have gone through the steps above you are ready to have your modem dial up KI (for information on modems see Chapter 2). After connecting to KI, you see a "?" prompt. This is KI's request for you to input something. The first command you use is "Begin MAGA1." This tells KI to move you to the desired files; MAGA1 is the abbreviation for the database. You are whisked there and given a second "?" prompt. You are now ready to enter your search statement, so you simply type it in and press return. You will then see the search run by the host computers in seconds. The results will be displayed something like this:

128 FAX
101 FACSIMILE
578 HOME BUSINESS
S1   12 (FAX OR FACSIMILE) AND HOME BUSINESS
?

Your search has been run and 12 citations have been found that meet your criteria. Those documents have been labelled "S1" or "set 1." It's time to see your results. Turn on your printer capture or your communications program's "save to disk" option. At the "?" prompt, type "DISPLAY S1." Your first citation (consisting of the article's title, author, magazine date and page, and an abstract of the contents) will pop into view followed by another "?" prompt. You then see if you are getting what you are looking for or not. To see the next citation, simply type "D" (for "display") again. The second citation will appear, and so on. You get the idea. There are some finer points to the process, but after a few hours with the manual and some online practice, you will be able to get most of what you need.

CHOOSING AN ELECTRONIC DATABASE

With the ever-increasing number of databases and information systems available, how should you go about choosing which system is best for your needs? Some considerations follow.

BIBLIOGRAPHIC OR FULL-TEXT?

The vast majority of databases available today are bibliographic in content. You can retrieve only an article's title, journal, data of publication, author and a brief 200 to 300 word abstract of its contents. Often, depending on the skill of the abstractor, these short summations are enough to give you the basics of the paper. If the article really smacks of something useful, you can try and find it locally. By knowing exactly where to look, even if you do have to make a trip to the library, you can save time. If the service is "bibcit" (*bib*liographic *cit*ation) only and you are not located near a well-stocked library, look for a system with the ability to order reprints of the articles you need directly online.

Once you place an order for a reprint, the database service contacts one of the dozens of document delivery agencies who will send their field representatives to a library where the document—regardless of how esoteric it may be—is housed. They then pay the copying fee and royalties involved and send

118

it along to you, usually by Express Mail or fax. You are billed, usually, right on your database account for the delivery, which can run from $8 to $15 per article, depending on length and method of delivery.

In the very near future, more and more databases will be available in full text. It is obviously the wave of the future. As more publications become available digitally, they will be added to the available databases. Even so, older articles will be the last to come online in full text, as they will have to be keyed in manually. Document delivery services will remain important to you for at least several years.

FULL-FEATURED (COMPUSERVE) OR INFORMATION-SPECIFIC?

Once you assess your information needs, you will need to decide which type of information provider you need to subscribe to. If your needs for pure information are limited, but you do want to take advantage of E-mail, fax transmissions, and the news wires, you may need only to subscribe to one of the general-interest systems, such as CompuServe. CompuServe offers all these facilities and more. With CompuServe's Executive News Service (ENS), you can store certain topics and have the system search the available news sources (including *The Washington Post,* Associated Press, and Reuter's) for stories that address the issues you have profiled.

As the ENS scans the wire reports each day, it extracts just those stories that fit your interests and then stores them for your reading at any time. CompuServe also offers a "gateway" to the EasyNet system (profiled later in this chapter) to dig out "hard-core" information when you need it. CompuServe's E-mail system can also cross-communicate with MCI Mail, so associates on that system can send and receive mail on CompuServe. One more added benefit is that you have access to hundreds of special interest groups (SIGs) where you can get expert advice on computer and professional interests. Business-related SIGs abound (including a Work from Home SIG, and areas covering public relations, entrepreneurship, and consulting). SIGs are frequented by other professionals working in related areas, and, by leaving questions in their individual message bases (just like E-mail, only the messages can be read by anyone using the SIG), you can get advice on many areas of concern in your specific business.

If, on the other hand, you need only access to information, you may want to choose a straight information system such as DIALOG, BRS, Dow-Jones News Service, or Mead Data General. These systems offer much more in the way of information and are set up to handle just that. Few frills are included, though several systems include E-mail services, at least to other users of their databases.

SUPPORT FEATURES

These information storehouses (databases) are becoming much more sophisticated in their support of the users. When their market consisted of, primarily, librarians and other trained specialists, support was not a big concern. These users would attend a 2- or 3-day training session and would, thereafter, require little else to be able to extract everything they and their bosses needed. Today, with the users expanding to include the bosses, themselves, as well as many other untrained information-seekers, the systems are dealing with a new market made up of people who need more than a quick tour of the database. The end-user has changed and so have the systems. Today, you can expect to have several areas of support:

- *24-hour customer support lines*   Most of these lines are toll-free. You can call and receive guidance as to where to search on the system and what phrases to enter; in fact, just about any problem that might come up can be solved. Those who handle these calls are often former librarians themselves or others equally trained in information science. The help they provide is superb.

- *Newsletters*   Most of the systems today have a monthly or bimonthly newsletter. They vary in size (DIALOG's *Chronolog* is a magazine that numbers dozens of pages monthly; the Dow-Jones *DowLine* is a glossy magazine), but all update you on additions to their services and offer search tips and examples. Sometimes there are some offers for free time on selected databases.

- *Training*   A third way that these systems support their new breed of users is to offer training seminars. The larger systems, such as DIALOG, offer training at regular intervals in the larger cities across the country. Smaller, more specialized systems may offer training sessions only in their home cities. For big-contract users, many systems will provide training on site. For the user who does not have the time to attend a training session in person, several databases have produced videotapes which instruct the users in the basics of how to use their facilities. The tapes walk you through building a search and then implementing it on the system. These tapes are, for the inexperienced person, an invaluable introduction to database searching.

- *Software*   As mentioned in Chapter 3, an increasing number of these electronic systems are producing their own communications software to facilitate your connecting to them. The programs vary greatly in sophistication. Some systems provide only a simple terminal emulator to at least get you connected to their mainframes. Others offer sophisticated packages that will allow you to construct your search requests offline and save them to disk. Then the software will call the system, enter your search request, collect the material received, and disconnect—all without you having to touch the keyboard. Outside developers are also involved in the hunt for the "perfect interface." Several communications packages are produced by so-called third-party companies and can be used on the databases to ease search costs and headaches.

- *Documentation*   Documentation consists of the instructional materials provided by the systems. These materials are getting better and better as the systems become more and more open to the nonprofessional searcher. The materials offered vary from system to system. They may include such things as search manuals (which provide examples of searches and how to move about the databases offered, how to use wildcards, etc.), quick reference cards (which summarize techniques in a shortened format), and a catalog of databases (usually with descriptions of what each database contains).

ACCESS TIMES—24-HOUR OR LIMITED?

Most of the major systems are available continuously, 24 hours a day. Their access charges are probably lower for evening and weekend use. Some databases, such as Knowledge Index, are available *only* in the evening and weekend hours. If your needs are not urgent, you will probably want to confine your activities to these non-prime-time hours to reduce costs.

USER-FRIENDLINESS—MENU-DRIVEN OR COMMAND OR BOTH?

When these systems first went online, the primary users were professional searchers. As a result, the interfaces with the users were pretty stark, with little more than a prompt for the user to enter commands. But as the databases became more and more aggressive in marketing to the novice, the structures were modified to encompass menus that simplified search activities. With menus, the choices are presented in a numbered sequence, and the user simply enters a number for his or her choice rather than having to memorize individual commands. While menus greatly facilitate getting a new user up and running, as you become more experienced you'll find that they start to become a nuisance and slow you down. The current status of most systems allow for searching either in a "command mode" or a "menu mode." DIALOG, for example, allows you to use its complicated command structure if you are a veteran or to drop into menu mode (called the "DIALOG Business Connection") if you are a new or infrequent user.

UPDATE FREQUENCY

While most database are updated as frequently as weekly or monthly, the currency of information can vary. The database descriptions usually list whether a database is updated weekly, monthly, or quarterly. While usually not a major concern, sometimes knowing how current the information you are going to retrieve can make a difference as you choose systems.

COSTS

The charges for using these systems still remain one of the more complicated aspects. Of course, the simplest scheme would be, simply, a flat hourly charge, such as that used by Knowledge Index. Unfortunately, such simplicity is the exception rather than the rule. You may be billed hourly charges, a charge for each citation retrieved, variable charges for individual databases used, as well as telecommunication surcharges (which can vary). Calculating your costs per search can sometimes be more complicated than using the systems themselves.

ACCESSIBILITY

There are usually several paths to connecting with the major systems. Some of the larger ones have their own communications networks with hookups being accomplished by a local phone call in most large cities. These are usually the cheapest as far as charges are concerned. Obviously, these systems want to encourage you to use their phone lines to use their facilities. After all, they are paying to maintain these dedicated lines. If you are not near a local network number, you can usually gain admission through one of the ubiquitous Telenet or Tymnet numbers. Using these "packet-switching" networks (see Chapter 2) usually entails added cost. A third way often available is to use a 1-800 line to call directly into the system. This is frequently the most expensive method of all because the network often bills 800 usage at a premium rate, but it may be your only alternative if you live in a rural area.

GATEWAY: AN EASIER WAY

There are alternatives to these command-oriented systems. While a flexible (albeit, often complex) command system is powerful and provides precision in searching complex topics, for the infrequent user, they can be quite intimidating. There is a simpler way. EasyNet, marketed by Telebase Systems (134 North Narberth Avenue, Narberth, PA 19072), is a simple, pay-as-you-go system that provides you with access to over 700 databases that run across several database systems. Called a "gateway," EasyNet will connect you to the databases you need through one call. With one call, you are connected to the information expanses of BRS, DIALOG, Pergamon-Infoline, Wilsonline, VU/TEXT, NewsNet, and other systems, which encompass virtually the entire spectrum of available databases.

How does a gateway work? You simply call a single number (either a

1-800, Telenet, or Tymnet) and you are connected to the EasyNet system. After entering your assigned password, you get to work. All the charges incurred are billed to your credit card. Once you are hooked up, you are presented with a menu. You can choose one of several options. EasyNet I is the simplest route. The system, based on the topic you wish to search, chooses the relevant database for you. It does so by presenting you with a series of menus to define such things as whether you are searching for subject, person, place, or organization. Then, based on your choices, subsequent menus follow to further define your desired topic. For instance, if you chose "subject" from the first menu, you are given a second level with these possible subjects: current events, business/economics, science/technology/computers/medicine, law/trademarks/patents, social sciences/education, art/literature/entertainment, religion/philosophy.

Other menus are based on selections made at menu level 2. For example, if you choose "Sci/Tech, Computers, Medicine" at level 2, the next set of selections allows you to choose whether you want agriculture, biology, chemistry, engineering/technology/computer, earth sciences/energy, mathematics/physics, or medicine/allied health.

Once you have defined your narrowed search area, you are asked at another menu whether you wish to search from research and popular magazines, newsletters, books, or encyclopedias. Finally, you enter your search topic. Any word or logical series of words will be sought in the database EasyNet chooses for you. You can use the logical connectors AND and OR as discussed previously in this chapter.

If you are more knowledgeable and have experience with a specific database, EasyNet II allows you to pick which of the individual databases you want to have searched. Picking your database will speed your search (and lessen costs) because by doing so you avoid the introductory menus used to confine your search.

You can also choose to do a "Company Name Scan," which takes a specific company name you input and shows you just which databases contain facts about that company. You can then go back to EasyNet II and go right to where the information lies.

If you get stuck or confused, EasyNet is right there to help. Besides the traditional help screens available for you to read at any point in your search, there is also "live" (in computer terms, "real time") assistance available. Search professionals located at the Telebase headquarters in Bryn Mawr, Pennsylvania, are availble to you 24 hours per day, 7 days a week. To have one of them break in and start communicating with you across your modem, you simply type "SOS" at any point in your search. Your "call" will then be answered. Someone will type "May I help you?" (or some such message) on your monitor. That is not a menu; it is a real person typing. You can then type back your question or problem and have that person help you with it. This is a unique form of personalized assistance not found on any other database system. You can use these professionals to help you formulate your search statements or to direct you to the best database in which to search for the information you require. Don't hesitate to ask for help. SOS can save you a lot of frustration, time, and money. You'll get exactly what you want and get it fast.

Once you have sufficiently defined your database needs and your search terms have been entered, EasyNet will call the system you have defined. This is the gateway part. It allows you to have a "subscription" to dozens of database systems without the individual sign-up charges and annual fees that each individual company imposes. EasyNet calls, connects, enters its password for that system, moves to the desired database on that system, and relays your search request in that system's unique command language. It collects what-ever is retrieved and disconnects from the host, and then it presents you with the citations it has found. If you want to see any of the articles' abstracts (or their full text, if available) EasyNet will call the system back and retrieve that material for you as well. All automatically, and all while you remain connected to EasyNet.

To illustrate what we've been talking about, let's do an example search on the EasyNet I system (in its incarnation as Western Union's InfoMaster service[1]). We will go screen by screen for the most part and make comments as we go along. You will see the advantages of such a simplified system as well as some of its shortcomings.

PRESS	TO SELECT	★ Main Menu ★
1	InfoMaster-I	System helps select the database
2	InfoMaster-II	You name the database
3	Company Scan	Data on companies
4	SmartSCAN	Scan a group of databases
5	Investments	Stock quote service
6	NEW USER?	Instructions, database directory, pricing
H	for Help, C for Commands	

->

This is the main menu for the InfoMaster system. It presents your available choices at this initial stage. One of the most unique features is the "Company Scan" option which directs that all the databases are to be searched for articles

---

[1] The EasyNet system is also offered by CompuServe. Its version of the system is called IQuest.

124

covering a particular company. The "→' "" on InfoMaster is your cue that it's time for you to make a choice or input a response. Since we want to highlight the InfoMaster I system, we enter "1" followed by the Enter key.

PRESS	TO SELECT
1	**Business**
2	**Science & Technology**
3	**Medicine & Allied Health**
4	**Law, Patents, Trademarks**
5	**Social Sciences & Education**
6	**Arts, Literature, Religion**
7	**Entertainment & Travel**
8	**Persons**
9	**News**
H	**for Help, C for Commands**

→

The next menu we are presented begins the InfoMaster process of narrowing down what it is we are looking for. We chose "1" for business.

PRESS	TO SELECT
1	**Accounting**
2	**Banking & Finance**
3	**Companies**
4	**Economics**
5	**Industries**
6	**Insurance**
7	**Management**
8	**Marketing**
9	**Real Estate**
10	**Taxation**
H	**for Help, C for Commands**

→

Again, the narrowing process continues with this next menu. This time, we choose item 8 for "Marketing" journals.

PRESS	TO SELECT
1	**Search a database**
2	**See list of databases**
3	**Scan group of databases**
H	**for Help, C for Commands**

→

InfoMaster is sufficiently prepared now to focus the search territory. It now offers to either begin the search process, see a list of the databases preselected for us, or to input our search terms and have Infomaster scan the whole collection of databases and then let us choose which one to use. We choose to look at the scan facility, so we enter "3."

PRESS	TO SELECT
1	**Explanation of Scan**
2	**List of Databases in Scan**
3	**Start Marketing Scan**
H	**for Help, C for Commands**

→

This is the menu for the scanning section. Let's see just what scanning is on InfoMaster by choosing item 1 from this menu.

> **Scanning is a convenient feature that lets you enter your search topic just once, then scans several relevant databases and shows you which one(s) contain information on the subject of interest to you.**
>
> **After scanning the select group of databases, the system displays an enhanced menu that shows you your search topic, the databases scanned, and the number of records covering your topic in each database. This cross-database scan and the resulting enhanced menu are billed as one standard search according to the published price schedule.**
>
> **Once you have reviewed the scan results, you can search the database(s) of your choice by making your selection(s) directly from the enhanced menu. Use H for help from this menu to see database descriptions that will help you choose the best databases for your information needs. Each search performed from the scan menu will be charged as a standard search, including surcharges where applicable.**

Here, InfoMaster gives us a brief description of just what the scanning procedure entails. We will see how it applies to our search immediately. At this point, we are presented with the scanning menu again. This time, instead of entering "1," we enter "2" to view which databases have been selected for us. They are as follows:

LIST OF DATABASES IN MARKETING SCAN

Dialog Databases:

ABI/INFORM - Monitors major business and management magazines (mostly English, some foreign) for timely articles which would help support the manager's decision-making process. Lengthy abstracts.

Business Dateline - Provides the full text of articles published in regional business publications throughout the U.S. and Canada. Covers electronics, retailing, management, transportation, real estate and financial institutions.

Findex - Indexes market and industry research reports available from U.S. and foreign publishers on all subjects. Corresponds to the printed FINDex: The Directory of Market Research Reports, Studies, and Surveys. Abstracts available.

FINIS - Contains abstracts of articles about marketing activities and products of organizations in the financial services industry. Also covers regulatory agencies.

Industry Data Sources - Includes articles, market studies, statistical reports and other publications covering industries and products. Drawn from U.S. and foreign sources. Short abstracts provided.

Infomat International Business - Provides coverage of international business news articles from business newspapers and journals worldwide. Abstracts are all translated into English.

McGraw-Hill Publications Online - Contains the full text of several leading business and technical magazines, including Aviation Week & Space Technology, Business Week, Chemical Week, Data Communications, Electronics, Engineering News-Record, Inside NRC, Nuclear Fuel, and PC week.

National Newspaper Index - Indexes most sections of the Christian Science Monitor, the New York Times, and the Wall Street Journal. Also indexes international and national news stories written by Washington Post and Los Angeles Times writers. References only.

Newsearch - Preliminary holding file for publications indexed in NATIONAL NEWSPAPER INDEX, MAGAZINE INDEX, LEGAL RESOURCE INDEX, MANAGEMENT CONTENTS, LC MARC, and THE COMPUTER DATABASE. Records appear within days of publication and are held until loaded in the appropriate database. Mostly references, some abstracts, full text of PR Newswire.

PTS F&S Indexes - Covers company, product, and industry information worldwide. Includes information on corporate mergers and acquisitions, new sociopolitical elements. Also reports on factors affecting future product demand, end uses, and production, as well as trends in business and finance, corporate management, and labor relations. References only.

PTS Marketing & Advertising - Provides information on the advertising and marketing of consumer goods and services. Abstracts included.

PTS New Product Announcements - Includes full text of U.S. and international company news releases announcing new products and services of all types.

PTS PROMT - Indexes worldwide business literature on new products, foreign trade, market data and more in major industries. Updated daily. Abstracts included.

Trade & Industry ASAP - Contains articles from journals relating to trade, industry, and commerce. Draws from about a quarter of the journals in TRADE & INDUSTRY INDEX, but provides full text. Also contains releases from PR Newswire.

Trade & Industry Index - Provides current and comprehensive coverage of major trade and industry journals and periodicals in all industries. Indexes information in agriculture, taxation, wholesale and retail trade, forestry and other areas. More comprehensive than TRADE & INDUSTRY ASAP.

PRESS   TO SELECT

1   List of Databases in Scan
2   Start Marketing Scan
H   for Help, C for Commands

→2

Enter your marketing topic
(e.g., DIRECT MAIL; PR OR PUBLIC RELATIONS).
Type H for more help.
(or type B to back up)

→(facsimile or fax) and marketing

Is:
(FAX OR FACSIMILE) AND MARKETING
  Correct? (Yes/No) → Y

The next menu eliminates the choice of seeking an explanation of what scanning is as we have already used that choice. It's time now to get to work. We enter "2" to start our scan. We are prompted for our search terms. We want to search for both *facsimile* and *fax* and hook both onto the second term, *marketing.* So, we place the two in parenthesis, separate them with the OR operator (so that an either/or situation exists) and then add "marketing" connected with the AND operator. The search phrase simply shortens what we are really looking for which is "facsimile and marketing" OR "fax and marketing." Let's see what we find. We are then given the following warning from Western Union about liability and responsibility:

128

We have no reason to believe that errors exist in the data or services furnished. If there are any such errors the parties hereto have no liability for any consequential, incidental or punitive damages. No warranty, either expressed or implied, including but not limited to those of merchantability or fitness for a particular purpose are made. Any liability is limited to the amount paid by the customer to Western Union.

System is now searching a group of databases, copyrighted 1989 and made available by Dialog Information Services, Inc.

Scanning Dialog databases.

Accessing network ....Completed.
Accessing Database Host ....Completed.
Logging on....................................Completed.
Logging on (second step) ....Completed.
Selecting Databases ....Completed.

Each period equals one line of scanned data. This may take several minutes...
....
....

Scan completed.

Press (return) to see your results . . . →

This is where the fun begins. You see, step by step, the gyrations InfoMaster goes through to find your data. It calls up the host system (in our case, DIALOG Information Services in Palo Alto, California), enters its password, selects each of the databases we have preselected, and searches each database for the prescribed terms. Since DIALOG also offers a scanning feature, the process moves quickly. When our scan is completed, InfoMaster disconnects from DIALOG and comes back to us.

Marketing profile for: (FAX OR FACSIMILE) AND MARKETING

PRESS Data Type	TO SELECT	Occurrences
1 abstract	ABI/INFORM	84
2 full text	Business Dateline	261
3	Findex	10

129

→

Our scan is now listed. There are additional choices available (notice menu item A), but these will suffice for illustration. Notice the variability in the number of hits for our search phrases in the databases. Also, note that the kind contents of each database are listed. Some are reference only, meaning that all that is available, usually, is an article's title and author and the journal name, issue, and page. Abstract databases have all that plus a brief summary of each article's contents, which generally runs 200 to 400 words. Full-text databases are just that: every word down to descriptions of the photos included (but not the photos themselves) are available. Since the McGraw-Hill database looks active (103 citations meeting our search criteria) and is in full text, we choose that one for our final search destination. We do so by entering "7" at the prompt, and we are then informed by EasyLink that the system is searching the McGraw-Hill Publications Online database through DIALOG Information Services, Inc.

   Accessing network . . . .**Completed.**
   Accessing Database Host . . . .**Completed.**

Logging on ....Completed.
Logging on (second step)...........Completed.
Selecting Database ....Completed.
Submitting Search ....Completed.

**There are 103 item(s) which
   satisfy your search phrase.**

We will show you the most recent 15

We now see InfoMaster going through the same process that it used in the scanning phase—logging onto the system. However, although we do not see the difference, InfoMaster selects only the single McGraw-Hill database this time and inputs our search phrase for us. It collects the first (the most recently published) 15 citations and disconnects. It collects them in the shortest format available, which is a reference-only format, in order to save money for Info-Master. If InfoMaster were to collect all 15, in this case, in full text, it would lose money if we did not want to pay for them all.

Here is the way the first 3 of the 15 citations offered are presented. The content appears to be relatively close to what we are looking for:

Heading # 1
0103017
The shots seen round the world: Videoconferencing and *facsimile* are just the start. Keep an eye on your network traffic: An imaging revolution is under way.
Data Communications   December, 1988; Pg 94; Vol. 17, No. 14
Journal Code: DC   ISSN: 0363-6399
Word Count: 4,960

BYLINE:
Robert Rosenberg, DATA COMMUNICATIONS

Heading # 2
0103006
Casting a net of messaging to overseas sites: A large manufacturing company linked its worldwide sales and distribution staff in a hybrid public/private electronic mail network that let users stick with familiar interfaces.
Data Communications   December, 1988; Pg IS21; Vol. 17, No. 14
Journal Code: DC   ISSN: 0363-6399
Word Count: 2,963

BYLINE:
Robert Kramer and Gerald Schloss, FMC Corp., Chicago, Ill. and

James G.
Meade, Words Co., Fairfield, Iowa

Heading # 3
0102991
***Fax* travels 'dedicated' routes . . . links into electronic mail.**
. ....
Data Communications   **December, 1988; Pg 170; Vol. 17, No. 14**
Journal Code: DC   **ISSN: 0363-6399**
Word Count: 159

Heading # 4
0091050
THE PORTABLE EXECUTIVE: FROM FAXES TO LAPTOPS, TECHNOLOGY IS CHANGING OUR WORK LIVES.

These are brief reference-only presentations of the retrieved citations, which include a limited look with the title, journal, volume/date/page, and the word count or length. The author (''byline'') is also presented. By collecting this brief set of data first, InfoMaster let's you see if your search is on target. If it is, you can then get the full text of the citations you need. If it isn't, you can revise your strategy at a minimum cost.

PRESS	TO SELECT
1	**Review results again**
2	**See full text article**
4	**See additional headings**
5	**Start a new search / return to scan occurrence menu**
6	**Leave System**

Note: 1 full text article(s) may be retrieved at no additional cost.

-> 2

The available heading numbers currently range between 1 and 103.

Please enter the heading number(s) of the full text article(s) you wish to see. Separate each with a comma. (e.g. 1,5,6)
-> 4

At this point InfoMaster presents several options. You can see the list of the first 15 citations again with option 1. Or, you can choose to retrieve one or more of the citations in the first list in full text. Third, you can have InfoMaster go back and get the next 15 citations from the 103 it found with your search. Or, if your results were off base and not what you were after, you can elect to start a new search with a revised set of terms. Finally, if you want to get offline and think it all over, you can exit here with option 6. For our example, we like citation number 4 and want to see the full text. We signal this to the system by choosing option 2. We are then prompted for which article(s) we want to see. We enter "4" and sit back and watch.

InfoMaster now goes through the process we saw earlier of accessing the network, logging on, and entering our search request. But this time it signals DIALOG to display citation numbers not in reference-only format, but in full text. InfoMaster collects this display, disconnects from the system, and returns to us with the results. Here is a brief excerpt of how that full-text article would be presented. Every word is presented.

Heading #4

0091050
THE PORTABLE EXECUTIVE: FROM FAXES TO LAPTOPS, TECHNOLOGY IS CHANGING OUR WORK LIVES
Business Week   October 10, 1988; Pg 102; Number 3073
Journal Code: BW   ISSN: 0007-7135
Section Heading: Special Report
Word Count: 3,563

BYLINE:
Geoff Lewis in New York, with Jeffrey Rothfeder, Resa W. King in Hartford, Mark Maremont in London, Thane Peterson in Paris, and bureau reports

TEXT:
Meet Lionel Goetz, portable executive. Chairman of Pan Atlantic Re Inc., an insurance underwriter and reinsurer with operations in Britain, Ireland, Bermuda, and the U. S., Goetz is rarely in his White Plains (N. Y.) office. But with electronic mail, *facsimile* machines, a personal computer at work, another at home, and a laptop for travel, the 45-year-old lawyer is always in touch. He can read and answer electronic mail from anywhere. For the latest headlines, he logs onto a news service. To buy or sell stock, he enters his orders by computer. "When the IBM PC came out, I bought one right away," Goetz says. "I decided that I was going to move forward with the technology—or I was going to be obsolete."

Or take Clifton E. Haley, president of Budget Rent a Car Corp. in Chicago. Back in 1986, a cellular conference call he made to two

executives on their way to separate golf outings in Tokyo helped him get the financing Budget executives needed to do a leveraged buyout from Transamerica Corp.

Since then, Haley has made advanced technology a way of life, a tool to help him "run the company 24 hours a day, seven days a week."

After we have collected our article, InfoMaster re-presents the menu of options seen earlier—specifically, to review results again, see another full text article, see additional headings, start a new search, or leave the system. We choose option 6 this time to quit InfoMaster. We are returned to the main Western Union EasyLink Service Menu, shown below.

> **Logoff 0450005 5Feb89 18:39 EST**
> **Thank you for using InfoMaster**
> **CONNECTION TO YOUR DESTINATION BROKEN.**
>
> **EASYLINK SERVICE MENU**
>
> **1   EASYLINK INSTANT MAIL SERVICE (IMS)**
> **2   FYI NEWS (FYI)**
> **3   DIRECTORY INFORMATION SERVICE (DIS)**
> **4   ON-LINE CONVERSATION SERVICE (OLC)**
> **5   INFOMASTER DATABASE SERVICE (INFO)**
> **6   EASYLINK MEMORY MAIL SERVICE (EMM)**
>
> **70   HELP FOR EASYLINK SERVICE MENU**
> **75   HELP FOR ON-LINE CONVERSATION**
> **80   NEWS ABOUT EASYLINK**
> **90   SIGN-OFF FROM EASYLINK**
>
> **ENTER NUMBER OF SELECTION DESIRED (RETURN) 90**

We enter "90" and disconnect from our host.

INFOMASTER COSTS

Your costs are based on four surcharges. First, the connect charges to Info-Master. These are 15 cents per minute ($9 per hour) for Tymnet or Telenet access. It is 35 cents per minute for their 1-800 WATS line (plus 20 cents per call). Second, there is a flat $8 fee per search. These charges are waived if nothing meets your search specifications. This charge includes displaying either the 15 most recent references and 1 full-text record (if on a full-text database) or the 10 most recent citations in a purely bibliographic database, whichever is applicable. Next, there are charges for each additional set of 15 (full-text database) or 10 (for a bibliographic database) titles ($6), for each additional full-text article ($6), for each added abstract ($2), or for each photocopied article from a bibliographic citation ($10 plus $5 handling per mail order; $20 for express delivery). Finally, some databases have an additional surcharge of $6 or $25 per access. There is an annual $25 subscription fee which also includes a subscription to Western Union's EasyLink E-mail system. InfoMaster is not cheap, but it is, for the once-a-month or so user, a very effective alternative way to access a host of databases.

Making the choice between using a gateway system like InfoMaster and using a more complicated collection of databases such as Knowledge Index or DIALOG is a difficult one. One industry expert compares the two with traveling by bus or by car. With a gateway—the "bus"—you don't have as many decisions to make and you don't have to know the route to your destination. But you give up a considerable degree of control. With the "car"—DIALOG or the other more traditional database collections—you have to control the system every step of the way yourself. But, once you learn the path, you can make choices that can lead you to just what you want without as many detours. It boils down to how much time you want to invest in your information retrieval activities. If you are willing to put out the effort, learning the intricacies of a system like Knowledge Index or a DIALOG can give you more power and specificity. If you want to leave the driving to someone else, InfoMaster can be a useful alternative.

THE NEW WAVE

Online research is fast and, when done correctly, complete. It can give you an idea of where to look for more information in more conventional forms. It is the wave of the future available now. If you are serious about your business and believe that up-to-date information and intelligence are important to its success, get used to doing research in this fashion. Electronic libraries are expensive, and for now there is no way around that. But think cost-effectiveness. If your time is worth $30 per hour, digging through a public library for three hours to find a specific bit of intelligence will cost you $90. If you can get the same information in a few minutes by computer without ever leaving your office, you'll almost surely spend less than $90, even on the most expensive databases. One business executive comments, "We asked our managers for a list of magazines that they would like to have available to them in our library. When we totaled up the subscription charges, we found that these exceeded an annual subscription to one of the large database systems and our average monthly access fees. Because of that analysis, we decided to be totally 'electronic.' '' The same sort of appraisal may apply for your activities.

Regardless of whether or not you decide electronic access is right for your business, you should be aware that this universe exists. In all pursuits in life, there are times when these information sources will be needed. In many pursuits, they will be essential. As you progress along the road to learning how to use electronic information, you will hear more and more about this new form of library. Eventually, the systems will become usable by the average modem-literate person. When they do (and it will not be too far in the future), you will be ready.

TEN INFORMATION SYSTEMS YOU SHOULD KNOW ABOUT

1. DIALOG

Services: DIALOG, DIALOG Business Connection, Knowledge Index
DIALOG Information Services, Inc.
3460 Hillview Avenue
Palo Alto, CA 94304
800/334-2564
TELEX: 3344999 (DIALOG)
TWX: 910-339-9221

Summary: DIALOG is quite possibly, the largest and most diverse database network in existence. Once difficult to master, recent enhancements in services—notably, the menu-driven ''Business Connection'' interface— have lessened the burden for the novice user. In business since the 1970s, DIALOG offers well over 300 separate databases to 86,000 or so subscribers in 86 countries. Now owned by Knight-Ridder, DIALOG covers the entire range of business, science, education, law, medicine, and news information. Knowledge Index (see Chapter 5) is a reduced version that has a limited number of databases available and is accessible only at night and weekends.

Costs: Subscription is free. Annual maintenance fee is $25. Online charges vary from database to database; individual databases range up to several dollars per minute. Searches may incur costs for number and format of records displayed, as well as time on the system (varying for which mode of access is used). Knowledge Index charges a flat $24 per hour regardless of the database used. DIALOG also produces its own lne of CD-ROM disk versions of several of its more popular databases.

Software: DIALOGLINK

2. BRS

Services: BRS, BRS/After Dark, BRS/Colleague
BRS Information Technologies
1200 Route 7
Latham, NY 12110
800/227-5277
TWX: 710-44-4965

Summary: BRS is smaller than DIALOG, offering about half the number of individual databases, but most of the major databases are available on both systems. BRS/After Dark is BRS's answer to Knowledge Index. It is a smaller system available only during restricted hours and at reduced rates. BRS/ Colleague is a collection of databases and services specifically of interest to health care professionals.

Costs: There are no start-up costs, but a $75 annual fee is charged. There is a one-time registration fee of $75 for BRS/After Dark. On the full service, connect and display charges are variable from database to database. There is a $20 monthly (mandatory) minimum usage fee for BRS/Colleague and $12 for After Dark.

3. DOW-JONES NEWS/RETRIEVAL

DJNR Service
P.O. Box 300
Princeton, NJ 08540
800/522-3567

Summary: Just as you might suspect from the producers of *The Wall Street Journal* and other business and financial news, the DJNS is geared for the investor and business person. With its full-text databases, you can search the full text of *The Wall Street Journal* (from January, 1984), *Baron's* (from January 1987), *The Washington Post* (from January 1984), and *Business Week*, among other publications. The investment and stock market information can hardly be matched by any other source—electronic or otherwise. Superb support features with glossy bimonthly magazine (*DowLine*) and frequent flyers and updates. The user manual is updated and sent annually, free. By some estimates the second largest online system as far as subscribers go (300,000 subscribers), DJNR also has a college-selection database, travel services, and movie and book reviews.

Costs: Standard membership is $29.95 and includes five free hours of access time; corporate membership is $49.95, which allows multiple passwords and eight free hours of access. There is a $12 annual service fee. Access rates for per-hour charges vary based on time of use and modem speed but, comparatively, are quite reasonable and range up to $72 per hour.

Software: Several packages are offered by DJNR, more for collecting and evaluating stock portfolios than to facilitate access for other functions: Dow-Jones Market Manager and Market Manager PLUS, Market Analyzer PLUS, and Market Microscope. These are strictly for automated stock portfolio management using data downloaded from DJNS.

4. NEWSNET

NewsNet, Inc.
945 Haverford Road
Bryn Mawr, PA 19010
800/345-1301

Summary: Unique in the database industry is NewsNet, which offers the largest electronic collection of specialized newsletters available. The newsletters cover over 30 industries and number over 300 individual periodicals. NewsNet has exclusive electronic rights to over half the newsletters, so they won't be found elsewhere except in their printed form. In fact, 25 percent or so of the newsletters are not even available in print. They exist only in electronic form and only on NewsNet. Sophisticated SDI (see Glossary), or clipping service, is available. Also available are national and international newswire services and TRW Business Profiles.

Costs: The monthly subscription charge is $15 per month ($120 annually). Online charges are dependent on time used and modem baud speed of access. They range from $60 per hour at 1200 baud up to $90 per hour for 2400-baud access during prime time (8 A.M. to 8 P.M.). Additional charges are applied by the various newsletters (up to several hundred dollars per hour) but may be waived if you subscribe to the printed version of the newsletter.

5. VU/TEXT

VU/TEXT Information Services, Inc.
325 Chestnut Street, Suite 1300
Philadelphia, PA 19106
800/323-2940

Summary: A subsidiary of Knight-Ridder, VU/TEXT is one of the premier "electronic newsstands" in the world. Over 30 newspapers are online and searchable in their full text. These include *The Washington Post, The Detroit Free Press,* and *The Chicago Tribune.* The AP newswire also runs through VU/TEXT. But VU/TEXT doesn't stop at the dailies. It also offers access to such premier business databases as ABI/INFORM, Disclosure, and PTS/PROMPT.

VU/TEXT can be a difficult system to navigate, as it is often without menus to guide you along.

Costs: One option is a $60-per-month minimum usage fee. A second option is a $10-per-month maintenance fee and access charges that are $10 to $20 higher than those of the first option. Charges vary between the various database areas but access charges of approximately $80 to $90 per hour seem to be the average.

6. DIALCOM

Dialcom, Inc.
6120 Executive Blvd.
Silver Springs, MD 20852
800/435-7342

Summary: Often thought of as strictly a sophisticated E-mail service (with nearly 300,000 subscribers), Dialcom also offers a full line of databases. Its gateways to BRS and Dow-Jones News/Retrieval and other databases offered directly make Dialcom a serious information provider as well.

Costs: Electronic messaging service is billed at $14 per hour, and each 1000 characters sent or received is 5 cents. Additional charges that depend on which network is used to connect to the system may apply. Database charges are variable.

7. QUESTEL

Questel, Inc.
5201 Leesburg Pike, Suite 603
Falls Church, Va 22041
800/424-9600

Summary: Questel mainly supports the pharmaceutical and chemical industries. For example, the DARC system can search databases for chemical structures. Trademark databases covering an international registry are available.

Costs: There is a $15 annual fee. Connect charges vary, depending on the database, from $30 to $170 or more. Display charges per document viewed are levied.

8. NEXIS/LEXIS/MEDIS

Mead Data Central
P.O. Box 933
Dayton, OH 45401
800/227-4908

Summary: Isn't it ironic that one of the largest paper manufacturers in the world also wholly owns this electronic information giant? Specializing in full-text information, the Mead triad covers an immense range of information resources. NEXIS is the general information "head" of the beast. It includes the full contents of *The New York Times* (since 1980) and over 120 other publications—a total of nearly 10 million articles. LEXIS is the famous legal database specifically for law professionals. MEDIS is the medical counterpart for the health industry. If you absolutely and positively need full-text information and need it immediately, there is no better place to turn—unless, of course, you live across the street from the Library of Congress. Support features are superb, with tutorial disks and online practice areas available.

Costs: There is a $50-per-month subscription charge. This is not a monthly minimum that usage charges are applied against but rather a charge over and above usage. Search charges are approximately $30 per hour and assorted "per search" charges are another $10 to $20.

Software: LEXIS/NEXIS Communication Software

9. ORBIT

Pergamon ORBIT Infoline
1340 Old Chain Bridge Road
McLean, VA 22101
800/241-7229

Summary: Small, select, and highly specialized are the descriptive terms best applied to ORBIT. It contains over 60 bibliographic databases, and half are available only through ORBIT. Don't look for menus here; the system is fully command-driven. That translates into your doing some significant study before you attempt to tackle its use. Good manuals and training seminars are available.

Costs: Several subscription packages are available, and no monthly minimum or subscription charges are applicable. Access charges vary, as usual, for the database used, but not for the time of day of use. Database charges range from $50 per hour to $300 per hour.

10. INFOMAGIC, INFOSERVICE

I.P. Sharp Associates, Inc.
Suite 1900
2 First Canadian Place
Toronto M5X 1E3 Canada
800/387-1588

Summary: I.P. Sharp, A Toronto-based electronic information veteran, produces a vast array of reports covering, principally, aviation, economics, finance, and energy. The reports are generally full of hard-core, numeric data, a format Sharp is famous for in the online industry. There are over 120 databases on the system, not all from Sharp. InfoService is menu-driven, and InfoMagic is a collection of Sharp's reports.

Costs: A $100-per-month minimum charge is applied, but don't panic. Access charges are a basic $5-per-hour fee. Other charges may apply. Info-Magic reports cost from $3 to $7 each.

FINDING AND USING AN INFORMATION BROKER
by John H. Everett

■■ There is absolutely no denying that there is a wealth of valuable information out there, and it's readily available to anyone who is willing to take the time to learn how to use the systems on which this information resides. But for many entrepreneurs, sitting in front of a monitor exploring the depths of DIALOG or other online systems is not the most productive use of time. These people need, but usually cannot afford, a professional researcher on staff.

Perhaps this is where you find yourself: intrigued by the world of online information but without the resources to hire staff and without the time to learn and do it yourself. What can you do? Fortunately, an industry has emerged, parallel to the development of the online industry, that can answer this question. This new breed of entrepreneur is the information broker. Known by many names (independent information professional or consultant, fee-based information service, free-lance librarian, etc.), this specialist has access to the kinds of information you've read about here and is ready to work with you to meet your information needs.

MORE THAN JUST A KEYBOARD OPERATOR

When you hire an information broker, you're hiring more than an "information wizard" who holds the keys to this magic kingdom and will grant you access for a fee. In the early days of the industry, a broker could make a good living in this way, but today the broker is offering a great many value-added services in addition to access to the information systems.

The type and degree of value-added service will vary from broker to broker, and the availability and scope should be one of the criteria you use in

John H. Everett is an information VAR (value-added reseller), coauthor of *Information for Sale: How to Start and Operate Your Own Data Research Service* and *The Information Broker's Handbook: How to Profit From the Information Age,* editor of "Information Broker" newsletter, and Assistant Forum Administrator of the Working From Home Forum on CompuServe.

selecting a broker and agreeing to the services you'll receive. Often, the value-added service will take one (or more) of the following forms:

1 *Conducting a reference interview.* In some instances (perhaps in many), you won't know exactly what information you need. You'll have a problem, such as the need to make a decision, and you'll take that problem to an information broker. By talking with you, the broker should be able to help you define your problem in terms of the information you need in order to solve that problem (make that decision).

2 *Knowing where to look.* It shouldn't be necessary for you to approach the broker with a list of databases to be searched and the key words to be used in the search request. At a minimum, the broker should be familiar enough with your information needs to be able to use the appropriate information resources and fashion the search request. And the broker should be able to use both electronic and traditional sources of information, depending on the specifics of your project. If your information need requires online searching, manual research, telephone interviews, focus groups, on-the-street interviews, or public records research, your broker should be able to do any of these things or arrange to have it done.

3 *Familiarity with the subject area.* While many brokers are generalists and offer their services in a variety of areas, more and more are specialists, serving a particular market with a specific type of information. If you have a specialized need, say, for example, a patent search, it is essential that you find someone with extensive patent searching experience. Otherwise, you'll be paying for someone's learning curve (or worse, for someone's mistakes).

4 *Finding the right amount of information.* If you're interested in reading about a specific subject, say, the use of passive solar energy in the design of home greenhouses, you really don't want everything that's ever been written about solar energy. You want only those few articles that directly address the specific situation you're interested in. Occasionally, a client (or a broker) will mistake quantity for quality. Are 100 articles relating to your subject really better than 10 articles that are exactly on the topic? Helpful hint: It's usually a good idea to tell the broker approximately how many articles you expect as a result of the search.

5 *Analysis and recommendations.* With a subject specialist, you might also expect more work following the initial search. An experienced competitive intelligence specialist can analyze the results of the search, pull out and highlight the relevant information, summarize the results, and, often, make recommendations. How much of this analysis and recommendation you request (and use) is up to you.

6 *Creating a complete information package.* Very few brokers will today consider a list of bibliographic citations to be a complete information product. When you have an information problem, you probably wouldn't consider a reading list to be a solution to that problem. While many brokers work alone or in a small group, through networking with other information specialists they can provide you with a full range of services, including both online and manual research, document retrieval (getting copies of the full text of relevant articles, either online or manually), postprocessing search results into a highly readable and useful package, and follow-up services to keep you current on your chosen topic.

WHAT KINDS OF QUESTIONS CAN AN INFORMATION BROKER ANSWER?

There are as many different kinds of questions as there are information brokers, but perhaps a few examples of questions asked of and answered by The Rugge Group will help you understand the ways in which you can use the services of an information broker.

Q: What is the market for Christmas trees in Hawaii?

A: An entrepreneur was interested in exploring the possibility of exporting Christmas trees to Hawaii from the West Coast. He wanted to know how large the market for Christmas trees was in Hawaii and how that market was being served. This project did not require an online search, but The Rugge Group was able to contact the right people in Hawaii to determine that the opportunity the entrepreneur was hoping for was not there. For a few hundred dollars, the client was able to make a business decision that saved thousands of dollars.

Q: What's been written recently about the dangers of hiring security personnel without proper pre-employment screening?

A: The client that asked this question is a security firm that was interested in selling pre-employment screening services to private security firms. The client wanted recent articles that pointed up the danger of not using such a service before hiring security guards. The more sensational the article, the better suited it was to the client's purpose. The Rugge Group was able to use a number of newspaper and magazine databases to provide references to and the full text of several articles on this topic.

Q: What is the average development cost for a software package?

A: The Rugge Group performed an online search of the trade press to identify leading software developers and to find articles on the cost of developing software. Major software developers were interviewed to determine the time and dollar costs involved. The final report to the client consisted of a bibliography of relevant articles, the full text of selected articles, and a narrative report detailing the interviews with software developers.

Q: How can the archdiocese of a major Southwestern city better serve the local Hispanic population?

A: This major research project, involving 400 personal interviews and focus groups (in four dialects of Spanish), required The Rugge Group to survey Hispanic print, radio, and television media to determine the relative costs of reaching the target population and to analyze the relative effectiveness of the various events. This project involved extensive telephone work, but very little online searching.

Q: What are the current statistics on the "upscale bread" market?

A: The client needed statistics to support a venture capital proposal and business plan. The Rugge Group performed an online search of the business and trade press and identified the top five companies in the upscale bread market. Executives with these five companies were interviewed to solicit their opinions of where the market was headed. The client was furnished with a complete bibliography, selected articles, and a narrative report. As with many projects, this effort required both a search of online sources of secondary information and collection and analysis of primary information through interviews.

Q: Are there any adverse effects related to the anesthetic known as Nafimidone? A client had been involved in the clinical trials of this drug and was believed to have suffered physical impairment from the experience.

A: While there were many levels to this project, the initial effort was an online search of MEDLINE and related databases, looking for articles relating to the adverse effects of Nafimidone. Later efforts involved identifying expert witnesses, examining the process by which a new drug is approved by the Food and Drug Administration (FDA), and filing Freedom of Information (FOI) requests to obtain critical documents from the FDA and the National Institute of Health.

This is only a small sample of the kinds of projects The Rugge Group can handle, but you should have a better idea of how you can use an information broker in your business. Don't discount the benefits of using a broker without first talking to one. Any competent broker will tell you when you need his or her help and when you don't. In most cases, asking "Can you help me with this?" is free, and it may open up opportunities and possibilities that surprise you.

FINDING AN INFORMATION BROKER

If you are convinced that you need an information broker, how do you go about finding one? Often, the answer to that question is as close as your library. In fact, sometimes it is your library. Many public and academic libraries now offer fee-based information services, and you shouldn't overlook this as an option. Libraries will often also have lists of information brokers in the area to whom they can refer patrons whose information needs exceed the resources of the library (perhaps your library doesn't offer online searching, or maybe their turnaround time is too slow for your needs, or possibly they don't have a searcher on staff who is experienced in your field).

Burwell Enterprises of Houston, Texas, publishes *The Directory of Fee-Based Information Services* annually. This directory lists hundreds of information brokers offering a wide variety of services in virtually every subject category. If your library doesn't have a copy, or if you think you'll be making regular use of the directory, you can order a copy directly by contacting Burwell Enterprises, Suite 214, 3724 F.M. 1960 W., Houston, TX 77068 (713/537-9051). There's also a professional association of information brokers, called the Association of Independent Information Professionals (AIIP), that can help you locate brokers in your area. You can reach the AIIP through The Rugge Group, 46 Hiller Drive, Oakland, CA 94618 (415/644-9654).

If you're online already, you can visit the Working From Home Forum (SIG) on CompuServe. This forum has a section of its message board and library (section 4) devoted to the topic of database research and information brokering, and many active brokers can be found there. In addition, the AIIP is online there, too, so you've got two resources in one. To get directly to the Working From Home Forum from any prompt on the CompuServe system, use the command "GO WORK."

And, finally, you can always use old reliable—the Yellow Pages. In many larger cities, the Yellow Pages has a category for "Information Brokers." If your town has yet to reach this stage of enlightenment, you can also check under "Library Research & Services" or "Information Bureaus" (an unfortunate category for brokers), or the specific subject area (such as "Attorneys' Service Bureaus," "Legal Research," or "Market Research").

CHOOSING AN INFORMATION BROKER

Despite appearances to the contrary, finding an information broker may be the easier half of the battle. Selecting the broker who is right for you may be the more difficult decision. As you go through this process, bear in mind that you are not required to hire the first broker you meet, nor the broker with the niftiest marketing material, nor the broker with the lowest fees. You need a broker who can give you the service you need at a price you can afford. The Rugge Group always gives a firm price quote on a project and sets a not-to-exceed budget before beginning any searching.

For many people, the decision to select one professional or service firm over another is one that doesn't get the same time and consideration used to select one pair of shoes over another. That is unfortunate, for the former decision is so much more important than the latter. Yet people pick a bank based solely on location or cute television ads, and they may choose an attorney or physician for the same kind of reasons. If you choose an information broker without doing your homework, you're risking a lot on superficial characteristics.

By investing a bit of time to find the right information broker for you and your information needs, you'll save time and money in the long run. Take the time to interview, in person, the information brokers in your area (geographic and subject). Make sure you'll be doing business with someone you like, with someone who understands what you need and can provide it, with someone who will do what it takes to complete your projects on time and within budget. If you're not comfortable with your information broker, you won't be comfortable with your information.

Your information needs are not always simple and straightforward, and meeting those needs will often be a complex process. But the intelligent use of your own resources (professional networks, your own experience and expertise, trade journals you read regularly, trade shows you attend, etc.) and the services of a competent information broker will usually combine to meet successfully even the most perplexing information need.

If you have any questions about information brokering or if you'd like to consult with me about the services of information brokers, please feel free to contact me at the following address: Response Time, Suite O-69, 314 MacArthur Commons, Irving, TX 75062; CompuServe: 75515,1144; DIALMAIL: 18847; MCI Mail: 213-2464; GEnie: J.EVERETT1.■■

6

Voice Mail

VOICE MAIL IS HOT

After all the discussion of electronic mail (E-mail) in the previous chapters, you may be surprised to know that there is something even newer to contemplate. According to *Government Computer News,* Lawrence S. Cohan, director of innovative office systems for General Services Administration (GSA), predicted that "In some year in the future, voice mail is going to have as much of an impact on office automation as word processing has already had." Cohan, noting that someday voice mail will outdistance E-mail, cited the advantage that voice mail offers over E-mail, which is that voice mail uses an ordinary touch-tone telephone. As a result, it is more readily accessible to people without the keyboard skills necessary to use E-mail.

According to the *Government Computer News* article, Cohan mentioned the advantages of voice mail, which include the minimization of time-wasting "telephone tag" and the composition of more succinct messages, which also saves time otherwise lost in chatting about hobbies, families, and other topics not relevant to the purpose of the call. Cohan insisted that once people use voice mail, they become hooked on it. The largest group of users—by a substantial margin—is women, although none of the experts are able to account for this. Cohan believes that voice mail looks even better when the disadvantages of E-mail are considered. Cohan cited two of E-mail's disadvantages to be (1) that there are several different E-mail systems on which one message may have to be sent to reach all correspondents and (2) that the speed of the message is lost if individuals do not regularly check their electronic mailboxes.

According to an in-depth report from the New York consulting firm Frost and Sullivan, "An estimated two-thirds of all phone calls are less important than the work they interrupt." The 353-page report on the benefits and future of voice mail stated that "Costs savings [from voice mail] are numerous and include direct savings from the reduced number of calls, shortened calls, and movement of calls to lower rate periods. In many cases too, a voice message can substitute for a memo or letter at less cost." The same report predicted a 60 percent annual growth rate for voice mail to run through the 1990s.

According to Frost and Sullivan, large businesses have been the first to adopt these systems, accounting for 52 percent of the 1987 market. Systems based on personal computers (PCs) account for 1 percent of the total. The least expensive systems today cost around $200 and consist of a printed circuit board that is inserted into a microcomputer and is controlled by a software program. The report states that voice messaging system sales in 1987 reached $300 million and could reach $3.2 billion a year by 1992. More than 45 companies offer voice-messaging systems. IBM/Rolm leads the market with a 30 percent share.

Venture Development Corporation's (One Apple Hill, Natick, MA 01760) report, "The U.S. Voice Mail/Response Industry: Beyond Telephone Answering to Integration into the Office of the Future," predicts that domestic sales of voice mail systems will increase at an annual average growth rate of 30 percent over the next five years. The technology, according to the report, can save companies time and money and is renewing interest in what was once considered a luxury industry.

What is this technology that these news items are raving about? A very simple but immense advance over the traditional answering machine. It is, in essence, a programmable computer system that allows callers to select what information they wish to receive (listen to). The information or message is stored on a computer disk just as if it were stored on the more familiar cassette tape you probably have in your answering machine today.

What separates the two systems—voice mail and an answering machine—is the options offered to the caller. On the conventional answering machine, a caller dials in, is answered by a message, and is asked to leave a message. With voice mail, the additional options are myriad. The caller can, for example, input a code (perhaps, the last 4 digits of the caller's phone number, sent by pressing one or more than one of the keys on a touch-tone phone) and then be given a second message stored specifically for that caller. Messages can be customized for individual callers. The caller may then be asked to leave a message which is subsequently stored for listening when the owner calls back in.

The voice mail device can also be programmed to deliver an entire series of messages or to ask questions and accept a caller's response to all of them. Surveys can be carried out. Orders can be taken. The equipment can store hundreds of phone numbers itself and can call each number in sequence and deliver a sales pitch that the recipient can control with his or her own push-button phone at home. In this fashion, complex telemarketing strategies can be carried out, automatically and totally unattended. The device can also transfer a call to another number. The voice mail system can even record a message and, after the caller hangs up, can call someone at a different phone and deliver the recorded message to the listener there. Voice mail is a much more complete and flexible system than is a standard answering machine. Interruptions can be avoided. Since it takes three times as long to recover from an interruption (get back to business) than it takes to deal with the interruption itself, and since, according to "Teleconnect" (April 1987), half of all business calls are for the simple one-way transfer of information, voice mail makes sense.

A MARRIAGE MADE IN ELECTRONIC HEAVEN

The concept of voice messaging is a marriage between the ability to record human speech digitally—in a form a computer can read—and the touch-tone telephone. With this combination, the caller can control various functions of a computer, and the computer, in turn, can serve as a relay system for voice messages.

Digital voice recording on a computer has been around for many years. It is only in the recent past, however, that the quality of the recordings has been high enough to make them generally useful. With the development in the 1960s of the tone phone (as opposed to the dial or "pulse" phone) and its widespread adoption, the union was complete. With the rapid increases in computer processing speed and disk storage capabilities, voice mail has moved out of the confining realm of mainframe computers and into the more available world of the PC.

The final development that makes voice mail worthy of note in the pages of a book for the small or home business is the price changes. Instead of stratospheric prices of the early systems—reaching into the hundreds of thousands of dollars—PC-based voice systems are now available for a few hundred dollars. System pricing is mainly based on capacity. The software that actually controls the message-handling capabilities is quite sophisticated even in the least expensive systems. What separates the $300 system from the $20,000 system is, simply, the number of incoming phone lines the network can support. If you have only a single phone number to support, a PC system may be the complete answer. If you have more than two or three different numbers or a complex PBX (private branch exchange) multiline net, you are going to have to move up the cost ladder but not necessarily out of the world of the PC.

VOICE MAIL APPLICATIONS

With this in mind, here are a few examples of how voice mail is being used already:

- A voice mail system is being used by the Professional Comedians Association to facilitate bookings between comedians and club agents. By calling in once a week, comedians can store information about what nights they will be available to work (as each day is "read" to them by the voice system, they enter a "1" on their touch-tone phone if they are free that night, "0" if they are not) and in what areas of the country they are able to work. Then, each week, the information is printed out and sent to booking agents around the country.

- A realtor in Indiana uses a voice mail system to control and facilitate calls from clients to their agents. Since most of the realtors are in the field all day, contacting them can be difficult. With the voice mail system, as a client calls in for an agent a message is generated and left in the system in that agent's secure area. The system then calls the agent's beeper to indicate that mail is waiting. The agent can then call in, enter his or her personal code, and receive the stored messages.

- According to the *New England Insurance Times* (February 4, 1986), insurance agents are using voice mail to do cold calling to generate leads. Recipients of calls who offer a positive response are asked to leave their names and phone numbers. The agents then follow up.

- *Financial Planning* (June 1986) reported on how a voice mail system helped a Massachusetts financial services firm by doing cold calling and delivering detailed messages about the services available to the firm's customers.

- An Arkansas cardiologist, to better market his services, installed a "Heart Watch Hotline" that allowed people from all over the state to call a WATS line and choose from a menu of short health tips. He changes the menu choices of the message weekly to keep caller interest. Of course, the doctor's name and phone number are prominently included in the messages.

- The *Market Chronicle* of May 1986 reported on a stockbrokerage in Texas that has a voice mail system in operation to deliver market information and outlooks, and also to accept stock orders to buy or sell 24 hours a day. For clients who work odd hours, it is the only time they may be able to get to a phone to initiate the transactions they desire.

- As reported in *Medical World News* (June 1986), a dentist in Massachusetts uses a voice mail system to call his patients scheduled for the following day and deliver a friendly reminder of their appointments, and to reinforce the value of their regular check-ups. The staff calls during the day to remind the patients "in person." Patients who are not at home during the day are called by the voice mail system in the evening hours. The patients hear their doctor's own voice (digitized), but amazingly real) reminding them of their upcoming visits. It can even remind specific patients to "not eat after midnight" or "bring your medications with you"—all in the dentist's voice.

- The *Computer Dealer* (February 1986) tells of a subsidiary of NCR that introduced an IBM clone and wanted to do something extra in the area of product support. To do this, the subsidiary installed a voice mail system. With it, dealers of the computer can call anytime, leave their questions, and have a reply from the technical staff the next day when they call back in. Individual answers to the dealers' queries are stored in each dealer's private mail area, which is accessible with the individual's identification (ID) code.

In general, voice mail applications fall into one of four categories. First, there is the classic voice mail delivery system. This could be for a single business with several employees. Or, the setup could be for multiple users in several businesses. For example, one computer could establish a customized answering service. Each business could buy or rent a mailbox, and a message or series of messages could be delivered to the business's callers. Each mailbox number is given at call in. If a caller wants Crystal Plumbing, for example, he or she can choose Crystal's mailbox number, listen to a short advertising blurb, and then get a chance to ask a question. If the caller indicates the need to have a service call, the voice mail can call the plumber (wherever the plumber is) and forward that message. As the plumber moves from house call to house call, he or she can call into the system and change the forwarding number for messages. The service could be leased out to 10 or more businesses (limited mainly by the host computer's disk storage capability) and could be available 24 hours a day. Such a business might be able to undercut the costs of an answering service.

Second, there is what one might call strictly an interactive, informational voice system which enables callers to control what information they want to listen to. A home repair (or car repair, or household emergencies, or poison control, etc.) voice mail hotline could be offered. The system could be set up as a marketing tool for almost any sort of business. Just as videotex (see Glossary) is a medium for presenting information as visual display on a computer monitor, "audiotex" could be a spoken alternative.

A third application for voice mail is inbound telemarketing. With this application a user calls in and directs the system to deliver whatever commercial advertisement the user desires; the caller also may be able to place an order over the system as he or she responds to various questions. For example, a single voice mail system could serve as a regional shopping guide. Merchants could buy ad space, and a general menu of goods and services could be produced. "Press 1 for restaurants, press 2 for automobile dealers" and so on. Then when the caller selects an area of interest, he or she could be routed to another set of menus. Merchants could pay $35 to $50 a month and change their ad's message (2 minutes) each month, or weekly for an added fee; both the merchant's and the system's owners could advertise the system. The voice mail system could also log inquiries from people who wanted a sales representative of a particular business to call. This sort of application is already being used in many areas of the country. It is particularly effective for marketing opportunities that change rapidly, such as real estate, job placements, and automobile sales.

The last application, outbound telemarketing, is a setup in which the voice system itself initiates contact by dialing a series of numbers. Then it switches into a system similar to that for inbound telemarketing. One might describe this as the phone equivalent of junk mail.

These are the general applications of voice mail. Some specific capabilities offered by modern voice mail systems may include:

- *Electronic phone books*   You can store phone numbers to be called on a specific time and date and have the equipment deliver a series of messages. The series can be controlled by the receiver by pressing a touch-tone keypad in response to questions.

- *"Smart" call handling*   The voice mail system can answer a call and deliver a greeting and instructions. A frequent caller can be assigned a voice "mail box." By entering his or her code (again, from a touch-tone phone), the caller can hear a series of messages specifically for him or her, spoken in your own voice. If such callers desire (and you wish), they can press another code and have their calls forwarded to another number. Calls can be screened in this way so as to eliminate work interruptions from trivial calls and yet allow the important callers to get through.

- *Dictation*   Some systems allow you to call in and dictate over the phone a message that can be transcribed by you or your secretary later. However, since digitized voice recordings consume a large amount of computer disk space, to use this facility to any extent you will need to have a computer equipped with a large hard (fixed) disk drive.

- *Calendar*   Some voice mail systems have a built-in calendar function.

You can, for example, program the system to call you a month from now and deliver a prerecorded reminder to attend an important meeting.

SYSTEM SPOTLIGHT: THE WATSON VOICE INFORMATION SYSTEM (VIS)

Watson (Figure 6-1) was introduced by Natural Microsystems (6 Mercer Road, Natick, MA 01760; 800-6-WATSON) in 1984. Since then, the Watson modem and voice mail technology has been extensively reviewed and well-received by the industry, as well as by the consumers.

WATSON ALONE

As the bare unit, Watson comes as a full-length board (strictly for the IBM line of computers and compatibles) that is installed in one of the slots inside the computer's chassis. Once it is secured on your computer, you have both a functional Hayes-compatible 1200-baud modem (or, optionally, a 2400-baud modem) and an instant voice mail system. You plug the Watson into a standard RJ11 phone jack, connect the phone directly to the Watson, and you are ready to begin. The software is then installed on your hard disk drive. Installation is simply a process of running a program on the software diskettes, which transfers the programs from diskette to hard drive.

Once you have the hardware plugged in and the software safely transferred to your hard drive, you can fine-tune Watson. You call up the software and configure the initial settings. By pressing ALT-F6, you can tell Watson to answer after a certain number of rings, to hang up (when dialing out) if no one

Figure 6-1 Watson modem and voice mail system.

answers after a given number of rings, etc. You can also configure the data compression to be used for the system for each card file. What does that mean? Since the VIS stores all voice information on your hard drive, for a complex system disk space is at a premium. You can get about 45 minutes of high-quality (low compression) recording for 10 megabytes of disk space. One set of choices might be to have the outgoing messages recorded at low compression (of the highest voice quality but also consuming the most disk space) and have the incoming messages saved at high compression (tolerable voice quality but taking up less disk space). You might run the risk of having a garbled message or two if someone really speaks poorly, but if your system's activity might be high and the incoming traffic active, you may have to risk it.

The basic Watson comes with many sophisticated capabilities. In its simplest incarnation, it can be an answering machine. It will accept incoming calls and deliver a standard "we can't come to the phone right now—please leave a message" greeting. You can use the greeting that comes with the package (delivered in a pleasing female voice) or record your own using a phone plugged into the system. At the other end of the spectrum, Watson can be your receptionist. It can be set up to answer the phone, deliver a standard or individualized greeting, and accept a message. Then Watson can call you at another phone number and deliver the message it just received. For security, you can have Watson wait for a code to be entered on the remote phone and play back the message only after the right code has been entered. As you travel around, you can call in from wherever you are and change the number you want to have messages sent to. With the built-in calendar, you can configure Watson to call a number at a specified time and date and deliver a message reminding you of an appointment. Watson can also function as a dictation machine. You can call in and dictate a memorandum to be transcribed later.

As mentioned, Watson also serves as a Hayes-compatible 1200-baud modem. Watson comes with a communications program included in the package. Because it follows the ubiquitous Hayes standard command language, you can also use virtually any other communications software with the modem as well. You can use Watson for E-mail or information access. Thus, you get two electronic systems in one.

One final benefit of the Watson package is software that enables you to call in from the modem of a remote computer and take over control of the Watson-equipped computer. Suppose you have Watson on your computer at work and a plain modem at home. You come home from work on Friday and decide you want to revise a spreadsheet or word processing document over the weekend. If you didn't have Watson and you didn't remember to bring a copy of the file on disk from work, this scenario would mean a trip back to the office or no work that weekend. With Watson, however, you call in to Watson at work and press a sequence of keys on your phone (which includes a security code you designate), and Watson will switch to its modem function during the same call. You can then have your home modem establish a digital connection with Watson's modem. At that point, you have several operations available to you. You can have Watson send or receive any file that exists on either computer. You can also delete files on the Watson host computer. You can execute any DOS program on the office computer—even copy files to a printer—all from your home outpost.

WATSON WITH VIS

As you can see, for the $199 price tag, you get a great number of capabilities with the standard Watson. For an additional $199, you can get a great deal more. Natural Microsystem's "Voice Information System" (VIS) software turns the Watson Voice Mail system into an intelligent, caller-controlled voice information system. With a bare bones Watson system, you have a sophisticated, highly intelligent answering machine. With the VIS option you have an interactive voice system, capable of asking questions and delivering answers based on the responses of the caller.

The VIS option for Watson comes with additional software on diskette and a specially equipped version of the standard Watson communications board. The board is equipped with a special piece of "firmware" (see Glossary) called a PROM chip. By outward appearance, the card looks just like the standard Watson and is installed into a computer slot no differently. Likewise, the software is transferred from disk to hard drive. To develop any kind of information delivery system, you need to use Watson VIS with a hard disk drive, 20 megabytes or larger. Since the messages that will be delivered are digitized and stored on disk space, you have to have adequate storage capacity to use the VIS effectively. Try to choose a hard drive with a relatively fast access time as well. Access time is usually measured and reported for drives in milliseconds. The lower the number, the faster the drive reads and writes information to the plates that make up the hard drive. Slow hard drive times will make the switching between messages seem a bit slow and a little jerky. But even with slow drives, it is only a minor point, and most listeners probably won't notice.

For our example, we will set up a simple information system; nothing more than a call-in system. Users will call in and, through a series of spoken menus, be directed to the information they want. We will not make use of the out-dialing capabilities of the Watson system.

After the installation process, setting up your Watson VIS requires another process involving setting up a series of "cards" for each of several files. Watson has separate files for a phone book (to maintain personal directory of names and phone numbers which can be used for outgoing message delivery), an outgoing message file (most important for the application we will implement here), an incoming message file (a new card is added every time a call is accepted by the system), a calendar file (to create and maintain an appointment diary), and a dictation file. Each card in the files has five fields of information. The first is the time-date field. It is only used when there is to be a timed "dial and deliver" sequence (for instance, in telemarketing). For example, you can have Watson "wake up" at 6:00 P.M. and start a sequence to dial a set series of phone numbers, deliver a series of messages controlled by the recipient of the call, and record the recipient's responses. Since the strategy for this example was for incoming calls, this field was not used.

The second field is the addressee name field. For outgoing dialing, Watson will look for this field in the phone file and use the number to call out from there. For our example, this field was used to enter a VIS command for our "answer-only" system. The third field is the number field, which, again, is important for dial-out sequences only. For our purposes, we used it as a second command field. The next field is the ID code field. You can number your cards here and refer to them in the VIS command language—much like a "GOTO x" command in BASIC. The final field is the key field. It allows you to identify which card starts a VIS sequence and which cards are follow-up cards. For our information delivery system, only the outgoing messages were of significance. If the *file, card,* and *field* terminology sounds like a database, you are right. Watson's VIS is a database with the stored information (digitized voice recordings) accessible through the VIS programming language. Nothing more, nothing less.

The feature that separates the VIS from the routine Watson is the set of programming instructions added with VIS. With this set of commands, you can sequence your outgoing message file to request and respond to key presses from a touch-tone phone and to move to set messages based on a series of responses from the caller. The following is a simplified segment of the outgoing message file that was set up for a Healthline system showing how each card directed the caller's session. A flow diagram for the process is presented in Figure 6-2. *Note:* The "Card #" is given for illustration only and does not appear on the actual VIS cards.

Time/Date Field	Addressee/ Command 1 Field	Phone Number/ Command 2 Field	ID Code Field	Key Field
Card #1				
	NEXT: ? 1080	NEXT: GOTO 2	1	A
	NEXT: ? 720	NEXT: GOTO 3		

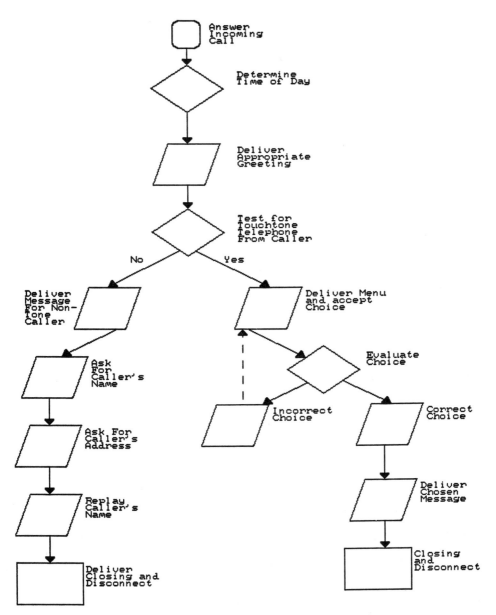

Figure 6-2 *Flow diagram for Healthline system.*

Explanation: These commands instruct Watson to check the number of minutes that have elapsed since the previous midnight. Watson first checks to see if it has been more than 18 hours (1080 minutes or after 6:00 P.M.). If so, it jumps two cards (to card #3). If it has not been 1080 minutes or more, it next asks if it has been greater than 720 minutes (12:00 noon) since the previous midnight. If that condition is true, VIS will jump to card #4. If neither condition is true, VIS simply moves to the next card in sequence (card #2). Note the "A" in the Key Field. This identifies this card as the first in an *Autoanswer* sequence. All incoming calls are handled with the card sequence beginning here.

Card #2
              NEXT: JUMP 3   **C**

Explanation: The voice message recorded here was "Good morning." The "C" in the Key Field will appear in all the following cards. It means that these cards are a continuation of the VIS card sequence started with the "A" card. The command "NEXT: JUMP 3" instructs VIS to jump to the third card in the sequence after this voice message is delivered. That is, jump cards 3 and 4 to card #5.

Card #3
              NEXT: JUMP 2   **C**

Explanation: The voice message here was "Good evening." We "JUMP" now to the second following card (card #5).

Card #4
              NEXT: JUMP 1   **C**

Explanation: The voice message here was "Good afternoon." "JUMP" to the very next card (card #5).

Card #5
        NEXT: TEST 3
    C

Explanation: The voice message with this card is "If you are calling from a touch-tone phone, please press any button now." We "NEXT" execute the "TEST" command, one of the unique features of the VIS software. It waits 10 seconds for the caller to press a button on his or her touch-tone phone. If a button is pressed (the condition is true), VIS jumps to the third following card (card #8). If the condition is false (no button pressed), VIS assumes that the caller has a rotary dial phone and goes to the very next card.

Card #6
        NEXT: CALL @11900
    C

Explanation: The message here is "We're sorry, but without a touch-tone phone you are unable to control this information system. Please answer the following questions so that we may send more information about the HealthLine to you in the mail." The "NEXT" command sends the caller to a subroutine beginning at card 11900 (see below). (For those of you familiar with BASIC, this is analogous to a "GOSUB" in BASIC: A GOSUB branches a program to a subprogram, performs that segment's function, and then returns to the main program at the next command.)

Card #7
        NEXT: HANGUP
    C

Explanation: VIS has returned from the routine at card #11900 and now delivers a voice message that states: "Thank you for calling. Remember: when you call again, use touch-tone telephone." The "NEXT" command is simply to hang up the phone.

```
Card #8
          NEXT: NUMBER 1                              11500 C
              NEXT: + 110      NEXT: JUMP @0
```

Explanation: This begins the user-directed session. VIS delivers the voice menu: "Press 1 to hear about heart disease, press 2 to learn about cholesterol" and so on. VIS has already determined that the caller is using a touch-tone phone. The first command—"NEXT: NUMBER 1"—allows Watson to accept one digit pressed from the push-button phone. If more than one number is pressed, only the first number pressed is accepted. Watson then adds 110 to the number pressed. The third command is a "JUMP" to the card number coinciding to the number pressed plus 110. If a choice is made that does not have a corresponding card number, VIS moves to the next card (card #9). In this example, item choices 1 through 6 are valid.

```
Card #9
          NEXT: JUMP −1                                      C
```

Explanation: The voice message here is "Sorry. That is an incorrect choice. Please try again." The command that is issued will "JUMP" back to the preceding card (card #8) and redeliver the voice menu.

```
Card #10
          NEXT: JUMP 6                              111 C
```

Explanation: The user has pressed menu item 1 and now receives the message on heart disease. Once the message is delivered, we "JUMP" to the sixth following card (card #16).

```
Card #11
          NEXT: JUMP 5                              112 C
```

Explanation: Item 2 was selected from the menu and the second health message is delivered. When completed, we jump five cards—again, to card #16.

Card #12
              NEXT: JUMP 4   **113 C**

Explanation: Health message 3 is delivered; jump to card #16.

Card #13
              NEXT: JUMP 3   **114 C**

Explanation: Health message 4; jump to card #16.

Card #14 .
              NEXT: JUMP 2   **115 C**

Explanation: Health message 5; jump to card #16.

Card #15
              NEXT: JUMP 1   **116 C**

Explanation: Health message 6; jump to the next card.

Card #16
              NEXT: HANGUP   **C**

Explanation: Watson has delivered the chosen message and now delivers a "Thank you for calling . . ." final message. The "NEXT" command is "HANGUP."

Card #17
                    NEXT: RECORD 15   **11900 C**

Explanation: This is our "GOSUB" called from card #6. VIS delivers the message "After the tone, please say your name." VIS delivers a tone and then records to disk whatever the caller says for 15 seconds and goes to the next card.

Card #18
                    NEXT: RECORD 30   **C**

Explanation: The voice message now asks the caller to say his or her address. It records for 30 seconds to disk. Next card.

Card #19
                    NEXT: RECORD 20   **C**

Explanation: The voice message asks for the caller's phone number and records for 20 seconds. Next card.

Card #20
                    NEXT: CALL RETURN   **C**

Explanation: This is the final card in the "GOSUB." Watson says "Thank you for your cooperation" and does a "RETURN" to card #7.

As you can readily see, programming the Watson VIS system will require you to learn about the available commands and place them in the appropriate cards. This is the one instance in this book where an application does require "programming." While not the easiest of tasks, thoroughly reading the manuals (there are three) will allow you to start experimenting. An example of an automated "dial and deliver" program is included in the VIS manual.

Since you may not be totally enamored with the prospect of programming Watson and the VIS system, Natural Microsystems has made available a simpler alternative, at least for setting up a voice-based E-mail system. The "Business Central" template is a set of preprogrammed VIS cards that establish a set of voice mailboxes. The "Administrator" is an interface that guides you through setting up the "Business Central" mailboxes, using menu choices rather than the VIS programming language. There are also predefined packages available for a medical office and an automobile dealership.

The VIS option makes Watson flexible and programmable, and lends it immense potential. The simple application presented here only touches on the possibilities. A similar caller-directed sequence can be delivered as a "dial-up" program as well for telemarketing. You could easily add an electronic mailbox module as one of the menu choices. The manual for the VIS option explains the commands available adequately. Unfortunately, there are not enough example sequences for my taste. The cost for Watson with the VIS option is now under $400 (on some streets). For the marketing professional—in all walks of life—it can be a superb tool. For a demonstration, you can call the Watson demonstration system at 1-800-6-WATSON.

THE HUMAN TOUCH

One of the obvious objections with voice mail is that it suffers from the same impersonal approach that answering machines have been accused of. There are many who, revolting at technology, refuse to talk to these "inhuman devices." Voice mail will, undoubtedly, face the same similar rejection as it becomes more prevalent. Customers may turn elsewhere.

A hint at how the problem might be handled in the future has been developed by the Headquarters Companies. Called Automated Human Voice Mail, which is a good descriptive term, it is an innovative combination of human contact and digital technology. It allows for the human touch to be added to the efficiency of electronic voice technology.

Imagine an answering service that handles your incoming calls for you, allowing you to avoid unwanted interruptions to your work. Your calls are answered by a pleasant, live, human operator. Callers are told you are not available at the present time and asked to "please leave a message." The operator then asks for your caller's name, number, reason for calling, etc. As the replies are received, the operator has activated a voice mail system which, like Watson, records your caller's responses in your electronic mailbox. The caller's only contact is with the human operator.

The "automated" part happens only on your side of the operation. When you call in to check for messages, you don't get the human operator—you get the voice mail system. You input your security codes and press the appropriate phone buttons to start receiving your new messages. They are played back from the digitally recorded speech in the caller's voice, just as they were spoken. You can hear the inflections, urgency, and even messages in foreign languages if that is how they were spoken. None of your time is spent with the human operators. Only you face the high-tech side of the system; your callers do not. This system offers an ingenious combination of high-tech (on your side) and "high-touch" (on the client's end). One would have to think that answering services will be going to this system more and more to enhance efficiency. After all, half of the work of the operators is eliminated. Instead of answering your calls and relaying your messages, they handle only customer calls. The computer handles yours. The computer can also call and forward messages to your phone immediately after they are received, if you choose that option.

WORD OF WARNING

Remember: *Try before you buy.* Test the voice mail system you choose on your phone network before you make a purchase. For a single-line, single-PC-connection user, this warning is not etched in stone. You are unlikely to have problems with such a simple set up. However, if you have a multiline office, particularly if the office has a PBX with rotating lines, it is absolutely imperative that the system be tested in-house. Adjustments may have to be made for the voice mail or the PBX itself. If the marriage cannot be electronically consumated, you need to know so before you commit the time and money to the system.

7

A Reasonable Facsimile

A facsimile machine is a must, often more useful than the telephone. Many foreigners are more comfortable communicating in written English than speaking over the phone.

—Hal Plotkin, *Inc.'s Guide to International Business*

It is a simple idea, really. Imagine that you have a page of paper which contains print. The print could be anything: simple text, photographs, drawings, hieroglyphics, it doesn't matter. Now, imagine laying a very fine mesh screen on top of the paper. The mesh contains tiny boxes or openings at a density of 200 horizontally per inch and 200 vertically per inch (for you mathematicians, that's 40,000 per square inch).

Now, you fix the screen on the paper, and you have a friend across town fix a second screen on a blank piece of paper. The two of you will look at the boxes on the printed page one at a time. You call your friend on the phone and you agree that if the box on the printed page is dark, you will say "one" and your friend will fill the corresponding box on her blank sheet with a black ink pen. If the box is white, the two of you have agreed to call that a "zero," and your friend will not mark her page. You have agreed that you are going to count horizontally across each row and, when you reach the end of the row, you will go down to the beginning of the next row and count across it. Can you see that, once you have tediously gone across and down the entire page, your friend's paper will now contain a rough facsimile of your page?

According to Ken Joy, writing in *Marketing Computers* magazine ("Fax Leads Growth in Office Automation," June 1988), 1987 sales of facsimile (fax) machines exceeded 465,000 units. Sales for 1988 were projected to double those figures, and more than 2.5 million units were expected to be in place by

1990. it has been estimated that Sharp Electronics, one of the leaders in American sales, moved 12,000 machines a month in late 1987. More than 50 percent of the telephone communications between the United States and Japan are fax machine transmissions. According to reports by International Resource Development, Federal Express could lose as much as 30 percent of its overnight courier business to fax machines. Telex traffic across Western Union lines has decreased almost 50 percent since 1984. And here is the bottom line: Transmitting six pages of fax during late-night hours (after 11:00 P.M.) is 94 percent cheaper than Federal Express overnight service, 90 percent cheaper than an MCI overnight letter, and 91 percent cheaper than the U.S. Post Office's Express Mail service! Now that is cost-effectiveness!

Who is buying these devices? Not just big business. According to market researcher CAP International, small businesses (fewer than 100 employees) will have 1.1 million fax machines up and running by December 1989.

SLOW MATURATION

Like voice mail technology, facsimile transmissions are nothing new. According to most accounts the underlying technology was invented by a Scottish physician, Alexander Bain, in 1842, although *World Book Encyclopedia* attributes it to F. C. Bakewell, a London inventor, and his "copying telegraph." Bain's crude electromechanical device could translate wire signals and print an image on paper. The "printing" was effected by a pendulum swinging across a chemically treated piece of paper. The devices, however, evolved ever-so-slowly.

In the 1940s, facsimile transmitters were used by the Allies to send weather and troop maps. But the devices in those days required more than a bit of technical finesse. The paper to be sent was gingerly rolled onto a cylinder, and the transmission process—which took six minutes or more—often produced nothing more than an unsightly black smear at the receiving end. Needless to say, there were few applications that warranted such aggravation.

By the mid-1960s, there were about 40,000 fax machines in the United States, all produced by Bell Telephone. They were 100-pound floor models which were allowed space only in the mailrooms of the largest of corporations.

When the Federal Communications Commission's so-called Carterfone decision (a ruling in 1967 that allowed connecting devices other than those made by AT&T to be placed on Ma Bell's phone lines) opened the doors to competition for devices, the marketplace started heating up.

As so often is the case, a U.S. manufacturer (in this instance, Motorola) leaped out with one of the first non-AT&T machines, but it was quickly outpaced by the Japanese. Ricoh Co. Ltd. of Japan had financed a California firm's application of digital technology to the problem of transmitting images. The U.S.-based company developed a method which not only improved the quality of the image but greatly increased the rate of transfer. The Japanese quickly commercialized the technology and just as quickly dominated it. (It is easy to understand why the Japanese have been so quick to adopt fax technology. Their very ornate alphabet, featuring thousands of characters, is difficult to transmit using keyboard-based ASCII standards, and some of their business messages are still handwritten. The ability to transmit graphics just as they are makes fax the ideal medium for sending Japanese documents. In fact, today the fax machine is becoming a common home appliance in Japan.)

As fax machines began to proliferate, the protocols used to transmit their images were standardized. The Consultative Committee in International Telegraphy and Telephony (CCITT) (see Glossary), a section of the United Nations that meets in Geneva, set forth its first standards for fax communications in the mid 1960s. The first set of standards was called Group 1, and it allowed for image transmissions through an analog signal at about the equivalent of 300 baud (see Chapter 2), which meant a page flew across the lines in about six minutes. As the machines were improved, the Group 2 protocols cut transmission times in half and used digital signals. In 1983, the currently popular standard, Group 3, was approved. Group 3 provided for data compression (reducing the amount of image data that must be transmitted, by a factor that ranges from 5 to 10) and transmission speeds up to 9600 baud; it cut the time required to send a page to less than a minute. The Group 3 standard also allows for two degrees of sharpness of image: standard, which is 200 dots per inch (dpi) horizontally and 100 dpi vertically, or fine, which is 200 dpi both ways.

Sending images with the finer resolution approximately doubles transmission time, but it can greatly improve the image, which is a nice capability to have available when quality is important. (Fine resolution is actually a higher resolution than most television screens, but doesn't appear to be so because of the "smear" factor that TVs use to fill in missing dots.) A Group 4 CCITT standard, which was approved in 1984, allows for greatly improved resolution (300 by 300 dpi) and remarkable speeds (a page in about five seconds). However, since machines that meet the Group 4 standards are prohibitively expensive (generally, over $5000) and require special, dedicated digital phone lines that must be leased, it will be some time before they gain use apart from the most demanding circumstances. Such machines probably will not become common until the proposed fiber-optic Integrated Services Digital Network (ISDN) is entrenched early in the 1990s (see Chapter 9). See Table 7-1 for a comparison of fax speeds according to Group 1, 2, 3, and 4 standards.

TABLE 7-1.
Fax Speeds for Group 1, 2, 3, and 4 Standards

Group	Speed for 8 1/2″ × 11″ Document
1	6 minutes
2	3 minutes
3	Less than a minute (less than 30 seconds for most Group 3 machines)
4	Less than 10 seconds

Note: Speeds only apply with machines in the same class, e.g., Group 3 machines transmitting to Group 3 machines, etc. If you connect a Group 3 machine to a Group 2 machine, expect it to take 3 minutes to send a document.

Fortunately, all of the standards are "backwardly" compatible, which means that a Group 3 fax can send to both Group 1 (about 150,000 machines) and Group 2 (about 45,000) machines, and Group 2 machines can communicate with Group 1 machines. The reverse, however, is not true. Also remember: When faster machines communicate with older (slower) machines, the transmission speed drops back to that of the slower machine.

WHAT'S THE BIG DEAL?

What has made fax machines so hot for the small business lately is that they are now affordable. With the development of cheap thermal-printing transceivers and marked improvements on speed, fax machines are now practical. Rather than the $10,000 investment they were in the late 1970s, machines are now available for just over $1000, and the price is dropping rapidly as competition grows. While Canon is often credited with producing the first "personal" or small-business fax machine, more than 20 companies now produce fax machines suitable for personal or small-business applications (see Figures 7-1 and 7-2). The names of the manufacturers are, along with Canon, familiar ones— Sharp, NEC, Konica, Hitachi, and Murata. Japan accounts for virtually all producers.

Why is fax such a hot topic these days? Well, there are several reasons why this technology is becoming so popular. First, and probably foremost, is that fax machines are easy to use and virtually maintenance-free. Unlike computers, which can still be difficult to start using productively, fax machines are as easy to use as a touch-tone phone and a photocopy machine. A standard fax machine is a self-contained, unimposing device that looks like it belongs in an office. In actuality, it is composed of three units, a scanner, a modem, and a printer. The scanner reads the original sheet of paper and breaks the image up into a series of lines. Along each line as the image is scanned, the points along the line, called *pixels,* are tested for either black or white, on or off, 1 or 0. The scanning goes on, line by line, for the length of the

Figure 7-1 *Murata Business System's new family of fax machines for the retail marketplace. Each unit incorporates a fax machine, a telephone, and a copier.*

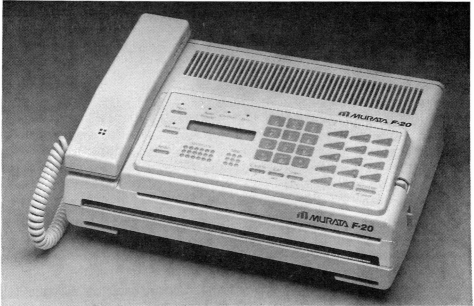

Figure 7-2 *Murata Business Systems F-20, which claims to be the "world's smallest fully featured facsimile machine."*

page. The string of digits thus generated is sent out through the second component of the the system, the modem. The modem dials the phone number of the receiving fax machine, and a connection is made. The sending fax conveys the image—converted to its digital form—to the remote modem and hangs up. The receiving fax then kicks in the third part to the puzzle, a printer, and translates the digital data back into the pixels that make up the transmitted image.

For you, the user, it's even simpler. You simply dial the phone number where you want the document to end up, slide the pages in the back of the machine, and it's off. (And with the new machines, most of this is done automatically for you.) Receiving a fax transmission is even easier. You just plug the machine into a standard RJ11 modular phone plug, put paper in it, turn it on, and leave it. As fax calls come into your machine, the replicas (facsimiles) will be automatically churned out and placed in a tray for you to pick up later. What could be simpler?

A second appealing feature of fax is that it is fast. Unlike regular or even overnight mail, facsimiles arrive immediately.

Third, fax is powerful. Not only can you send plain text, but you can also send virtually any type of printed matter. Contracts complete with signatures (that are often legally binding), prescriptions, plans, graphs and charts—anything that can be scanned—can be moved through fax. Fax breaks through the language barriers of printed electronic text. Fax is graphics-based and deals with images rather than characters or words. You can send English, Chinese, Japanese, or Russian characters through the same fax machine and mix them at random. If you still write notes by hand, fax can handle them without difficulty. It just doesn't matter. As long as it shows up on paper, it can be faxed.

Fourth, fax machines are well-standardized. Unlike modem use, there is no need to grapple with baud rates, parity, echoplex, or data bits. No need to agree upon file transfer protocols or subscribing to the same electronic mail (E-mail) system to transmit materials. All fax machines play by the same rules, and, since they do, users have no need to concern themselves with the actual rules. All you really need to provide a fax machine with is an image to scan and a phone number to dial. The machines, themselves, handle all the rest of the handshaking (see Glossary) and identification. Virtually every fax machine can talk with every other fax (with the exceptions noted previously).

Last, but certainly not least, is that fax transmissions are cheap. Transferring a one-page document by fax costs the same as a one-minute phone call to wherever the document is being sent (a minute is the minimum billing unit on most phone systems—a page would be cheaper than a one-minute call if there weren't a minimum, because the true transmission time is usually less than a minute). Unless you are sending more than 50 pages, you'll probably pay less than the price of an overnight carrier. If you wait until the phone rates drop at night, sending a fax can even be cheaper than first-class mail.

The comparison chart presented in Table 7-2 may help put your communications options into better perspective.

FAX FEATURES

Before you make your buying decision, you should study the fax machines available. Specifically, you should look for the features described on the next few pages.

PAPER HANDLING

There are two considerations here that concern paper handling. First, how does the machine accept documents that you want to transmit? If you have documents that often exceed one page, you will want to look for a fax machine with automatic document feeding. With this feature you can put a multipage text (5- to 30-page stacks) into a bin and have the machine scan each page, send it, eject that sheet, load the next page, scan and send, etc. Without automatic feeding, you will have to sit and manually load each sheet each time, which is a tedious process, especially if it is recurrent.

Second, consider the type of paper the machine uses. Ideally, plain bond paper in single sheets, automatically fed—sheet by sheet—is best. It is the cheapest way from a paper cost standpoint, and it generally makes the best copy. Unfortunately, this feature is only found in the high-end (over $3000) machines. Most fax machines use thermal paper in 8½-inch, 98-foot rolls

TABLE 7-2.
Communications Options and Cost Comparisons

Delivery Method	Time	Cost	Comments
U.S. Mail	2–3 days	$.25	No Sunday or holiday delivery; no way to track arrival.
Express Mail	Overnight	$8.50–$12.00	Must call to arrange pickup or take to a central location.
Telex	6–10 minutes	$2.00 (approx.)	No graphics; may have to be keyed in by an operator.
Telephone	Immediate	Variable*	No hard copy; no pictures. Must be able to "connect" with party.
Facsimile	15–45 seconds	Variable*	Operates 24 hours per day, seven days per week.

*Variability depends on time of day and duration of call. For fax, even in prime-time hours, the time to transmit a single page generally translates to a cost of $.30–$.50 nationwide.

(more expensive fax models accommodate longer, wider rolls). Thermal paper is coated with a chemical that turns black when heated. The fax print head heats the paper in response to the signals it receives and produces black dots on the paper. Dot by dot, the transmitted document is reproduced. The paper is thin, smooth, and difficult to write on. The image on this type medium tends to fade and yellow with time and, particularly, with exposure to strong light or some kinds of plastics and organic solvents.

Many businesses immediately make a photocopy of all incoming faxes to plain paper and discard the originals (and, thus, consume even more paper). Also, without an automatic paper cutter, you have a rolled up mass of paper to deal with at day's end. If you have minimal traffic, this is a manageable problem—you simply cut the sheets with scissors or a paper cutter. But if your activity level is high, you will almost certainly want a cutter (which adds bulk and weight to the machine) to do your work for you.

TRANSMISSION SPEED

If your fax needs are extensive and you send to distant locations, you will want a machine with the fastest speeds possible to minimize long-distance tolls. Transmission speeds range from 10 to 45 seconds or more per page. Speed will also be dependent on what you are sending: documents with graphics take longer to scan and send.

BROADCASTING

If you have the need to send the same document to more than one location, you should buy a machine with the broadcasting feature. Broadcasting allows you to input a list of phone numbers and have the machine sequentially call each number, transmit the document, hang up, and then call the next number on the list and send the same document there (see Figure 7-3).

For example, suppose you have several buyers and have a change in your price list. You can transmit the same list to all your buyers automatically. As is the case with most features, price will determine capabilities—particularly, within the same manufacturer's line of machines. For example, the Canon FaxPhone 25 (retail price around $2695) can broadcast seven pages to up to 15 locations. The FaxPhone 20 (retail price $1995) will handle three pages to up to 16 locations. Some of the newer fax machines allow broadcasting for 100 different phone numbers.

While broadcasting is a real boon to those who use it appropriately, it has also led to one of the growing scourges of the fax world: "junk fax." Just as junk mail fills your mailbox, junk fax can tie up your phone line and waste your costly paper. The only way to avoid the problem is to be selective about whom you give your fax number to. Here is another prediction for your collection:

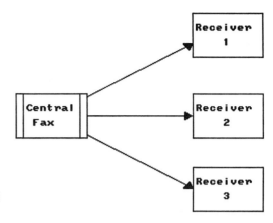

Figure 7-3 Broadcasting from a central fax machine.

Donn Parker, a consultant at SRI International in California, predicts that the next high-tech "plague" we will face will be "fax graffiti"—people sending annoying and, possibly, obscene messages via fax machines (*Personal Computing,* May 1989).

POLLING

Polling is the opposite of sending. The polling feature enables a machine to call up other fax machines and "ask" if these remote machines have documents waiting to be sent to the polling machine. If so, the polling machine can request that the document be sent immediately. For instance, a traveling regional salesperson can, when it is convenient, have his or her machine call a central office and check for any waiting documents. If there are any, the salesperson can then have the faxes sent to his or her current location. Some machines offer "automatic turnaround polling," which allows the machine to transmit documents to the remote machine after completion of the polling operation without a new phone call having to be made.

BUILT-IN COPIER

Some fax models can double as low-volume thermal copiers. But don't be too enamored with this—the quality is poor, and you still have the same problems with thermal paper that were mentioned earlier.

PHONE SYSTEM

Most of the fax machines available include a phone system so that they can allow access to voice calls as well as fax transmission. You can talk to the receiving party before or after you send a document without having to make a second call. But therein lies a problem. Sending fax messages poses no problem with such a shared line as long as you do not pick up the phone handset while a fax is being sent. Some units have a signal button that can be used to tell the machine that you want to "go voice." A tone then sounds on the remote machine for the remote operator to switch to voice. Some machines have a speaker for line monitoring that allows you to hear the fax and voice coming over the line. Models may include a jack for an external phone or answering machine to be connected to the fax machine.

Counting Connections. Now is a good time to discuss one of the problems a small business, particularly if it is a home business, will have to work with and resolve. With all this electronic connectivity, how many phone lines are you going to need? If you have a modem, a fax, and, of course, a voice line or two, you can see how things can get complicated and expensive. Ideal situation? Get separate lines for all functions. Less than ideal but workable? Several options exist.

Of course, you should not mix voice lines, generally, with electronic lines. Modems and fax machines answer and make phone calls with some awful noises that sound like something between an air-raid siren and an injured cat. Customers and associates will remember the sound for days (sometimes from the resulting ringing in their ears). In particular, don't mix a voice line with a call-waiting option with a modem line. The call-waiting signal will disrupt and frequently disconnect your modem from your network.

But separate phone lines cost money. (If all the lines are being used, regularly, frequently, and actively, your business is probably going well enough that it is able to afford them.) When you use a fax a couple of times per day (but every day) and your modem in the morning and afternoon, you do need to spring for a dedicated data line. Yes, the modem and fax can share the line but not, of course, be in use at the same time.

Now you have your two lines. What if you need to expand your voice capabilities? Can you use your data line for occasional incoming calls? Yes, with the right setup. There are a couple of devices available that allow you to have a fax machine and a phone connecting to the same phone line. One is the Line One Fax/Phone Switch from the Extel Corporation (3005 MacArthur Blvd., Northbrook, IL 60062; 312/205-3311; $375). You plug this box into the phone jack and the phone and the fax into it. Then, when that line gets an incoming call, the device determines whether it is a fax signal or a voice call and directs it to the appropriate peripheral. The Line One can also work with your answering machine. Another switching device is the Faxmate 168 (Dragoon Corporation, 1270 Avenida Acaso, Unit F, Camarillo, CA 93010; 805/987-4911; $79.95). A few of the newest fax machines have this capability built right in. If the incoming call is a fax call, the fax kicks in; if it is a voice (or, really, if the fax "handshaking" sound is absent), the fax's phone will ring. There are devices that can accept a fax, a modem, and a phone and can tell which signal is which when a call comes in.

Fax and Modem in One.   One of the most imaginative ways to deal with the problem of mixed lines, at least with fax by personal computer (PC), comes from Touchbase Systems (160 Laurel Ave., Northport, NY 11768; $699). Their new WorldPort 2496 Portable Fax/Data Modem (see Figure 7-4) offers two data reception options—fax and modem—all in one unit. The small (less than five inches long and three inches wide), battery-powered device is able to distinguish an incoming fax signal from an incoming modem or voice signal. The software provided with the unit will interpret the incoming phone signal and accept a fax image or file transfer by modem. Conceivably you could run a bulletin board system (BBS) on your computer to handle E-mail or file transfers and have fax access running on the same phone line. You could have the fax and modem line in one and your second line could be for voice. Problem solved; two lines would be sufficient.

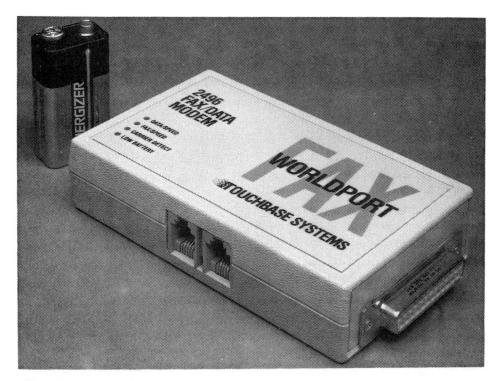

Figure 7-4   *The Worldport 2496 Portable Fax/Data Modem. (Photograph courtesy of Touchbase Systems, Inc.)*

TIMER TRANSMISSIONS

Some of the higher-priced machines offer programmable transmissions. You can have a timer start your transmissions in the evening hours when phone rates are lower. These capabilities are usually limited, however, in comparison with the capabilities offered by PC fax boards (see "PC Fax," in this chapter).

RELAY BROADCASTING

Relay broadcasting is also a feature found, generally, in the more expensive models. Also known as "store and forward," this feature allows a fax machine to transmit a document to another fax (usually only a machine made by the same manufacturer), which, in turn, can store the document in its memory and then transmit the document to other facsimile machines in its network (see Figure 7-5). This can reduce telephone costs and more evenly distribute the work load between locations.

LIQUID CRYSTAL DISPLAY

An LCD display on the machine can show such things as the date, time, machine status, and error codes for operating guidance.

DIALING OPTIONS

Many machines now offer storage of a variable number of frequently used fax phone numbers. They can then be called up automatically with the touch of a single key. You can, of course, also manually input the phone number on the keypad. Most machines also have at least rudimentary radial features.

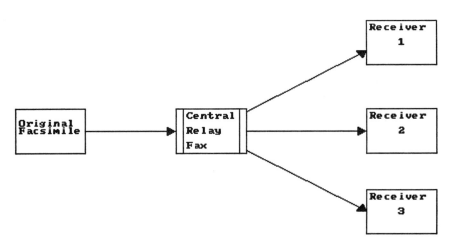

Figure 7-5 *Diagram of the relay broadcasting feature available on some fax machines (also known as "store and forward").*

COPY OPTIONS

Some machines offer the ability to reduce or enlarge original documents prior to their transmission as fax.

ACTIVITY LOG

Some machines offer the ability to make a report of your fax transactions. You can specify how often you want an action report (for example, after every 15 exchanges). The report sometimes includes all the details of each transmitted and received document—including number dialed, connected time, number of pages, error count, etc.

HALFTONES

If you send and receive illustrations or, particularly, photographs, you will probably want a machine that offers the ability to print more than just off and on dots. This feature, called "gray scaling," allows the printout to display the more subtle details of photographs. Some machines offer 8, 16, and, at the highest end, 64 shades of grey.

PRINT RESOLUTION

We mentioned that the Group 3 CCITT standard allows for two degrees of scan and print resolution, standard and fine. Moderate-to-high-price machines offer both, but cheaper units may offer only the standard 200 by 100 dpi (sometimes listed as 196 by 96 dpi).

DOCUMENT SIZE

You will need to decide whether you will only be dealing with letter-size documents or if you need larger pages (such as the wide computer printout paper) as well. As mentioned, the larger machines sometimes can reduce these larger documents so that a letter-size machine can accomodate them.

CONFIDENTIAL COMMUNICATIONS

When you send a document to a remote fax machine, it is subject to being seen by as many pairs of eyes as have access to the machine. Several of the latest machines have a way to get around this obvious problem. For the Sharp fax machines (at least their FO series), this is called "confidential communications." This feature allows you to send a document to another Sharp machine and specify a passcode to be attached to that document. When another Sharp machine receives the document, rather than printing it out immediately, it will store the image in its memory. It will print out only a notice that a confidential document was received and was stored successfully. Once this notification has been received, a security password (a preset 4-digit code) must be entered before the fax can be printed out. For the higher-end Sharp machines (the FO-700, 800, and 3200), there may be multiple codes and even multiple secure "box numbers" for receiving documents.

Now that you are aware of current fax capabilities, which machine to buy for your business falls, again, to your specific needs. Price variability is tremendous, but fortunately, since competition has heated up, price is based more on capabilities than on brand name. Besides price, the other consideration, as in buying any piece of equipment, is how well the unit can be supported locally. Since fax machines are easy to install and require little maintenance, buying through mail order can bring significant savings in many cases. Mail order is a safer alternative for buying a fax machine than it is for buying a computer.

PC FAX

If you have already installed a PC in your business, you are well on your way to having a fax system. By adding a relatively inexpensive "PC fax" board to your computer, you can get extensive fax capabilities for, generally, less than you would pay for a comparable stand-alone fax machine. With certain caveats.

What are these systems? A PC-fax system consists of a computer board that is installed in one of the slots inside your computer's chassis and also the software that directs the fax system's operation. The hardware can be thought of, simply, as a modem that acts in a way that is quite similar to the modem you use for other digital communications (see Chapter 2). In fact, you can buy a fax board that can pull double duty and perform as a modem as well as a fax device. However, instead of using an ASCII standard that the usual modems use to send E-mail and such, the digital signals from these boards conform to the fax standards. They transmit, not ASCII characters, but rather a picture, in what is referred to as "bit-mapped" graphics. Instead of sending along codes for each letter of the alphabet used in a document, fax simply sends signals that code for hot and cold (dark and light) spots on a page. The only coding used is that of the CCITT standard. Rather than knowing how to "converse" with other computers, the fax boards have learned the lingo of the fax machines.

At the basic level, the differences between standard fax machines and PC fax are apparent. With a stand-alone fax, you feed a document into a machine, tell the fax the phone number to dial, and then stand back and let it go. An incoming fax just pops out already printed for you to read whenever you get to it—automatically.

With a computer-based fax, the material you send comes directly from your computer. It never has to be printed out and read into the fax from a paper copy. Let's look at a simple example. The mechanics will certainly vary from system to system, but the generalities prevail. Suppose you want to send a letter by fax to a client. You sit down at your trusty PC and compose your correspondence on the computer with your word processor. As discussed with E-mail, when you have finished with your letter you store it on your disk in an ASCII format. Again, you do this in order to remove the formatting codes unique to the various word processors that, when transmitted electronically, can mess things up at the receiving end. Once you have your file stored safely on disk in the correct format, you are ready to fax it. You load the software that controls your fax board, tell it which file on your disk you want to fax and where you want it to go. That's all. The software reads the file on your disk, converts it to the proper format for a receiving fax to understand, dials the designated fax's phone, and transmits the document. As you can see, a couple of steps in the usual fax process are eliminated with PC fax. Instead of writing the letter on your computer, printing it out to your printer, putting the paper copy into the fax, and so on, you transmit it directly from a file. No printing is required, and there is no need to feed a paper document into the fax machine.

To receive a fax is just as simple. The PC fax answers the phone for the incoming fax and, as the transmission continues, the facsimile data is stored on the computer disk. When the transmission is complete, you can view the document you have received right on your computer monitor and print out a copy right on your computer's printer.

PC fax, or, as some call it, "virtual fax," has some features that are different from those you have read about above in connection with stand-alone fax machines. PC fax is limited in several ways, but it also, for the right user, has some interesting possibilities and cost-savings potential. Here is how the two processes stack up.

DISADVANTAGES OF PC FAX

Requires Printer.   PC fax requires a printer in order to get a hardcopy of your received faxes. This, of course, is a minor problem, as there are few computers in the business setting that are not hooked up to a printer of some sort. And seldom is the quality of the printed fax limited by the printer used. With the new 24-pin dot matrix printers and, better, the laser printers, the quality of output far exceeds that taken off a fax machine.

May Require Scanner.   If you frequently need to send copies of preexisting documents (for example, forms completed by hand or on a typewriter and not created on your computer), you will need a scanner. As mentioned, a standard fax machine consists of a modem, a scanner, and a printer—all combined in a single unit. A scanner, in the PC sense, is a device that plugs into the computer and can take a digital photograph of a document placed upon its scanning bed. The scanner and computer interaction is directed by software which is provided with the scanner. The images, thus scanned and captured, are stored in the computer's memory chip and on its disk drive as a storage file. Virtually all of the fax boards available today can use images read in by a scanner and stored on computer disk.

Unfortunately, the current crop of fax boards are limited by which scanners they support. Scanners from various manufacturers have not been well standardized as to the format with which they read a document and store it as a file on disk. With the various ways of representing a printed document's graphic "facsimile" on disk, PC-fax boards may or not be able to read a file created by an individual scanner and convert it to the proper fax data needed for transmission to another fax. The second major consideration is the cost of the scanner, itself. Scanners are very expensive. They range in price from $1000 to $15,000. When you figure this into the total cost of a PC fax system, you almost always exceed the price of a mid-level all-in-one fax machine. Third, you have another piece of equipment to install, find room for, and learn how to operate. Most scanners come with a board that has to be plugged inside your computer in order for the hardware to be able to communicate with the computer. Scanners also have their own software that must be installed on your computer, as well as manuals to read and commands to learn. All of this adds another magnitude of complexity (compared to using a stand-alone fax) to what should be a simple process.

The bottom line is this: If a majority of your fax transmissions are of paper-based forms and other materials not created on a computer, the PC fax market is, currently, simply not cost-effective for your needs. If, on the other hand, you find yourself writing your letters on a computer, printing them out, and sending them off on someone else's fax, you will probably benefit from a PC fax.

Software Is "Ram-resident." The software that runs these PC-fax boards is "ram-resident" or "terminate and stay resident" (TSR). What that means is that the program is loaded into a segment of the computer's memory space and remains there, out of view until you need it. When it is called up—either by your pressing a "hot key" or by its sensing an incoming fax on the phone line—it will take control of your machine as the file is received. "Take control" can mean some nasty things. It can mean anything from freezing your computer screen and locking up your keyboard so that you have to stop working on whatever it is you are doing until the fax process is finished to just slowing down how your computer handles whatever it is you are doing. Since fax transmissions are fast, this is only a minor nuisance. However, there is one circumstance that can be catastrophic. If you are saving material to disk just as a fax comes into your computer, when the fax software takes over control you have the distinct possibility of losing some of your work being saved to disk.

Another problem with TSR software is that it can sometimes be incompatible with other software, particularly other TSR-type programs. When software "competes" for the same specific memory locations in a computer, what generally happens is that the computer stops or "locks up." When this occurs, you have to restart the computer. These electronic "collisions" can be a problem.

By the time this book reaches you, PC-fax software will probably have been improved to eliminate most of these problems, but do be aware of them. In fact, newer generations of PC-fax boards will probably eliminate these problems altogether. Second-generation fax boards will probably have their own microprocessor chips and will work independently from your computer's controlling electronics. With its own set of chips, a fax board can merrily accept and send fax signals without interfering with you or your computer's activities. At this writing, there are at least two such fax boards already available (see "PC-Fax Manufacturers" later in this chapter).

Can Be Slower Than Dedicated Fax Machine. While many PC-fax systems say they will transmit files at 9600 baud, this is only true on AT-class [using a central processing unit (CPU) that is an Intel 80286 chip] or faster (using the newer generation 80386 chip) machines. A machine based on the older 8088 or 8086 chips simply cannot drive the fax board to achieve the faster transmission speeds. This is based primarily on a computer's ability to run the fax's controlling software—which is constantly reading and processing disk files as it transmits or receives a fax—quickly enough, rather than on a problem with the fax boards. If your computer—PC fax does transmit at less than 9600 baud, there is no problem with sending or receiving documents from another fax machine, since fax machines can drop back to slower transmission speeds if they need to. However, if you send a lot of documents, particularly with several pages or with complex graphics, the slower speeds can cost money through longer phone connections. Of course, when you receive documents, the sender pays the higher phone bills.

Some high-end (above $1000) fax boards that carry their own controlling microprocessor can handle the faster transmission speeds regardless of what computer CPU they are working with. Examples of these boards include Intel's CoProcessor board, The Complete Fax/9600, and Panasonic's Fax Partner. The cheapest boards cut costs primarily at the expense of speed. The $395 JT-Fax from Quadram and the $595 Omnium PC Fax System cannot handle anything above 4800 baud, regardless of what computer they are connected to.

More Difficult to Use Than Dedicated Fax Machine. Despite the fact that the software that directs PC-fax systems is relatively simple to use, using PC fax remains more difficult than using a dedicated fax machine. Unlike standard fax machines, which almost anyone can use, with PC fax you have to have some computer experience to use the fax effectively. Even installing a fax board into your computer is more difficult than setting up a dedicated fax machine. A fax board may still have tiny dip switches that have to be set to various combinations of off and on settings before you plug it into your computer. Like everything in the computer word, the manuals and instructions also vary in clarity and completeness, so PC fax might present an additional challenge.

Requires Extensive Computer Hardware. Associated computer hardware requirements can be a concern with PC fax. Already mentioned is the problem with communications speeds based on the computer's CPU. You must have a hard disk drive attached to your computer. Not only does the software that runs the PC fax take up room, but also the files that are handled by PC fax have huge storage requirements. A simple page of text in ASCII format stored by your word processor may need 2 to 4 kilobytes of disk storage. That same file, converted for fax output, may occupy up to 10 times that much disk space. Further, if your system receives a file that contains a lot of graphics from another fax machine, it may gobble up nearly 1000 kilobytes (which is equal to one megabyte) of room on your disk. Even temporary storage of incoming faxes on a hard drive (before you print them out or archive them to other storage media) will require a large (and expensive) hard disk drive in your system.

Computer Must Remain On. To be able to receive a fax at any time, your computer must be turned on constantly. Since more and more fax transmissions are being timed to take advantage of non-prime telephone rates, this often means that you will have to leave your computer on all night. Now, before you say that's impossible you should know that many computer experts will tell you that you should leave your computer on 24 hours a day regardless of whether you are waiting for a fax or not. There is a prevailing opinion that the wear and tear on a computer's chips from turning a machine off and on each day is greater than the stress of leaving the machine on at all times, routinely. Some experts will tell you that if your computer has a hard disk drive, this is particularly true. Most hard drive failures occur just when the computer and drive are being turned on or turned off. This is when the hard disk's head that reads and writes data to the disk drops down to rest on the disk (on older model hard drives). This process, more than any other, appears to be what makes the drive the most likely to "crash" or lose data and become inoperable. So, if your only problem with the thought of leaving your computer and fax on at all times is the worry that you may burn out your computer, you may be wrong on that point.

ADVANTAGES OF PC FAX

Faxes Printed on Bond Paper. You will print faxes out to your printer, which uses standard bond paper, so you won't have to work with the ugly, shiny thermal paper of conventional fax.

Can Send Word Processing Files Directly to Fax. Most PC-fax boards allow for your sending word processing files directly to a fax. Since most of your documents are probably created on a PC-based word processing system already, you no longer need to print out a document prior to transmitting it via fax. By eliminating a step, time is saved and paper consumption is reduced. For sending the occasional quick fax, jotted off on a word processor with no graphics bells and whistles, it is a very convenient and quick process.

Fax Output Looks Better. Fax output transmitted from a PC-fax system to a standard fax machine will probably look much better than what is output when the a document is sent from a standard fax. Why? With standard fax-to-fax transmissions, the document you send must first be scanned by the sending machine and then printed out by the receiving one. Both processes can degrade the quality of the image. With a PC-directed fax system, you skip the initial scanning process because the document is sent directly from your computer's files. If you send a file from one PC fax to another PC fax and the resultant file is printed out on a high-quality laser printer, you can achieve some remarkable quality. Now, realize that even faxes sent in this manner are bounded by the 200-dpi restrictions of Group 3 fax. Even if your document is output to a laser printer capable of 300-dpi print quality it will still be only 200 dpi by 200 dpi in its final form. Nevertheless, when scanning is eliminated at the initial stage, the final transmitted product, printed on bond paper, is certainly a refreshing improvement over the hard-to-read, rolled-up thermal paper of standard fax machines.

Programmable. One of the real advantages of the PC fax is its programmability. While broadcasting to multiple recipients and timed transmissions are currently found only in the higher-end standard fax machines, these capabilities are bread and butter for even the cheapest PC fax. Directories of commonly used fax numbers can be created and stored on your computer. The directory can then be searched for the fax number you want. You can also set up groups of fax numbers to be used for a broadcasting session of a single document. You can set up a timed transmission with ease for a broadcast session or for sending specific document files to a series of individual destinations.

Portable.   Imagine that you are on the road. You find yourself in East Padocah, Wyoming, and you need to send in an order for 1000 widgets to Widgets 'R Us. Do you have to be out of touch with facsimile technology? Not a chance. Quadram (One Quad Way, Norcross, GA 30093; 404/564-5666) makes a portable fax unit that can attach to virtually any IBM-compatible PC to send and receive fax messages. Suppose you are at a buyer's office and the buyer shakes on the deal. You ask if you might use the secretary's computer for just a few minutes. They both have a cup of coffee, and you connect the small, external device that connects on to the computer's serial port. You don't have to open the computer or do any fancy electronics work. A simple connecting cable, provided with the unit, is sufficient. Plug in the phone line and power plug and slide in your software on your disk, and now you are off and running. You can send a fax placing an order in a minute and disconnect.

If you are one of an increasing number of business people who travel with a laptop computer, you are in even better shape to use fax. Just slip back to your hotel room and plug it all in there. You don't even need a printer on the road. The software with the JT-Fax Portable will show your fax documents right on the computer screen so you can read them without a hard copy.

Miscellaneous.   Careful shopping can often turn up some interesting abilities and additions to some fax board products. For example, The IntelliFAX (Brother International; $999) and Microfax (Xerox Imaging Systems; $695) boards come with 1200-baud, Hayes-compatible modems built in. The IntelliFAX system includes the communications software needed to run the modem. For an additional $295, you can get a 2400-baud modem with your Connection CoProcessor board (Intel PCEO; $995).

DEVELOPMENTS

Some fax boards offer another sometimes-valuable feature. If you have two PCs equipped with the same brand fax board, they can often be connected through the phone lines and files can be transferred between the two machines at 9600 baud. This is the same sort of transfer you can do with a modem (see Chapter 2). Fax boards are built around a 9600-baud modem and almost all use the same set of Rockwell chips. The transfer protocols they use meet CCITT fax standards, rather than the ASCII transfers that modems adhere to. If the fax board offers this option (Intel's CoProcessor, Microlink's Fax LC96, and The Complete PC's Fax/9600 do), you can have the software dial up another computer equipped with the same type fax board and transfer word processor, spreadsheet, database, or any other type computer file. The transfer speed, 9600 baud, is about as fast as you can wrangle from standard phone lines.

The problem, though, is that, just like the current crop of high-speed 9600-baud modems (without fax capabilities), the devices will only talk to a twin. Only fax boards made by the same manufacturer will communicate in this fashion. An Intel CoProcessor will only communicate with another Intel board. It cannot communicate with The Complete PC's Fax/9600, even though both offer the function. This incompatibility among brands will, hopefully, change soon, as the industry is moving toward standardizing transfer protocols. One must suspect that if there is some type of agreement on the transfers, the next generation of fax boards will offer this as a standard feature.

Another development that will necessitate some careful shopping is the ability of the individual fax boards to handle varying file formats. When fax boards first appeared, they were little able to send anything other than standard ASCII text files—the kind generated by word processors. As they matured, they next incorporated the ability to send files generated by graphics or "drawing" programs. This meant that you could send anything you could draw on your computer. The most popular art programs—PC Paintbrush, PC Paint, and Dr. Halo, among others—were supported to a varying degree. Next came support for various scanners. Which file formats and which brand scanners (if any) are supported by a fax board is, currently, highly variable and quite likely to remain that way.

One development being spearheaded by some of the industry heavyweights is "Communicating Applications Specifications" (CAS). You may also see it referred to as the "DCA/Intel Communicating Applications Specifications" (DICAS). The CAS were put together by an informal group consisting of Intel (a major hardware producer) and software leaders such as Lotus, Microsoft and WordPerfect Corporation. The goal of the group is to develop a standard protocol for data transmission. The group is not trying to usurp the CCITT's functions. The CAS will enable a software developer to include in its program the ability to send data directly from within the running program out to either a modem or a PC-based fax. Of course, the hardware—modem or fax board—must comply with the CAS standards as well. Currently, the only product that fits the CAS is, as you would expect, the Intel CoProcessor fax board and, presumably, their add-in 2400-baud modem for the board.

The potential power and convenience of this development should be easy to visualize. Suppose you are working in, let's say, Lotus' 1-2-3 spreadsheet software. You want to send the figures for the current fiscal year to the home office's fax machine. With CAS developed, you might press a unique keystroke and call up the communications module programmed into 1-2-3. You would tell it to send the current set of data in fax format, give it a phone number, and allow it to get to work. You would continue merrily crunching numbers in 1-2-3, while CAS and your complementary fax board set about the task of faxing off the document on your screen. To further develop the scenario, you could send the same data to another computer (similarly equipped with compatible hardware) as a file—modem to modem—for the recipient to then work on within his or her computer's copy of 1-2-3. If other software developers accept the standard, you could, conceivably, fire data and facsimiles from any program at any time using any kind of data.

Unfortunately, it's mostly a dream at this point. The only hardware product to offer CAS is Intel's CoProcessor board and fax. As yet, there are no software packages that offer CAS capabilities. The impact of CAS has yet to be determined. While the support appears to be available, implementation seems to be a promise for the future. Even one of the supporters of CAS, WordPerfect Corporation, has offered an alternative. In association with Quadram and its JT-Fax line of fax boards, WordPerfect now offers a new software program that allows users to send and receive fax documents from within WordPerfect version 5.0 through a JT-Fax card. CAS is not involved in the transfer. The trend—either through CAS or other means—is clear. As the fax board market matures, you will be offered more and more ways to send and receive fax materials to and from more software packages.

PC-BASED FAX OR DEDICATED FAX?

With the availability of PC-based fax, the choice of which model to choose for your first fax has become even more complicated. PC fax will not replace the stand-alone fax machine for most business applications. The sheer simplicity of using a stand-alone machine will keep it at the forefront of fax activity for some time. However, there are some specific situations for which PC-fax boards may be worth a good look. For example, if you are a competent PC user already, you have overcome the major problem with fax boards—learning how to use them. With the combination of PC experience and relatively low-volume use, you are a good candidate for implementing a PC-fax system. PC fax becomes the prime choice for a system if what you fax is limited to text and graphics that you create with your computer already.

Another situation for which PC fax may be a viable choice is for the extremely heavy fax user. The programmability of fax software exceeds that available on all but the most expensive stand-alone units. The ability to broadcast to the numbers stored in huge directories on your computer can be hard to match with standard fax machines.

FAX WITHOUT A FAX MACHINE

FAX USING E-MAIL SYSTEMS

If your budget does not allow you to jump on the fax bandwagon just yet or if you rarely need to transmit by fax and cannot justify the expense for a machine, all is not lost. If you have joined the E-mail age, you can still send fax messages with just your modem. Western Union EasyLink, MCI Mail, AT&T Mail, and several other E-mail services will accept text messages, just like standard E-mail communications, but will direct them to a fax machine for you.

You simply compose the message with your word processor (see Chapter 4), upload it to the network just as you would any E-mail message, mark it for fax transmission (the method varies from system to system), give the carrier the area code and phone number of the destination fax, and the service takes care of the rest. Anything you can type in at your word processor will work just fine. Now, admittedly, this stretches the concept of facsimile a bit, since this is not really a replica of any document, other than one on your word processor, but it does allow you to enter the world of fax. Since fax machines outnumber E-mail accounts in many businesses, you can now communicate with a vast new audience through one technology. If you have mastered E-mail transmission, you have mastered sending a fax.

However, there are a couple of glaring shortcomings, currently, with this form of fax. First, you cannot receive fax transmissions through any of these E-mail-to-fax services. After you send a fax, return contact must be made by phone or E-mail. The concensus among industry experts is that this will change soon. Several networks are scurrying to be the first to offer incoming fax service, so it might be available by the time this book reaches you. The second limitation is that E-mail-to-fax cannot accommodate graphics in any form. There is no way to send a signature, a logo, a letterhead—anything beyond simple letters and numbers—by this route. Depending on your business, of course, this could be insignificant or it could be a fatal flaw to the system.

Costs for fax transmission are variable among systems. EasyLink charges 55 cents for the first page (1250 characters) and 35 cents for each additional half-page. CompuServe goes for 75 cents for the first 1000 characters (averaging 80 to 120 words) and 25 cents for each additional 1000 characters. MCI Mail's Fax Dispatch levies 50 cents for the first half-page and 30 cents for each additional half-page. AT&T Mail charges 55 cents for the first half-page (1500 characters) and 40 cents for additional half-pages. Virtually all of the major networks can send faxes internationally for a surcharge based on the destination country and message length.

FAX USING PC-XPEDITE

Xpedite Systems, Inc. (446 Highway 35, Eatontown, NJ 97724; 800/227-9379) is a new service that makes fax transmission and reception cost-effective for the infrequent user. If you already have an IBM or compatible computer, a 1200- or 2400-baud modem, and a printer, you are more than halfway to having fax capabilities. For $49 and usage charges, Xpedite provides the rest.

The rest, specifically, is a software program. The PC-Xpedite software is a dedicated terminal emulator (see Chapter 3) package that allows for the creation, transmission, and collection of fax documents that can be communicated to and from any standard fax machine worldwide. You can think of Xpedite as E-mail with a twist. Instead of communicating with ASCII files and messages, you can send and receive fax documents—letterheads, signatures, and all—straight from and to your PC. Incoming faxes can be printed out on your printer, just as you would with a dedicated fax.

This is the kind of magic we have become accustomed to in the "computer age." Through software "smoke and mirrors," the Xpedite software takes your ASCII file and transmits it through your modem to a bulletin-board-like facility in New Jersey. There it is translated into data bits that can be understood by a standard fax machine, and then the system transmits the converted document to the fax phone number you addressed your message to. On the flip side, you can have your fax-equipped customers use their standard fax machines to use the Xpedite phone system in New Jersey and send a fax there. It is stored on the Xpedite system, and when you check in by your modem, it is sent to your PC (again, by modem and an error-checking transfer protocol like XMODEM). Once you receive the fax, you use the print function of the Xpedite program to get a hard copy of the document. If you have used a modem for downloading programs from a BBS or network (or read Chapters 2 and 3), you can be up and running an effective fax system in a matter of minutes.

One quick caveat: Your correspondents need to know your Xpedite mailbox ID (mine, by the way, is "ALBRIGHT/MD" if you would like to send me a fax) and the phone number to direct their fax machine to call (my incoming fax number is 201-542-1266). It is important for your fax messages to have your Xpedite mailbox name on the cover sheet or first sheet of any documents sent to you. The Xpedite manual warns that, without this ID, your faxes may be delayed in getting to you or may "possibly not [be] delivered to your mailbox."

Xpedite comes with a two-diskette software package, an 80-page manual, and your ID codes. The latter include your Xpedite account number, mailbox, and password. You can run the program off two floppy drives or install it to your hard drive. Running from floppies is simply a matter of making copies of the two disks and typing "B : PCX" at the "A>" prompt. Hard drive installation is carried out from a batch program, making the process foolproof.

Once the program is installed, you will need to configure the system the first time PC-Xpedite is run. A screen is presented that asks for your specific hardware—which serial port your modem uses, whether you want pulse or tone dialing, and modem speed. You also input your mail box ID, password, and the phone number you have been instructed to call to receive your faxes. Once that is done, you are ready to get to work.

Major Functions.   The main menu lists all of the major functions available through the PC-Xpedite software. Briefly, they are as follows:

- *Prepare Mail* allows you to select the Xpedite service you want to use. Services available include, of course, sending a fax, but you can also use document, message, file, or telex services (see below).

- *Send/Receive Mail* activates your communications options to either send prepared mail (through the Prepare Mail option), to receive mail, or to do both.

- *Electronic Filing System,* the program's way of handling files, is one of the most innovative features of PC-Xpedite. You have an "In" folder, where all mail goes when received and an "Out" folder, where files you have prepared for transmission go.

- *Activity Logs* are files that keep track and allow you to view information about your incoming and outgoing mail and also provide a second-by-second summary of your last online session with the Xpedite system.

- *Configuration* options allow you to change the software parameters discussed above or your printer, screen color, etc. options at any time.

More Than Just a Fax Service.   Besides the described fax transmittal service, Xpedite also has other features and capabilities, as discussed below.

- Xpedite has a *document service* which allows for the sending and receiving of formatted documents created with any of several supported word processors. These include MultiMate, WordStar, DisplayWrite, Microsoft Word, and WordPerfect. And get this: The document file transmitted is converted or translated into any of the formats supported! For example, if you use WordPerfect and your correspondent uses Word, you can send him or her a WordPerfect file—all nicely tabbed and formatted—and, when sending it, have Xpedite translate the document as received by your correspondent into something Word can understand. You can, of course, use the file translation yourself. If you use a MultiMate at work and WordPerfect at home, send your file to Xpedite before you leave the office and have Xpedite translate it into WordPerfect format. When you get home, download the file and get to work on it. Of course, both sender and receiver must have Xpedite accounts to use this facility.

- Xpedite sports an *E-mail service* for subscribers to its system. This service is for pure ASCII transmissions.
- You can send *binary files* of any type to other Xpedite subscribers. Spreadsheets, data files, and programs can be exchanged on the system. Just give the file an address (the recipient's Xpedite mailbox ID), and when the recipient checks in for faxes and messages, the file will be sent right along with the other communications.
- You say you need *telex?* Xpedite has it—to anywhere in the world.
- With Xpedite you can create *online phone books* with the fax or telex numbers of your frequent outlets. Each phone book can have up to 35 numbers. You can give each phone number a "tag" of up to nine alphanumeric characters. Then, when you fill in the address for your message, you can use the tag (preceded by a "#") in place of the phone number. Xpedite will look in the appropriate phone book for the tag and plug in the corresponding phone number.
- Xpedite has a *built-in editor* for composing your transmissions. While limited to one screen (20 or so lines of text), you can access the editor from the "Address" screen by pressing F7 of the fax, telex, or message facility.
- Xpedite allows for *letterhead registration.* Once Xpedite has entered your letterhead into its system, you can elect to have your faxes sent with your letterhead included in the transmissions.
- According to the Xpedite documentation, "PC-Xpedite is the only electronic facsimile service that can send your *graphics* files to fax machines." You can, for example, create a letterhead with bold or enlarged characters and lines and graphics, "print" the file to disk, and upload the resultant file to Xpedite. When Xpedite transfers the file to the receiving fax machine, the output will have all the appearance of the graphics you use.

When you choose "Send/Receive Mail" from the main menu screen, Xpedite enters its "Online" communications module. You can choose to both send and receive, to send only, to receive only, to receive selected files or messages, or to send mail and pick from what is waiting to be sent.

Once your selection has been made, the communications program is activated and PC-Xpedite displays a split screen showing two dialog boxes. The top box ("Log In Dialog") explains what the modem is doing at each step, and the bottom box ("Modem") displays the commands actually being sent to the modem. For the initiated, you are viewing what amounts to a script file in action. It's all automatic. The files are either sent, received, or both as you have directed Xpedite to do. If you have chosen to receive selected files, once the connection is made and your "In" box has been scanned, you select online which files you want to have sent during this session. The binary transmission is via an XMODEM protocol with error-checking, and, since the files are compressed at the Xpedite center, it is very fast.

Once it has been received, your mail is placed in your "In" folder. From there, you can either print the document to a printer or, if it is a program or data file, you can have it decompressed by PC-Xpedite and converted to its native format for you to use elsewhere.

"Attack" Fax.   Xpedite has recently implemented a service that will be of keen interest to direct marketers, public relations firms, and advertising professionals. Dubbed "FaxCast," this service allows you to send a fax to hundreds of addresses based on an electronically submitted list of fax phone addresses. This is the same principle as broadcasting, discussed above. Rather than standing at a traditional fax and feeding in a fax document for each address, you transmit it as a single file to Xpedite. Xpedite merges the information through electronic "magic" and fires the faxes off to all the addresses you designated. Costs? These vary based on the times for transmission to the receiving fax machines (which is dependent, in part, on the graphics the document contains—letterheads, signatures, photos, etc.) and the length of the document. As a yardstick, Xpedite advertises that costs can be as little as 25¢ per recipient, presumably for a single page with little or no graphics.

Costs.   The PC-Xpedite software sells for $49 and includes a $10 credit for Xpedite service charges. Site licensing is available. Charges for sending a fax from your PC to a fax in the United States is based on transmission time measured in 6-second increments, with a one-minute minimum charge. For transmission within one hour ("express" delivery), the cost is 90¢ per minute; for off-peak (nightime delivery), the cost is 60¢ per minute. To receive a fax, it costs a flat $2 per delivery of incoming faxes, regardless of document length. For an extra $1, an Xpedite Systems operator will call and let you know that you have a fax waiting. International fax charges, which are based on transmission time measured at one-minute intervals, vary by country. You are billed for your connect time to the Xpedite system at $7.50 per hour (12.5¢ per minute). These charges apply when you are both receiving and sending a fax to their system. Some solid discounts are available for heavy users. Your mailbox is free. There is no minimum usage charge during the first three months. Thereafter, you are charged $10 per month, whether you use the system or not.

Summary. For the infrequent fax user, Xpedite and its PC-Xpedite software service is a superb alternative to buying a fax machine. PC-Xpedite's features make it suitable for many applications, from a simple E-mail service to file transfer, telex, the exchange of word processing documents between collaborators. Charges are reasonable and, even for E-mail and file transmission, is competitive with CompuServe and other national networks. It offers two nice advantages over traditional fax. First, the documents you receive are printable to a regular printer and paper. You do not need to worry about the thermal paper of standard fax machines. Secondly, for the small business with infrequent but unpredictable fax traffic, installing a dedicated phone line for fax is an expense few can afford. The $20 to $30 per month to maintain a separate line for a fax machine can be prohibitive. With PC-Xpedite, you do not need a dedicated line. With these two factors to consider, PC-Xpedite opens the doors to fax for the budget-minded small or home business already equipped for modem communications. The system requirements are IBM-PC, XT, AT, or PS/2 or compatible; DOS 2.0 or higher; 512K minimum (640K to use print facility from within PC-Xpedite; two disk drives or hard drive; 1200- or 2400-baud Hayes or compatible modem.

FAX ETIQUETTE

One of the most important rules to remember when using fax technology is to use a cover sheet. In a lot of businesses that receive faxes, the machine is shared by many departments. It sits in a room by itself or, worse, in the basement mail room. At variable intervals, someone comes by and collects the faxes that have come in, sorts through them, clips what appear to be the correct pages together, and distributes them to where they seem to be addressed. Without a cover sheet, the poor soul who must do the sorting, clipping, and delivering will have a hard time determining where the fax needs to go, much less how many pages are in each document.

A good cover sheet can solve these problems. Cover sheets can be as fancy or as plain as you like. At the most rudimentary level, a cover sheet can be a piece of paper with the "To:" and "From:" handwritten on it that is sent as the first page of your document. But, if you have a PC and a word processor, you can produce a standard form that will add some "class" to your fax (and your business). It could look something like this:

Urgent FAX! Please Expedite!
Please deliver immediately to:

Name _____ Dept. _____

Title _____ Phone _____ Ext. _____

Please forward copies of this fax to the following people in your organization:

NAME	DEPT.	TITLE

This is page _____ of a _____ page document.
Transmitted at _____ AM/PM on _____.

If the document appears to be incomplete, please call
_____ at _____ to have the fax retransmitted.

For return fax, use _____.

This fax was sent from: _____

_____

_____

_____

Note that several things are included on the form to make distributing
your transmitted fax much easier. First, there is a complete address of the
recipient. Be as specific as possible. If you know the floor, department, etc.,
include them. The intended recipient's phone number is important in larger

businesses. The fax clerk can call and let the addressee know that he or she has a fax for pickup.

Next, there is an optional section if you want the fax document to be distributed by the recipient to other members of the organization. This can save you the cost of sending the same fax to several people in the same company. Let the recipient make copies for distribution.

Third, and perhaps most importantly, the total number of pages in the document should be clearly identified. Label the cover sheet as page one. The date and time of the transmission is also important.

The next section is included to assure that the document was received in a complete and clear form. Transmission errors do occur, though rarely, and you need to give the fax operator a quick way to contact you if the fax was flawed or the page count incorrect. Use a voice phone number and a contact person, as well as a return fax number. You may want to include a line that says "Please call _____ at _____ to acknowledge reception of this fax." This immediate feedback will assure you that your fax has reached its destination.

Finally, there is the clear name and address of you, the sender. There is nothing more annoying than to get a beautiful, complete, correctly addressed document and have no idea where it came from. While your correspondents might be able to guess where your faxes to them came from, why take a chance? Make sure the cover sheet includes your name and address. You may also want to use a one line "RE:" or "In Reference To:" comment. If the fax concerns a contract number, a purchase order number, a previous fax document, etc., make a reference to that. Then the secretary, if there is one, can pull any referenced documents and attach them to the fax. When the reader gets the whole package, he or she can interpret the material and respond completely. Make it easy on everyone who must handle your faxes.

A couple of other considerations:

- When possible, give your documents adequate margins all the way around each page.

- Try to avoid sending documents with large dark areas on them. These might occur when you photocopy a page that has photographs from a book or magazine. The photos are "black holes." When sent by fax, they transmit very slowly (increasing your costs) and consume a lot of developer on your recipient's machine (increasing his or her costs). Remove them when possible.

- Make sure your original is as legible as possible. Don't send documents that have type smaller that 8 points or with a lot of serifs (the short lines stemming from and at an angle to the upper and lower ends of the strokes of a letter). They can cause a fax to be illegible at its destination. Consider retyping a document, if necessary. If the original is too light, consider recopying it using a darker copy setting.

NOT FOR EVERYONE

Fax, while certainly useful, is not for everyone. From a practical point of view, it is incongruous that fax machines have become so popular. If your only need is to send graphics to someone else with a PC, particularly if you are exchanging files from desktop publishing or CAD (computer-aided design) software to be modified or worked on jointly, it is probably cheaper to just equip both machines with a modem and send the graphics across as files. These can then be loaded into the graphics software at the other end and revised. As long, of course, as you are both using the same graphics software.

If you are sending long sections of text that are to be modified by the receiver and returned to you for additions, you are much better off using E-mail. Text sent by fax arrives on paper. Since it is sent in a graphic format, the transmission time is longer even at 9600 baud than that of simple text sent through a cheap 1200-baud modem. To be revised, the text must be manually retyped into a word processor or optically scanned through an expensive add-on device. With E-mail, it can be received as a file and loaded directly into the computer program. For pure textual information without the need for graphics, signatures, and letterheads, E-mail is probably the best. As one industry consultant puts it, "If all you need to do is look at something, a fax machine is the answer; but if you want to modify the material, E-mail is better." If, of course, both parties have access to the appropriate equipment and accounts.

So why is fax so popular? Fax is the simplest way to transmit text, with or without graphics. You don't have to grapple with baud speeds, data bits, or parity, It's a "plug in and go" operation. And, when something is effective and simple, it will always supercede more complicated technology, even if the latter is more powerful and efficient for some applications.

RESOURCE LIST: PC-FAX MANUFACTURERS

Ricoh Corporation
5 Dedrick Place
West Caldwell, NJ 07006
201/882-2000
Product name: ImageCard

Quadram Limited Partnership
1 Quad Way
Norcross, GA 30093
800/548-3420
Product name: JT-Fax, JT-Fax Portable, JT-Fax 9600

Panasonic Corporation
Pansonic Industrial Co.
2 Pansonic Way
Secaucus, NJ 07094
201/348-7000
Product name: FX-BM89+ Fax Partner

Pamirs Business International Corp.
550 Lake Site Drive #2
Sunnyvale, CA 94086
408/736-25583
Product name: Pamirs FA10

195

Omnium Corporation
1911 Curve Crest Blvd.
Stillwater, MN 55082
800/328-0223
Product name: Omnium PC Fax
  System

MicroLink International Inc.
4064 McConnell Drive
Burnady, B.C.
Canada V5A 3A8
604/420-0366
Product name: MicroLink Fax LC96

Intel PCEO
Mailstop CO3-07
5200 NE Elam Young Parkway
Hillsboro, OR 97124-6497
800/538-3373
Product name: Connection
CoProcessor

GammaLink
2452 Embarcadero Way
Palo Alto, CA 94303
415/856-7421
Product name: GammaFax

DEST Corporation
1201 Cadillac Court
Milpitas, CA 95035
408/946-7100
Product name: Facsimile Pack

The Complete PC
521 Cottonwood Drive
Milpitas, CA 95035
408/434-0145
Product name: The Complete Fax
and Fax/9600

Brother International Corp.
8 Corporate Place
Piscataway, NJ 08855
201/981-0300
Product name: IntelliFAX

Brook Trout Technologies, Inc.
110 Cedar Street
Wellesley Hills, MA 02181
617/235-3026
Product name: FaxMail 96

AT&T
1 Speedwell Avenue
Morristown, NJ 07920
800/247-1212
Product name: Fax Connection

Xerox Imaging Systems
1215 Terra Bella Ave.
Mountain View, CA 94043
415/965-7900
Product name: MicroFax

8

Miscellaneous Tips and Tricks

THE TELEX BONUS

BACKGROUND

As an added feature that opens your communications door even wider, several of the systems that host electronic mail (E-mail) also allow you to direct your messages to the vast telex network as well. To do so, you simply address your message to the intended recipient's telex address (not to the recipient's electronic mailbox). Then the message is sent to that person's telex terminal. If you plan to do any business in the international marketplace, you should definitely investigate the use of telex. Despite the fact that the telex market is shrinking at a rate of 10 to 15 percent a year—being replaced by more modern communications like E-mail and facsimile—it is still a major communications network in the world market. According to *PC/Computing* (October, 1988), the sheer size of the installed user base (1.7 million subscribers worldwide) means that the system will remain viable for years to come. Using E-mail for telex purposes makes even more sense, because it allows you to have the benefits of telex without the added expense of leasing a telex terminal that may be used infrequently.

According to Alfred Glossbrenner, author of the "bible" of telecommunications, *The Complete Handbook of Personal Computer Communications* (St. Martin's Press, New York; 1985), the telex machine was developed by

Siemans-Halske Company in Germany. Almost concurrently, the technology was embraced by firms in England (Creed and Company) and the United States (E. E. Kleinschmidt and the Morkum Company). The goal of technology was to remove the major restriction on using the telegraph which was, namely, that one had to know Morse code to use it. The idea was a simple one. Why not use something more familiar (i.e., the typewriter keyboard) to use as data entry (instead of the telegraph key) and have the machine itself translate the letters and symbols entered into transmissible code? In today's computer jargon, one could say that the teletype was a major improvement in the "user interface" to the telegraph's capabilities.

In the early days of telex (short for "*tele*printer *exchange*"), telex machines would take the typewriter input, translate it into a code that could be handled by the existing telegraph lines, and send it "down the wire." When the information was sent from another teletype, the receiver, instead of dealing with the dots and dashes of Morse code, could see the messages as they were typed out on a tape or paper in an immediately readable style. Telex technology has made great advances, and today the same phone lines that send our calls, modem transmissions, and faxes are also used to convey telex data. No longer is telex information confined to dedicated telegraph lines; now it can be sent along the ever-expanding network of phone cables to any telex address worldwide.

HOW IT WORKS

Every telex machine hooked into the system must have an "address," which is no different in concept than the address for which you receive paper or E-mail. Each address is usually assigned a standard "answerback" code. This is the name of the teletype addressee and, to continue the analogy, the telex number is the street address. The answerback code is used to identify the receiving machine to the sender so that "wrong numbers" can be eliminated. If you are trying to send a message to Saber Tool and Dye in Israel, whose answerback is known to be "stool-isr," and, when you connect to the remote telex, "blue-inn-ct" is answered back, you know you have the wrong address (and so does your machine).

Since some of the machines do use the common phone lines, the messages you send must be modified extensively before they can be successfully carried from telex to telex. This is the same problem that computer-to-computer communications encounter, as discussed in Chapter 2. A digital telex signal has to be converted to a modular signal in order to be carried over the phone lines. If you recall, the smooth, undulating sound signal characteristic of modular sound is easily carried across the lines. That is exactly the kind of signal the phone lines were designed to handle—specifically, the human voice. Whereas dedicated telegraph lines can handle the dots and dashes of the telegraph (nothing more than digital voltage spikes that magnetize and demagnetize the telegraph key), the phone lines cannot handle these non-modulated signals. Telex, like other computer communications, understands only digital information spikes and drops of electric voltage changes.

As you saw in our discussion of computer-to-computer communications, in a binary numbering system, only 2 numbers are used, a 0 and a 1. This system fits nicely into the electronic world inhabited by teletypewriters, as these machines can only understand voltage changes as information, usually either "on" (a positive voltage) or "off" (zero or negative voltage). Thus, the binary number system, with a 0 being "off" and a 1 being "on," is well-suited for this environment.

To recap, briefly, one binary digit can represent one of two numbers, either a 1 or a 0. If you string two binary numbers together, you have the possibility of representing four possible numbers: 00 (zero), 01 (one), 10 (two) or 11 (three). Suppose you string three binary digits together? You can then represent eight possible numbers. Mathematically, the number of possible numbers you can represent with any binary number can be expressed as "2 to the x power," where x is the number of digits in the number. So a 4-digit binary number can represent any number between 0 and 16.

Now, what does this numbering system have to do with the letters we want to send? First, the symbol generated by each punch of the teletype-writer's keys (be it an "A" a "Z" a "?" or whatever) is encoded into, commonly, the 5-digit binary code developed by the Frenchman Baudot. Under this code (currently dubbed International Telegraph Alphabet No. 2), a binary number of 5 digits in length is used to represent each of 32 letters of the alphabet and certain commonly used punctuation symbols. In simplest terms, instead of sending letters and periods and commas, the telex system sends numbers representing these letters and periods and commas. Just as the old telegraph used a series of dots and dashes to represent the alphabet, telex uses numbers.

If you have been reading closely, you have probably picked up on an obvious problem with using a 5-digit binary code to transmit text. A 5-digit binary number has 2 to the fifth power possible numbers. That, if my math is correct, allows for numbers up to 32 ($2 \times 2 \times 2 \times 2 \times 2 = 32$). The English alphabet alone has 26 characters, which leaves only six additional numbers to use to represent all the periods, commas, question marks, dollar signs, and colons, not to mention the 10 digits, 0 to 9. How can a 5-digit code work? Baudot assigned 2 of the 32 5-digit numbers to serve as "shift characters." In a transmission, these numbers change the code of the next several characters until another shift character is received. The shift characters allow for 62 possible character codes (64 minus the 2 shift characters). For example, the pattern

11011 [the "figure shift" number] 11001

will be read by the receiving machine to be the number 2. If the following pattern was received

11111 [the "character shift" number] 11001

the receiver would read the string as being the letter *W*. By coding and sending character shift and figure shift codes whenever appropriate, the Baudot code works quite well.

The Baudot code is still common in the European telex systems, which explains why only uppercase letters are typically allowed in the international telex network (if both uppercase and lowercase letters were allowed, they alone would take up 52 possible digits, too many to allot to just the alphabet, even with shift characters).

That is a brief explanation of the codes used for the telex system. Don't be overly concerned with the mechanics. Just as obscure combinations of dots and dashes stand for the alphabet and numbers in Morse code, various (and equally obscure) 5-digit numbers represent the same letters and numbers in the telex system. If you understand the discussion above, terrific. If not, you'll still be able to use telex.

SENDING TELEXES USING E-MAIL

There are a new set of rules when you use E-mail systems to send to telex machines. Some of the characters you would normally use with a full ASCII-supporting system (such as semicolons, exclamation points, and quotation marks, among others) are not understood by 5-bit telex. The problem with upper- and lowercase has already been mentioned. While several of the E-mail networks will automatically translate your mixed upper- and lowercase messages to all capital letters, and some even translate or remove the taboo punctuation marks, you still need to check. The best rule, of course, is to not use them to begin with. Another limitation is that telex will not accept lines longer than 69 characters (including spaces). You need to keep your lines shorter than that, and it is a good idea to use shorter lines even for standard E-mail. Finally, telex will not take messages longer than 100,000 characters (about 15,000 words). You will have to break up transmissions longer than that into separate passages. Just add a "more to come" notice at the end of each segment.

Don't overlook the appropriate use of telex. Most of the E-mail carriers allow for sending your E-mail into the worldwide telex network. AT&T Mail, EasyLink, MCI Mail, and CompuServe (among others) allow for telex transmissions.

SETTING UP A PRIVATE E-MAIL SYSTEM

If you find your business using E-mail to communicate with salespeople or regional managers in several different locations, you might find it more cost-effective to set up your own E-mail system. This is not nearly as difficult to do as it may sound, and it can save money. If you have several sales representatives scattered about the state or country, getting each an account on one of the commercial E-mail networks can be a costly undertaking. If you set up a central, private system, no accounts or fees need to be managed. Running a centralized electronic post office can simplify account management and cost containment.

You have a couple of options. One is to set up a simple network which handles only messaging. For IBM and compatibles, several packages exist. One, "PC-tPost" (Coker Electronics, 1430 Lexington Avenue, San Mateo, CA 94402; 415/573-5515), sets up your own mail station on your PC. It is really two packages: One is run on the central PC, probably at the home office. It accepts, stores and routes messages that come to it from users.

The second package, a dedicated communications program, is run by individual users. It allows them to compose their messages and send them to the central station quickly and efficiently. The central computer, running PC-tPost Central, also borrows a nice feature from the fax world (see Chapter 7). At intervals, the central computer can call the remote computers and poll them for any mail waiting to be sent in. If a message has been composed and queued for sending by the remote computer, the central unit can order it sent—accept and store it. You can save money by having the central machine call at night when telephone costs are low. Of course, for the process to work, the remote computer must be running PC-tPost and must be left on, with its modem attached to a phone line.

The second option is to set up a more complex system. If you have more than messages to send (for example, spreadsheet and other non-ASCII files) you need a system which can accept this data. If you have information that should be seen and responded to by all users, "bulletin board system" or BBS (see Chapter 10) software might be a good choice. Then, you can post all your messages and bulletins at a central phone number and have the other users call in regularly to retrieve their mail, upload files, leave messages for all to see, or send and receive private correspondence, when appropriate.

One of the fastest ways to get started is to get a copy of the *Complete Electronic Bulletin Board Starter Kit* by Charles Bowen and David Peyton (Bantam Books, $39.95). These two telecommunications experts have written several books on computer communications. This 430-page treatise includes the software and complete instructions necessary to get a BBS up and running with the minimum headache. The software, called RBBS, is one of the very best for the IBM and IBM-compatible family of computers. Most BBS software, compared to simple, dedicated messaging software, offers more features but also more complexity for users. If your needs extend beyond ASCII text, a BBS may be the correct choice.

With either system the only costs incurred are for the initial software and computer start-up, and, thereafter, only toll calls into the BBS. The estimated costs for the initial equipment—software and hardware—for the central, host unit is between $1500 and $5000, depending on what you need. For a simple, single-line system, the lower price would be about right. If you get into a more complex, multiple phone-line unit with large data storage, the costs rise significantly.

A FAX DIRECTORY

As fax machines become more and more common, you will need a program to keep up with the players. One is already available. FDP Associates (One Park Avenue, New York, NY 10016-5801; 212/503-4100) publishes a directory of nearly 100,000 fax numbers in the United States and abroad. *The Official Facsimile Users's Directory* costs $65.

USERS GROUPS

As mentioned in Chapter 3, users groups are gatherings of local computer enthusiasts held on a regular basis (more or less). Their internal organization varies from highly structured to highly informal. What these groups can offer you also varies, but they can always offer a level of expertise in using computers that is an invaluable resource for you, the computer user who is new to the computer world.

Computer groups began with a simple concept: sharing. In the earliest days of the PC, software was scarce. Users were usually computer professionals—the programmers themselves. The meetings allowed these "hackers" to gather and show their creations for the others to test and critique. Also, the software was shared, free of charge, with others. The face of the users group has changed with the increasing number of PC owners. Far from being just the elite groups of the past, groups today are increasingly for the user who, far from being a programmer, is simply someone who uses a computer for work.

Users still meet, though, to share knowledge, tips, and advice about what works for them and what might fit the needs of others.

Usually, users groups have a membership fee—$10 to $40 per year is common. For the fee, you get more return for your dollars than you get from any other investment in the world of computers. Usually, there is a group newsletter. This may be nothing more than a single photocopied sheet, or it may be a 100-page, typeset monster. Contents cover meeting dates, software and hardware reviews, programming tips, and "how-to's" for a range of topics.

Most groups maintain a software library. These are collections of programs that are either public-domain or user-supported (see Chapter 3). The group may charge a modest copying fee. The group library is an enormous resource where high-quality software can be cheaply acquired and tried out.

For all these benefits, though, the major value of a users group is its members. They range in age from kids to adults, in occupations from corporate executives to junior high students, and in computer experience from new owners to professional programmers. Almost anyone can find someone in the group who knows more about computers. Members ask questions and get help, and that is what the users group is all about.

How do you find a users group? If the owners you already know aren't aware of when and where a group meets, call the local computer stores. They will usually be able to direct you to a contact person. Don't be hesitant to ask around.

What if there is no local group? Not having a local group is becoming an unlikely possibility in all but the smallest of communities. If you have looked everywhere and found nothing, you can still get many of the group benefits by joining one of the larger groups as a long-distance member. You can get the newsletter, access to the software library by mail, and, sometimes, even a phone number to call for help. A few of the larger groups are listed below:

Alamo PC Organization
P.O. Box 65180
San Antonio, TX 78265-5190

The Boston Computer Society
One Center Plaza
Boston, MA 02108

Atlanta Computer Society
Box 888771
Atlanta, GA 30356

CACHE
6720 Palma Lane
Morton Grove, IL 60053

Atlanta IBM PC Users' Group
Box 28788
Atlanta, GA 30358

Capital PC Users Group
51 Monroe St., Plaza East 2
Rockville, MD 20850

Chicago Computer Society
Box 8681
Chicago, IL 60680-8681

Cincinnati PC User Group
P.O. Box 3097
Cincinnati, OH 45201

Columbus Computer Society
P.O. Box 1556
Columbus, OH 43216

Houston Area League of PC Users
Box 61266
Houston, TX 77208

IBM AT/XT Clone User Group
Box 15000/324
San Francisco, CA 94117

Kentucky-Indiana PC User Group
P.O. Box 3564
Louisville, KY 40201

North Orange County Computer
P.O. Box 3616
Orange, CA 92665

North Texas PC User Group
P.O. Box 780066
Dallas, TX 75278-0066

Orange Coast PC User Group
P.O. Box 6100-211
Costa Mesa, CA 92628

Pacific NW PC User Group
P.O. Box 3363
Bellevue, WA 98009

Palmetto PC Club
P.O. Box 2046
Columbia, SC 29202-2046

Pasadena PC User Group
711 E. Walnut St.
Pasadena, CA 91101

Philadelphia Area Computer Society
c/o LaSalle U., 20th & Olney
Philadelphia, PA 19141

Phoenix PC Users Group
P.O. Box 35637
Phoenix, AZ 85069

Pittsburgh Area Computer Club
Box 6440
Pittsburgh, PA 15212

Portland PC Club
The Galeria, Suite 529
Portland, OR 97205

Sacramento PC Users Group
Box 685
Citrus Heights, CA 95611-0685

San Diego Computer Society
Box 81444
San Diego, CA 92138

Silicon Valley Computer Soc.
2464 El Camino Real, #190
Santa Clara, CA 95051

Stanford Palo Alto User Group
Box 3738
Stanford, CA 94309

St. Louis UG for the IBM PC
P.O. Box 69099
St. Louis, MO 63169

Twin Cities PC Users Group
Box 10360
Minneapolis, MN 55458-3360

Triangle Computer Society
Box 3588
Chapel Hill, NC 27515-3588

Utah Blue Chips
P.O. Box 510811
Salt Lake City, UT 84151

BULLETIN BOARD SYSTEMS (BBSs)

AN INTRODUCTION

At several points in this book, the local BBS has been mentioned. BBSs provide an inexpensive way to try out communications software and hardware. But, more than being just a rehearsal area, the local BBS may also provide some of your communication needs.

What would you call a computer user who sets up a computer, modem, and disk drives for strangers to use for free? Pretty nice person, right? What about someone who also

- Installs a phone line and pays for its monthly charges out of his or her own pocket so that others can call and access his or her computer equipment?
- Provides storage space on his or her equipment for users to leave E-mail to others using the system?
- Spends several hours weekly maintaining the system, deleting old messages, providing new programs for downloading, and answering questions from users?
- Allows others to subject his or her expensive computer equipment to the rigors of nonstop usage, often 24 hours a day?

Most would agree that these benevolent souls are extraordinary. But that is exactly what thousands of computer enthusiasts do, nationwide, in increasing numbers every day. These patrons of the computer world are called "sysops" (for "*system operators*"), and their electronic sanctuaries are called "bulletin board systems," or simply BBSs.

The origin of the BBS can be traced back to Ward Christensen and Randy Seuss, who started the first such system in Chicago in the late 1970s. Since that pioneering effort, BBSs have been set up on practically every computer brand made. The "bulletin-boarding of America" has spread to the homes of thousands of computer enthusiasts. It is so pervasive now that it is difficult to find any metropolitan area in the nation that does not have at least one BBS accessible to local users.

What motivates this unusual group of benefactors to undertake the expense (in both equipment and time) necessary to establish such oases for others would make for interesting psychological study. The factors involved are probably as varied as the systems themselves. Whatever they may be, the sysop is a unique breed which provides a splendid facility for communication, sharing, and education among the computer zealots of the world.

THE ESSENTIAL BBS

BBSs usually share two common ingredients. Preeminently, they provide an electronic messaging service. Users who call in can leave messages addressed to either all other users or specific individuals. The mechanics of BBS-supported E-mail differs little from the commercial E-mail services discussed earlier. Messages are left by simply typing them in, line by line, or uploading them while you are connected to the BBS. (Note that since most of these systems do not have access charges, composing messages offline is not so imperative, unless, of course, you are calling a BBS through a long-distance call.) Then, when the addressee calls in at some later time, that person is "told" that he or she has "mail" waiting. The recipient can then elect to read and respond to the mail just as if it had come to them in the usual paper form.

Unlike traditional E-mail networks, messages can be left addressed to "All." These messages are useful in soliciting comments, opinions, or information from any other interested user. Depending on the mix among the users of a BBS—predominantly local users, or local users with a smattering of long-distance callers—the "message base" (the collection of messages stored on the BBS) can vary greatly in content. The messages may be strictly of local interest or may be of more general interest to all who might call in.

Whether a BBS is "dedicated" to a specific computer brand or topic also affects what can be found in the message base. While most BBSs do not prohibit users of other computer brands to use the system, some do have a distinct focus on one particular brand of computer or another. There are MS-DOS boards and Apple boards and Commodore boards, where users of these particular computer brands share detailed information in the message bases on the inner workings of their beloved brands. While the majority of the messages may not be of interest to you if you own another type of computer, you are welcome to make comments and ask advice on general computer equipment or even your unique machine. Computer users often own more than one brand of computer, and an Atari or Commodore BBS is very likely to have some IBM or Apple owners on it as well. There is no "discrimination" (except some good-natured kidding about which brand is superior to which) in the BBS computer world.

There are also BBSs that are not so much dedicated to computer brands as they are to specific areas of interest. There are health and medical BBSs, engineering BBSs, legal BBSs, handicapped BBSs, and Christian and psychology BBSs, among dozens of other topics of interest. This is not to say that only messages in these areas are appropriate—general computer queries and comments are always welcome on a BBS. It is just that these particular systems are usually frequented by professionals and lay people with specific interest and expertise in a BBS's special subject area. The BBS provides a special place for these individuals to discuss the problems, concerns, and opinions particular to their area of interest. These BBSs provide a splendid chance to obtain an expert's opinion. (Note: Never look for definitive medical or legal advice; you will not get it. Not because the users are incapable of rendering it, but because of the medical/legal ramifications involved. Be content to accept the information provided simply as advice from a friend and then act in a prudent fashion to obtain explicit, personal guidance from a qualified professional).

The typical BBS runs on a single phone line using a 1200- or 2400-baud modem. The system may be owned by an individual or a users group. Access is free. Most BBSs have a message area, for E-mail to other users, and a file section. The file section contains public-domain and user-supported software that you can download to your computer. Capabilities beyond these basics depend on what software the host system is running. Some BBS programs have multiple message and file areas, interactive games you can play while connected, and even ways to transfer messages left locally to other BBSs in other cities.

While the preceding description may be a portrait of the average BBS, there are a few that exceed the norm, some to a remarkable degree. Some BBSs have multiple incoming phone lines and can support several users at once. Others feature huge file areas with hundreds of programs available to users. These mammoth systems may have a subscription fee—often $20 to $45 per year—for using the system.

Just like the local users group, the BBS—local or in a distant city—can be a watering hole for the forlorn or confused computer user. BBS users can get the same high-quality, personal advice and assistance they can find in a users group. In fact, the BBS is an electronic equivalent of the local group. As with finding a users group, finding a BBS to call is usually as simple as calling a computer store. They often have a list of BBSs available in their area. If you have found a users group, they can also provide you with some phone numbers to call.

RULES OF THE ROAD

The first time you call a BBS, any BBS, regardless of where you got the phone number, make sure you call at a "decent" hour in the BBS's zone, preferably during daytime hours. Once you have confirmed that a BBS still exists at that phone number, then call whenever you can. The one-time expense of a prime-time phone call to a new BBS is worth it. If you don't make the initial daytime call, you may disturb a former BBS owner (or, even worse, someone who has just inherited a previously used BBS number) out of a sound sleep. Have a heart. Make sure a BBS is active before calling it in the middle of the night.

While we are discussing BBS etiquette, a few more words of advice are in order. When you call a BBS, always keep in mind that you are no less a visitor in someone else's home than if you physicially walked in the door, a stranger off the street. Always be on your best behavior. Avoid using profanity. Sysops are likely to delete any obscene remarks, as well as libelous or slanderous ones. That is their prerogative.

Use your real name when signing onto a system for the first time. Many sysops elect to verify new callers, so leave accurate information when you sign on. Depending on how the system is run, you might be granted limited activities the first time you connect to the system and your privileges will be liberalized after you are "verified." Verification may include leaving your name and phone number for the BBS owner to make sure you are not someone trying to leave obscene messages or disrupt their system. You may very well get a call from the BBS's owners to make sure you are not playing games. Don't feel like they are trying to invade your privacy. The sysops are just checking credentials.

The legal responsibilities of BBS owners is a current hot topic, and there are several court cases pending that will more clearly define the legal aspects of running a BBS. A prominent Chicago law school recently held a day-long seminar on just this topic. The responsibility of sysops to protect the private content of messages on their systems and, at the same time, screen messages for illegal activity (passing credit card numbers or MCI account IDs) puts the BBS owner in a quandary. How does the sysop maintain message privacy if he or she is to prohibit illegal communications at the same time? The sysops are somewhat under the gun, right now, so don't be affronted by their efforts to protect themselves.

Take time to participate. Be active. Don't be a one-way electronic conduit, signing on and downloading everything in sight. Leave messages, answer questions, and take the time to upload a program now and then. Sysops take pride in their message bases and enjoy seeing a lively interchange. They also like new software. However, do not upload commercial software. That is taboo on a BBS, as well as being blatantly illegal. Sometimes the sysop may not even be aware that the software is a commercial package. If the sysop innocently makes the software publicly available, he or she can be subject to legal prosecution. Contribute, but contribute public-domain (free) software only.

Once you access a few BBSs, you will find them to be a major source of information and new software for you. Exploring the BBS world can be a fascinating and rewarding experience. It is probably where you should start exploring the capabilities of telecommuncations. For free or next to it, you can practice with your modem and software before you tackle the costly commercial systems. The sysops won't mind—they enjoy the company. But use a BBS with the same courtesy that you would use any other public facility. BBSs are to be nurtured rather than exploited. Check them out—you will not be disappointed.

WHERE TO FIND INEXPENSIVE SOFTWARE

You can save thousands of dollars on software by checking out the vast collections of public-domain or "shareware" (user-supported) software. The first place to look is your local users group. Second, check a local BBS. BBSs often sport collections of variable sizes that can be downloaded by modem to your computer. If one of these resources is not available, all is not lost. An entire industry has sprung up based on the need to distribute these inexpensive treasures to a software-hungry public. Several mail-order houses make the software available at low cost, generally $3 to $6 for a disk full.

One of the largest and most respected software distributors is PC-SIG (1030D East Duanae Ave., Sunnyvale, CA 94086; 800/245-6717). You can order this company's 425-page catalog from your bookstore or directly from PC-SIG ($12.95 plus $4 shipping). The fourth edition of the catalog covers disks 1 through 705. A supplement ($8.95) covers disks 706 through 1124. That should give you an idea of how much software there is available in the public domain or shareware network. You can get the programs for $6 per disk.

Another distributor is Public Brand Software (P.O. Box 51315, Indianapolis, IN 46251; 800/426-3475 [800/IBM-DISK]). Public Brand Software publishes a quarterly 80-page catalog complete with ratings for the software— one to four stars—and descriptions. The catalog is free for the asking. The software is $5 per disk.

Other distributors include:

Public Software Library
P.O. Box 35705
Houston, TX 77235-5705
713/665-7017

Shareware Express
P.O. Box 219
San Juan Capistrano, CA 92693
800/346-2842

Always remember, when you pay the $5 or $6 for a disk of software, you are not paying the registration fee for the shareware software. You are only paying the cost for distributing it. You are still obliged to pay the author of the program the requested fee, if you choose to use the program. Think of the distribution cost as retail markup. The wholesale price of the software is still due to the author.

(ALMOST) UNIVERSAL E-MAIL

DASnet

In Chapter 4, one of the problems noted that users of E-mail services had to deal with was the lack of interconnectivity. Specifically, with the exception of MCI Mail and CompuServe's Easy Plex, you cannot send a message from one network to another. To correspond with someone, you both have to have accounts on the same system. While we wait on the CCITT (see Glossary) X.400 and X.500 protocols to remedy the problem, there is one service that offers some putty to fill the gap.

An interesting answer to sending across E-mail systems is offered by DASnet (DASystems, 1503 E. Campbell Ave., Campbell, CA 95008; 408/559-7434). For a monthly fee of $4.75 and a variable charge per message (depending on the length of the message and the destination), DASnet will forward your E-mail across systems—including ABA/net, AT&T Mail (see Chapter 4), BIX (an electronic edition of *BYTE* magazine), DASnet Network, Dialcom (another large E-mail network), EIES (from the New Jersey Institute of Technology), EasyLink (see Chapter 4), Envoy 100 (a Canadian service), FAX, GeoMail (a service for users of GeoMail software), INET, MCI Mail (see Chapter 4), NWI (a teleconferencing system run by Networking and Information), PeaceNet/EcoNet (a network operated by the San Francisco–based Institute for Global Communications), Portal Communications (a system used by members of the Sierra Club), The Meta Network, The Source, Telemail, ATI's Telemail (Japan), telex, TWICS (Tokyo, Japan), UNISON, UUCP, and The WELL (a popular conferencing and E-mail system). DASnet serves as the United Nations for 21 warring electronic mail systems. These networks allow DASnet to accept and forward messages to and from their subscribers. The subscribers are billed for their activity, which can vary depending on systems used and message length.

The way DASnet works is simple. There is no need to learn anything about another E-mail network to get your messages there to people on that network. You simply leave a message on your favorite network to the specified DASnet mailbox address and let DASnet know the address of the recipient on any of the other supported systems. The recipient does not have to be a DASnet subscriber. If you've made an error and sent to an ID or name that does not exist, DASnet will notify you within four to eight hours, and the text of your message will be returned. DASnet collects the messages on the various systems, connects with its account to the addressee's network, and relays your message. The correspondent can then reply, again using the DASnet account on his or her system, and the reply is billed to your account. DASnet maintains an account on each of the supported networks. Each account's mailbox is checked approximately every four hours by DASnet. If DASnet finds a message, the service transfers it to the appropriate recipient's mail system. Messages are billed per 1000 characters (about 20 lines of text). For example, an MCI Mail subscriber can send a 200-character message to a GeoMail subscriber for 64¢. An MCI Mail user can send a 2000-character message to a GeoMail recipient in London for $1.69. DASnet also offers fax (a typical one-page letter costs about $3.70 for domestic delivery and $5.70 internationally) and telex services (you even get a telex address for you to use as an address for others). With your subscription, you get a DASnet subscriber directory and a listing in the directory.

DIRECTORY INFORMATION

Another valuable way to deal with the lack of E-mail integration is to have a directory of E-mail users with their addresses and the systems they use. The National E-Mail Registry (Suite 110, Two Neshaminy Interplex, Trevose, PA 19047-9905) offers free registration by modem to anyone. You connect to their network via a 1-800 number and register with a password and two security codes (your mother's maiden name and the year of your birth). You then enter any E-mail, fax, and telex numbers you have. These are then placed into the Registry's database. To find another party, you call 203/245-7720 by modem. After entering your identifying account information, you enter the name (company or individual) of the party you seek. The database is scanned. There is a 50-cent charge for each successful search, and unsuccessful searches are free. You can buy 20 searches for $10, and unlimited use is available on the system for $95 per year. You can update your registry information—add or delete addresses for E-mail, fax, or telex—by calling 800/622-0505. While not an ideal solution to interconnectivity (you would still have to have some way to send messages to the individual on the systems they use), the National E-mail Registry gives us a view of the future: directory assistance for electronic addresses.

CD-ROM

In the next very few years, rather than using a modem and phone line to access the information stored on the databases of mainframe computers, it will be possible for you to access the information right at your desktop computer. The data will be stored on *your* computer—not on a remote one. The same technology that permits music to be generated from a laser-read compact disk is now being applied to textual computer-accessible data.

Called CD-ROM (*compact-disk, read-only memory*), these small disks can hold the equivalent of approximately 250,000 pages of text. Their storage capacity far exceeds the more familiar floppy or even hard disk drives. Instead of kilobytes (a thousand characters or so of text) or even a few megabytes (a million characters), these disks can hold hundreds of millions of characters. Their capacity to hold immense amounts of data (1500 times greater than a floppy disk) makes it feasible to place comprehensive databases, so large they could only be held on a much larger computer previously, on their surfaces. They can be easily mass-produced and are read by your computer through an optical laser drive attached to it. With CD-ROMs, you will no longer need to be concerned with accounts, modems, telephone lines, search fees, and passwords. The entire database will be yours—right in your own office.

Already there are dozens of business-related products available. For example, Ziff-Davis, a major publisher of high-tech magazines, has produced a CD-ROM disk that includes the most recent 12 months of 10 leading computer industry journals in full text and the most recent 12 months of computer-related articles from more than 120 computer, communications, electronics, and business periodicals (including the national edition of *The New York Times*) in abstract form. The disk has the full-text of *PC Magazine, PC Week, Lotus Magazine, Digital Review, MacUser, PC Tech Journal, Government Computer News, A+, MicroSoft Systems Journal,* and *Communications of the ACM* (a publication of the leading association of computer scientists). The "Computer Library" CD-ROM is available for $695 for a one-year subscription. It uses special software (Lotus' "BlueFish" search and retrieval software) to make finding the most specific information a breeze.

Disclosure (Disclosure Information Group, 5161 River Road, Bethesda, MD; 800/638-8076), a database that reports on companies that file their financial status with the U.S. Securities and Exchange Commission, is available on a CD-ROM database. Updated quarterly, the database includes detailed profiles of more than 11,000 companies whose stocks are traded on the New York Stock Exchange and the American Stock Exchange. You can search and analyze information from 10-K's, 8-K's, 10-Q's, proxy statements,[1] and shareholder reports of these firms. The cost: $3200 a year.

---

[1] Form 10-K's are reports filed annually by companies that describe the company, its chief officer, its market, balance sheets, statements of income, and sources and applications of funds. Form 8-K's are filed by companies within 15 days of a material occurrence, for example, a major acquisition. Form 10-Q's are filed quarterly and announce any significant company developments. Proxy statements are sent to shareholders when there is an issue to be voted on.

For demographics, try Donnelley's Demographics (Donnelley Marketing Information, 70 Seaview Avenue, Box 10250, Stanford, CT 06904; 203/353-7207). It includes the 1970 and 1980 census data, five-year projections, 160 key business statistics for each area, household demographics (number of households, income, occupations, etc.), and more. Data are searchable for almost any demographic area imaginable. It includes simple, menu-driven search software.

There are dozens more CD-ROM databases available as well. But, despite the attractiveness of having the data available to search leisurely and without time constraints, there are some problems. The main one is cost. According to Maureen Fleming, author of the *Information Industry Factbook,* published by the Digital Information Group, online services will continue to dominate electronic information for the next several years "because the price of CD-ROM titles won't decline enough to be cost-competitive to online." According to the *Factbook's* statistics, the average price of a CD-ROM title for professional markets—such as lawyers, accountants, and librarians—was $1829 (June 1988). Business/financial titles were even more expensive, at $8865 per title on average.

The bottom line right now is that CD-ROM simply isn't cost-effective for most information users. However, Fleming foresees that as the prices of CD-ROM titles decline over the next few years, more and more online users will shift over to CD-ROM. According to Fleming, "In five years, it is conceivable that nearly all of the online industry's profitable customers will shift to CD-ROM." The *Factbook* reports that CD-ROM prices declined nearly 13 percent from 1987 to 1988 to an average of $1883 per title for all kinds of titles, excluding titles on business/financial subjects.

It is clear that CD-ROM technology is feasible for certain special needs. For database access, it is cost-effective only for the high-volume research users. With desktop CD-ROM, competition between online providers and those producing the readable disks, themselves, should continue to lower the costs at both ends.

9

What the Future Holds

The "three C's" of modern business are *complexity, competition,* and *change.* These characteristics pervade electronic communications just as they do our personal lives and business lives. To keep pace, the modern business person must continue to learn and adapt. This includes mastering and applying current technology, as well as reading and remaining current on where the next generation of technology may lead. This chapter discusses some of the coming trends and presents the views of some of the experts in the industry. With this perspective, you will have a head start for planning for the impending developments and thinking about how they will affect your activities.

SIMPLIFICATION AHEAD

While the electronic information industry is growing by leaps and bounds (revenues were an estimated $1.9 billion in 1987 and are expected to double in the next five years), it is still much too alien for the general public. The complexities of the technology involved just to access the information networks is overwhelming for most. While this book has pointed out that the technology need not be overwhelming, there is no escaping the fact that it requires some degree of study and work to set up a computer for telecommunication. For busy professionals, this task is not something they approach with any real vigor. Until they do, those who take advantage of what is available will remain a small percentage of the total computer users.

The barriers to effective use of database systems do not stop with the technology itself. The networks remain just as difficult to use as they are to connect to. Initiated and structured for the librarian and information professional, their command structures remain totally nontransparent and nonintuitive. Voluminous user manuals which explain, or attempt to explain, arcane search languages are not something the average professional has the time to digest. The problem lies with lack of standards. Each information host demands users to follow its own command structure. Mastering one set of commands on one system will not carry over well to controlling another network.

The third factor which has limited the effective use of the existing information systems is their cost. The systems are relatively expensive to use, particularly when compared to the public library. Now, the information providers argue that these electronic libraries save you time over the traditional shelves and card indexes of the library. One advertisement boldly asserts that "trying to find information in a library is like trying to find your high school sweetheart by going door to door." While this is certainly true for the trained information professional, it is still difficult for the ordinary user to achieve such advances in efficiency and time savings. One of the drawbacks of the commercial information systems is that there are charges for time spent using the system, as well as for the information accessed. Usually, and paradoxically, the expenses are geared heavily toward time rather than information. The user is penalized for being inexperienced. As long as there are charges ranging as high as a dollar or more a minute for usage, all but the most efficient and experienced users will shy away.

Finally, there is an educational gap. There is a serious lack of awareness among the general public and professionals in all fields as to what can be accomplished through online information systems. The commercial database systems have not done an adequate public education campaign. Most potential users may have an idea that information can be accessed by computer, but they have little understanding of the speed and efficiency with which information can be retrieved.

Alfred Glossbrenner, the author of the "bible" of the information age, *How to Look It Up Online* (St. Martin's Press, 175 Fifth Avenue, NY 10010; $14.95), explains the problem this way:

> I believe that a significant number of people will master one or two databases completely and use them regularly. And I feel very strongly that there will be a great demand for professional searchers or "information brokers" capable of skillfully tapping a variety of online databases. But neither of these things will happen until the general "information consciousness" of managers and profes-

215

sionals is raised. Today, most managers aren't even aware of how badly they need online information, let alone how easily it can be obtained—once you know where and how to look.

With these four barricades separating the public from the electronic information systems, it is easy to see where things must move for the two to come together. And they will come together. What we will see in the future is a marked relaxation of the technological hurdles users must overcome to access the networks.

The success of the Minitel system in France is a prime example of how things can be done. Now, France has not traditionally been recognized as a leader in high-tech advances. But with Minitel, a videotex service, the French have certainly taught (hopefully) their American counterparts a few lessons. After all, with 4.5 million users on Minitel (compared to maybe 700,000 or so Americans using online systems in our country), somebody must be doing something right. Rather than selling information and leaving it up to the subscriber to find a way to access it, Postes Telephones and Telecommunications (PTT), the state-owned monopoly that controls France's postal and telephone services, provides a complete system to its subscriber. A simple terminal, sold cheaply and installed at no charge, is made available for the users. Certainly, the terminal does not have the power and data storage of a PC, but that is not the purpose. There are no modems or RS232 cards to install, no parity settings to deal with, and no complicated software to learn. It's a "plug-in and go" setup. The public has instant access with no technological preparation required.

Once the user is connected, the services provided are simple to use. Everything is menu-driven. If you can order in a restaurant or choose your floor in an elevator, you can use the system. The access charges are cheap. They are based on services accessed, more so than time online. You are not penalized for being a new, inefficient user. You pay for what you retrieve. And retrieve the French did (*do*)—from sports reports, to weather, to food prices, to online "chatting" (probably the most popular feature with the flirtatious French)—to the tune of 20 million or more calls per month. PTT earned $70 million in 1985, and that figure has certainly increased in succeeding years.

ADJUSTMENTS TO CURRENT SYSTEMS

The message to the American information industry is clear. Yes, there is a market for online information resources, and it can be tapped by relaxing the technological toll inflicted on its potential users. A system that is easy to access and use, affordable and full-featured, will have people flocking to the online information door.

What you can expect in the future is an increasingly simple interface between the information systems and the user. The systems themselves will simplify and, eventually, move toward standardization. That will allow functioning at two levels online: in a menu mode, for infrequent users, guiding them along every step of the way; and in a command mode for experienced users, allowing them to take advantage of the efficiency that will bring. I predict that the systems will increasingly move toward lower access rates, and they will be based more on information retrieved rather than time connected. You will be charged perhaps $2 an hour, but 10 cents for every 1000 characters that cross your screen. These changes will probably take place in the next few years.

Already, things are changing. Trintex, announced in 1984 as a joint venture between CBS, Sears, and IBM, has lost one of its original partners, but it has produced a product that may change the face of electronic communications. CBS left the triumvirate in 1986, but "Prodigy," as the new service was named, appeared on the digital scene late the next year. A full-fledged version was rolled out in early 1988. City by city, Prodigy has been expanded, and it has been well received where it has appeared. The system is expected to be available on a national basis in the early 1990s.

What makes Prodigy different from current electronic information and communications providers? First, Prodigy is true videotex. The computer screen is used to present text and images in a coordinated fashion. Current information systems, such as CompuServe and GEnie, deal with presenting text alone. True, CompuServe offers weather maps, but the point remains that the information is displayed purely as text. True videotex applies color, pictures, and text together in a page-by-electronic-page fashion.

Videotex is made possible by the software that comes with the Prodigy sign-up package. Presently, the program is available only for IBM and IBM-compatible computers. One of the problems with videotex has been that it is slow. To send across a modem and phone lines the computer codes necessary to generate a page of text with graphics takes longer than to send text alone. But, with the software, Prodigy is able to speed up things considerably. The Prodigy software stores a great deal of the codes necessary to display most of the graphics screens right in the disk at your computer. As a result, all it takes for the system to send a full screen is to send a few codes to fill in the appropriate text and color changes for each page. It still takes longer to generate a page of videotex than it does to generate text, but this format accelerates the process considerably.

STANDARDIZATION THROUGH ISDN

The development that will change the whole face of the online information industry is the Integrated Services Digital Network (ISDN) which will arrive by the turn of the century. The ISDN will replace our old analog-only phone system and provide a complete network, connecting us to every form of data imaginable and bringing it to our homes at the speed of light. ISDN is the brainchild of the Consultative Committee in International Telegraphy and Telephony (CCITT). That learned international body, which meets every four years, put forth the ISDN standard in 1984. It describes ISDN as "a limited set of standard interfaces to a digital communications network. The result: a network providing end users with voice, data, and certain image services on end-to-end digital circuits, using an international standard for interfaces that is accepted by communications carriers, users, and systems manufacturers."

In simple terms, ISDN really describes two systems. First, the Basic Rate Interface will work over existing, ordinary copper phone lines. It will be marketed primarily for the home and small-business user. The Basic Rate Interface will provide for three channels for data transmission. There will be two "Bearer" or B channels. These will transmit digital information at a rate of 64 kilobits per second (kbps), which is equal to 64,000 bits per second. If you think about what current modems and fax machines use (1200 to 2400 bits per second for the common modem and 9600 bits per second for fax), you can appreciate the speeds these B channels will offer. The third channel, dubbed the "Delta" or D channel, will operate at 16 kbps. It will be used, according to ISDN, to be the control channel for "housekeeping" and, presumably, error-checking and reporting. Because of the designation of the channels as "B" and "D," the Basic Rate Interface has also been referred to as the "2B + D" system.

The second ISDN standard will be for the heavyweight business needs. It is called the Primary Rate Interface and will provide twenty-three 64-kbps B channels and one 64 kbps D channel. For this reason, this interface is often referred to as the "23B + D" system.

Again, it all boils down to integration. ISDN aims to take the confusing array of wires that connect PCs, modems, and fax machines to the phone system and put them all on the same wire. The higher speeds of the ISDN standard will allow users with the right equipment to send high-quality faxes, near-CD-quality audio, and tolerably clear video images all on the same data pipe—and all at the same time. It is simply a patterned way of combining voice and data on the same network.

Stripped of the (necessary) jargon, exactly what will this new communication system mean to you? Again, Alfred Glossbrenner:

The future of computer communications, at least computer communications for a truly mass audience, lies in the television set and ISDN, or the Integrated Services Digital Network. ISDN is the fiber-optic network that makes possible two things—tremendous throughput of data and the multiplexing of many types of data for many different purposes over a single "data pipe." When ISDN networks become widespread, you will be able to plug your television, computer, telephone, and a variety of other appliances into the same receptacle in your home or office. There will be no need for modems to convert a computer's digital pulses into sound and back again for transmission over copper wire lines.

The throughput of an ISDN connection is, I believe, on the order of 64 kilobits per second, compared to the 300 to 9600 bits per second possible with today's modems and phone lines. This means that huge amounts of graphic and visual information can be communicated instantaneously, compared to the several minutes required to transmit a single graphic screen at today's speeds.

Now, imagine what this can mean from a home shopping standpoint. You're interested in cubic zirconia bracelets. So you turn to a shopping channel, where you are greeted by a menu. You press a key on an attached keypad to select jewelry. You then press another key to select bracelets. And here you find you have five to choose from. Keying each selection in turn causes a CD-ROM at the shopping service to spin and send you a brief television presentation on each piece. If you like, you can switch on your VCR to record all of the presentations, switch off, and make your decision at your leisure.

The result is a narrowly focused, completely customized interactive session with a remote "database" of, in this case, product information. But there is no reason why the same model cannot be used for "real" information—everything from sports scores to stock market statistics. The key point here is that while computers are heavily involved at every stage of the process, the resulting service is no more difficult to use than an automatic teller machine.

The possibilities, as Glossbrenner suggests, are endless. Fiber optics can handle upwards of 27 gigabits—a gigabit is equal to one billion bits—per second. That is the equivalent of 400,000 simultaneous phone calls and enough to handle hundreds of video channels, high-fidelity audio conversations, and computer files concurrently. The blend that will be possible between the television, the telephone, and the computer will allow interaction between host and user in ways we can only dream about now. Encyclopedias with digitized pictures, video-magazines with animation, electronic how-to books that can respond to your questions as you watch a procedure being carried out, and other scenarios will all be possible. How about a "sketch phone" with which users can discuss a project while each views the other making drawings on a digitized tablet thousands of miles away?

Before you simply file this away as some sort of electronic "Fantasy Island," be aware that several large-scale trials of ISDN are already under way. More than 10 of the "Regional Bell Operating Companies" (RBOCs) are working with AT&T on ISDN development. Such industry giants as McDonald's, 3M Corporation, and Shearson Lehman Hutton are already customers of ISDN technology. Computer vendors are also jumping into the ISDN puddle with both feet. IBM, Hayes Microcomputer, and AT&T have already released or are developing ISDN-related products. By the end of 1990, some 500,000 ISDN lines are expected to be in use.

While most experts agree that widespread application of ISDN systems is still at least several years ahead, it would still be prudent to keep your ear to the ground as the technology unfurls. It is not something that will be available only to the corporate giants. In fact, it may be most useful to the small business seeking increased networking with suppliers and customers.

ADVANCES IN COMMUNICATIONS

The second major area of development, besides standardization, will be in communications. While E-mail and online conferencing are already in use, they each must be considered to be in their infancy. Again, the limitations are the same—complex technology, compounded by lack of standardization and integration.

According to Cathryn Conroy, reporting for *Online Today,* an electronic news service available on CompuServe, awareness of and preparation for the future of the telecommuncations industry is happening even at the White House. The President's Council on Management Improvement has provided its projections on the economy, society, and the federal work force of the future. Some of its projections are presented below:

- The administration expects a continuing decline in the cost of hardware. Over the next 10 years, progress in large-scale integration of electronic circuitry will cut computer power costs by 50 to 70 percent.
- Processing speed of computers will increase to 5 to 9 times the 1987 level.
- Software upgrades will provide easier access to electronic networks and will enhance the ability to access databases quickly.
- Improved access will foster complex commmercial and governmental relationships, establishing an "information infrastructure."
- The government's biggest challenge will be in meeting the public's demand for more convenient services. By 1995, 60 to 65 percent of households will have an actively used computer, and people will interact with business and government from their homes.

While the government readies itself to deal with the inevitable changes and demands of electronic communications, the major hurdle the industry itself is working to overcome is lack of integration. As mentioned in Chapter 4, with a few rare exceptions, sending an electronic message from one network to a user of another network is impossible. To reach each other, correspondents must subscribe and confine their activities to a common host.

Interconnectivity already has standards, which are waiting to be implemented. In its 1984 session, the CCITT endorsed the X.400 communications standard. When the X.400 protocols are activated, E-mail transmissions may be sent from one network to another as easily as they are sent to subscribers on the same system. The key, of course, is how the addresses are recognized and handled. Just as paper mail and telephone calls can reach anyone in the world because of a unique address, X.400 defines how messages are to be addressed and how systems are to handle forwarding and receiving from system to system. In the United States, things are moving ahead with activating X.400-based connectivity. The National Bureau of Standards has organized an Open Systems Interconnection (OSI) Implementator's Workshop to get industry leaders together on the topic. The special interest group on X.400 has reached a prelimnary agreement on a version of X.400, and new products have already started appearing. Such industry heavyweights as DEC, Dialcom, Western Union, Xerox, AT&T, and IBM have moved ahead with new products which have been demonstrated at industry events.

Because you will have to know the unique electronic mailbox of your recipient before your message can be sent properly, the CCITT approved the X.500 recommendations at its November 1988 meeting in Australia. The X.500 protocol continues the X.400 transfer system but adds a universal "directory assistance." With this addition, if the address you need is not known to you, you can look it up electronically and address your E-mail accordingly.[1] "In some cases, such as electronic mail," the draft of X.500 said, "the entry will have some additional information, such as the types of information which the user's equipment can handle. If authentication is to be supported, then user password and/or credentials will be needed."

With implementation of the X.400 or X.500 protocols will come elimination of the major obstacle for universal acceptance of E-mail as a principal player in personal as well as business communications. When it becomes feasible to reach anyone in the world by electronic means, the other problems—the overly complicated technology and the costs—will obviously become worth overcoming. And X.400/X.500 will not stop with electronic mail. It will allow for electronic fund transfers, electronic mass advertising, and

---

[1] Actually, the X.500 proposal goes far beyond offering just an E-mail address. A person's entry could contain information corresponding to each of the communication methods by which that person can be reached. These could include a list of at least the following: telephone number, electronic mail, telex, ISDN, physical delivery (e.g., the mail system), and fax.

better circulation of all forms of information. The impact on the way people do business will be enormous.

FILE TRANSFERS

A hybrid of standardization is rapidly developing in the United States without sanction by the CCITT. It will, perhaps, become a major way for businesses of all sizes to communicate before there is anything approaching implementation of ISDN or X.400/X.500. Western Union, one of the major developers of the technology, recognizes this. They stated in a release in December 1988 that "our architecture today represents what X.400 proponents are hoping to have in place by 1992."

What is all the excitement about? It's "Electronic Data Interchange" or EDI. A simple definition of EDI is "a computer-to-computer and application-to-application interchange of business documents in standardized format for the purpose of facilitating business transactions." In simpler terms, EDI is basically a way for businesses to make paperless exchanges of forms—e.g., purchase orders and invoices—electronically.

While EDI is not new (it began in the late 1970s), it is gaining momentum in the business world and is already changing the way businesses interact. As usual in the United States—where competition and free enterprise are king—no universally accepted standard has emerged as yet. But that has not stopped many businesses—large and small—from activating EDI protocols in their businesses. Industry experts have taken the view that EDI is on the verge of causing a revolution in the computer industry. As rapidly as the concept is being grasped by the larger firms, it is only a matter of time before they begin to expect their smaller associates to be on the bandwagon. (More on EDI is presented under "Electronic Data Interchange" later in this chapter.)

FAX OF THE FUTURE

Another blend that is already on the horizon of reality is the cellular facsimile (fax) machine. NEC America Inc. developed a 10-pound car fax machine in 1988 that plugs into the cigarette lighter, uses the cellular car phone to transmit, and can double as a personal copier. It, reportedly, will sell for $2400 when it gets on the market. The new fax will be part of the mobile office known as the Trump Edition Cadillac. The rolling chief executive officer will have the fax, a portable computer, three car phones, and a paper shredder at his or her disposal—as standard features, of course. On the more realistic front, fax machines will continue to become smaller, cheaper, and transmit faster, using the Group 4 CCITT protocol. There are already briefcase-size fax machines on the market. Of course, the quality of the transmitted images will improve as well. With the $500 barrier soon to be history, fax machines will become a ubiquitous part of the home information system. They will be mass-marketed as general consumer items. K-Mart plans to be selling fax machines in 2200 stores by the end of 1989. Public fax will be available anywhere people gather. Northwest Airlines is installing credit card–operated fax machines at its terminals in 12 major airports. Even the U.S. Postal Service began testing the consumer fax machine at 260 of its 29,203 branches in June 1989. If the four-month test is positive, another 6000 to 8000 offices, mostly in urban centers, will also have the machines. Slide a Visa, MasterCard, or American Express card into a reader attached to the fax, and you will then be charged either per document or per minute, plus whatever phone charges you incur. *Consumer fax is here.*

GETTING COMFORTABLE WITH TECHNOLOGY

As pointed out in the Introduction to this book, accepting changes—even if they are vast improvements—is a slow process in our personal lives as well as in our business practices. Telegraph, telephone, radio, and television met with slow acceptance, and the same has certainly been true for the new electronic technologies discussed in this book. The sceptics point out the problems. But the optimists marvel at just how rapidly electronic and voice mail, fax, and CAIR ("computer-assisted information retrieval") have advanced onto the American business scene. Compared to the 40 or 50 years it took for the telephone, for example, to reach all the American homes, the pace of computer-to-computer communications has been a sky rocket.

There are several phases that we must go through as we accept any new technological development in communications:

1 We learn to accept the medium (over a period of time).
2 We become comfortable with the technology.
3 We begin to use the medium creatively.
4 The new medium becomes a major form of communications; we start to rely on it.

The phases are certainly not distinct in the entire industry at one time, but they are the stages that each individual and each business must go through. Some people and businesses are already comfortably into the final phase. Some are still lingering somewhere in the first phase. Most are somewhere in between. It can be safely asserted, however, that electronic data transfer is not going to go away. Electronic and voice mail and facsimile are not passing fancies. They are not fads. They are changing the very way we live and work. To not investigate how they work and how they can be used is to practice "ostrich intuition." Burying your head will not make it all just go away.

Despite the problems of today, the point remains: Regardless of the difficulties inherent in computer communications today, remaining on the fringes only delays the inevitable. Computer communications will become, increasingly, an essential component of your daily life. By exploring its possibilities now, you will become accustomed to its nature and its usefulness.

ELECTRONIC DATA INTERCHANGE
by Craig Mellor

■■   In today's business environment, intense competition is forcing business to look at new ways of doing business. Leaders are constantly looking for new methods that will allow their business to do things faster, cheaper, and better than before.

The problem with most approaches is that they often sacrifice one objective in favor of another. It's one thing to cut costs in your operation, but that often increases the time it takes to service the customer. Also, depending on how cost reductions are achieved, you may end up providing an inferior product.

Electronic data interchange, or EDI, is a tool that will allow you to achieve significant improvements in all three objectives (faster, cheaper, and better). EDI can speed up many business functions while cutting costs in a number of areas. By reducing unnecessary delays, you have more time to produce a better product and you can provide your customers with improved service. In today's competitive world, speed is a weapon you can use against the competition. Providing your product or service faster than the competition can not only win increased business, but it can also reduce sales loss due to price competition.

Before I describe what EDI is, I will first describe what it is not. EDI is not new and it is not dependent on any one technology. While the current term, EDI, may sound new, EDI has been with us since the late 1960s.

While EDI has benefited enormously from advances in technology, EDI is not technology-dependent. There are preferred ways to implement EDI in your business, but there are many approaches to choose from. The approach you choose should be derived from your business case, not a particular implementation or technology.

Craig A. Mellor is president of CAMCOM Systems Inc., a Detroit area consulting firm established in 1983 to provide strategic planning, design and implementation of communication solutions for its customers. Mr. Mellor is an acknowledged expert in network management and is a frequent speaker on the topic at national conferences and seminars: CAMCOM Systems, Inc., 18326 Fernlea Rd., Mt. Clemens, MI 48044; 313/286-1170

So what is EDI? *EDI* is paperless document transfer between companies. What's a document? A *document* is any form of communication, traditionally paper, sent between two companies. Examples include:

- Purchase orders
- Invoices
- Shipping notices
- Export/import information
- Carrier-to-carrier waybills
- Funds transfers
- Design specifications
- Health insurance claims

EDI is a data-processing concept that is independent of communication protocols or transmission media. EDI is a logical outgrowth of the standard computerization that has been going on *within* businesses for the last several decades. The type of electronic communication that has been used between departments within a business is now being extended to reach out to other business, or trading, partners.

EDI is computer-to-computer communication. Contrast this with one of the other forms of communications discussed in this book, electronic mail (E-mail). E-mail is person-to-person communications over a computer. A person creates a text message which is sent to another person. While this form of communications is electronic, it still requires people to create and interpret the messages.

EDI replaced human-readable paper or electronic-based documents with machine-readable, electronically coded documents. With EDI, the sending computer creates the message and the receiving computer interprets the message without any human involvement.

Let's take a standard business transaction, a purchase order (PO), and explore how and where EDI fits into the picture. Without EDI the process might look something like this:

1 The customer determines a need to purchase an item and creates a PO document. Often these documents are produced by a computer.

2 The PO is sent to the supplier via either the post office, Express mail, E-mail, or fax. (In any case, it takes a person at the supplier to receive and interpret that PO.)

3 The PO is then transcribed into the supplier's computerized order system.

An EDI implementation simplifies the process to:

1 The customer's computer system creates and sends the electronic PO.

2 The supplier's computer receives the PO and places the order directly into its own system.

What is clear from the example is that time is saved by eliminating the post office and people cost is saved by removing the people from the process. What is perhaps a subtle area of savings is the cost due to errors. How much would it cost if the order-entry clerk added an additional zero to the quantity field?

I'll discuss more benefits in detail later. First, let's look at the history of EDI.

THE HISTORY OF EDI

Since the 1960s, many companies have developed in-house computer systems and internal networks to streamline business functions. A typical example is the order processing system, which can process customers' orders with great speed. Still, the speed with which a business can respond is determined by the communication link between the company and its customers. That communication link consists of the postal service and the telephone and remains a slow and costly process.

Some business executives were working on methods to shortcut the conventional communication link. Electronic communications was a prime consideration in circumventing the paperwork-telephone problems, and it soon became clear that linking up to other businesses electronically had one major initial problem: information format. Very few companies use the same paper document format. One company's PO form looks different from another company's form. The same holds true with computer systems. Information stored in one company's computer system may be in a different format than that required by other companies' computers.

People can deal with format problems with relative ease. When an order-processing clerk receives a PO form in an unfamiliar format, it's not a difficult task to analyze the new form and interpret the required information. Computers do not have that ability and require information in a specific format and in an exact order. You do not want your system to interpret your trading partner's PO number as the quantity ordered. That could easily happen if the two companies do not agree on a format and sequence for the information they exchange with one another.

A supplier serving one customer can follow that customer's formats and rules for EDI. The problem arises when a supplier has to deal with different rules from different customers. Systems can be developed to interpret an electronic transaction from Company A differently from a transaction from Company B. This approach, however, is extremely costly to develop and maintain, and it doesn't solve the problem when Company C comes along and wants to do business electronically. A better approach would be to support standards that all customers and suppliers could adopt.

EDI standards are a set of formats and protocols, much like a language, that trading partners agree to use to communicate with each other. A good analogy can be found in the airline industry. All over the world there are airlines and airports in different countries. Pilots and crew may converse in their native tongue, but English is required for all aircraft-to-control-tower communications. Could you imagine the confusion if there were not standard language?

The Transportation Data Coordinating Committee.   The transportation industry recognized the need for industry standards early and formed the Transportation Data Coordinating Committee (TDCC) in 1968. The TDCC, formed as a nonprofit organization in Washington, DC, organizes data standards, formats, codes, and protocols for the transportation industry. The ground rules that the TDCC began its standards development with were:

- The EDI interface must be insensitive to computer equipment internal architecture
- The EDI interface should be responsive to end users' needs.
- EDI should leave the choice of communication speeds and services to the using parties to select.

Several hundred people worked in teams to develop the TDCC standards. These teams consisted of shippers, railroads, motor carriers, forwarders, ocean carriers, air carriers, and banks. The end product was the publication of the TDCC Electronic Data Interchange Standards. These standards were first used in the rail lines and later across motor carriers. TDCC estimates that 90 percent of all rail waybills were electronically interchanged between railroads by 1985. Today, the usage of TDCC's EDI standards include:

- Export/import information for international shipments
- Carrier-to-carrier waybill exchange
- Reservation or pickup requests
- Shipment information from shipper to carrier
- Freight bill data, carrier to payer
- Shipment tracing information
- Payment data (payer to bank, bank to bank, bank to payee)

Private Company Standards.   A few major companies, such as General Motors (GM) and Kmart, charged into the EDI arena and developed their own standards. GM's EDI involvement was an outgrowth of their "just-in-time" plant inventory approach. With just-in-time inventory, each plant stocks only those parts required for one day's production. Because of the low inventory levels, GM needed a fast, reliable way to order parts so that they arrived at the loading docks just in time for assembly. This inventory approach allowed GM to save millions in inventory costs, and EDI was the enabling technology without which just-in-time inventory would be difficult, if not impossible.

We should note here that while GM saved millions, the inventory costs didn't just disappear. The burden of inventory was shifted to GM's suppliers. Some of these suppliers were large enough to absorb these costs, but many were not. This put many suppliers in tough situations as GM was requiring EDI connections for suppliers providing production material to just-in-time plants.

To complicate matters even more, Ford and Chrysler adopted similar plans which led to confusion throughout the automotive industry. Also, several large suppliers, such as Rockwell, wanted to use EDI with their own suppliers. The question was, who's standard should they use?

Private Industry Standards. Relief came to the auto industry in the form of the Automotive Industry Action Group (AIAG), a trade association for the industry. The AIAG worked with the automakers and suppliers to develop an EDI standard for the entire industry. Other industries have taken the same approach of developing specific standards of their own. Industry-specific EDI standards development associations include the following:

Automotive Industry Action Group

General Trade Document Interchange

National Automated Clearinghouse Association

National Wholesale Druggist Association

Transportation Data Coordinating Council

Many other industries are also developing EDI standards and many are using the TDCC standards as a base. The Grocery Industry's Uniform Communications Standards and the Warehouse Information Network are examples of TDCC derivatives.

Even the collection of industry-specific standards is not enough, since few businesses operate in a single industry. For example, a telephone manufacturer in the communications industry must buy plastics from the chemical industry. Once again, the need for further standardization exists.

ANSI X12 Standards. The American National Standards Institute (ANSI) chartered a committee to develop inter-industry EDI standards. This committee, known as the X12 Business Data Interchange Committee, is using the TDCC standards as its base structure. The X12 committee has added many transactions to the list provided by the TDCC. The most common transactions are the PO and the invoice.

In addition, the TDCC is serving as the secretariat for the X12 committee. All data field names, types, formats, and lengths are defined in a data dictionary The TDCC maintains this data dictionary and provides quarterly updates. With the data dictionary available, everyone supporting X12 standards knows exactly what format each field or data element should use. For example, the standard PO number is defined as being from 2 to 30 characters in length. A 31-character PO number is not allowed.

Industries working with X12 standards include: telecommunications, electronics, chemical, auto, metals, textile, and aerospace. Individual industries may use a subset of the overall X12 standard. The format and meaning of the individual data elements remain constant, but different industries have chosen to implement some fields in a different order, or to exclude certain information that is not appropriate for their industry.

Conversion from industry-specific standards to X12 has not been easy. Once an industry has an investment in one approach, it takes a lot of time to convert to another. The grocery industry established its industry-specific Uniform Communications Standards in the early 1980s and has been the most notable holdout from X12 acceptance. The approach in the grocery industry has been, "If it's not broken, don't fix it."

Even with X12 standards, many EDI trading partners are finding it necessary to translate documents from one X12 subset to another. Additionally, as more companies move to X12, there is a great need to translate their standard X12 transactions into the industry-specific standards from whence they came. Conversion is often required in order to communicate with trading partners that have not yet made the step to X12. This translation of formats can occur either at the originator, the destination, or via a third-party intermediary.

HOW DOES EDI WORK?

EDI is implemented in software and is conceptually an interface between the sender's and the receiver's internal computer programs. These company-specific internal programs may be operating on different types of computers and may use different internal data structures. This interface between sender and receiver is implemented in at least the two trading partners' systems, and often in a third, intermediary's system.

We'll again use the transmission of a PO to illustrate how EDI works. The buying party's purchasing system generates a PO and passes it to the EDI software. The EDI software converts the internal data structure into a standard EDI transaction with the required fields supplied by the data dictionary. This transaction is then transported to the supplier, whose EDI software converts the standard transaction (using the same data dictionary) into the format acceptable to their order-processing system.

The TDCC and other vendors provide EDI software for mainframes, minicomputers, and personal computers. The TDCC leases mainframe software that is written in ANSI COBOL and is shipped on 9-track tape. TDCC provides the COBOL source code because few mainframe COBOL systems are exactly alike. Users may need to make some changes to the software to make it match their particular systems.

The TDCC software is "table-driven," which means that all translations between internal and standard data formats are defined in easily modifiable tables. You do not have to modify COBOL programs for translation. A portion of the EDI software, called the "Set Generator," converts internal format data records into standard transactions. These internal format records are produced by some internal system, such as a Purchase Order System. The Set Generator reads these input records and performs the translation according to the parameter tables and the information in the data dictionary. When the transactions are received by the destination EDI software, the receiver's data dictionary and parameter tables are used by the Set Interpreter to convert the standard format transaction into the desired internal format.

TRANSPORT ALTERNATIVES

EDI specifications do not require any particular type of transport. There are four general methods to choose from, as outlined below.

Tape/Diskette Transport. Transactions could be batched and recorded on formatted magnetic tape or diskette. The tape or diskette could be sent by the U.S. Mail, Express mail, or by a courier service. This transport approach might be the most cost-effective, depending on the application, but it is also the least responsive.

Point-to-Point Communications Lines. Point-to-point communications lines could be established between the trading partners using standard communications protocols. The connection could either be a leased or a dial-up line. A lease line is purchased on a monthly basis and is always available for transmission. A dial-up line is established just like a normal telephone call. When the sending party has something to transmit, the call is made and the data is transmitted. When dial-up links are used, senders typically batch up their transactions and at certain points make the connection and send an entire batch at once.

The dial-up approach is cheaper when the amount of data is low and sporadic. An expensive leased line can be more cost-effective if the number of transactions is high and fairly constant throughout the day. Also, faster line speed can be achieved with a leased line, and there is no dial delay or need to batch transactions. With a leased line the transaction can be transmitted as soon as it is created. For some applications, immediate transmission and reply may be appropriate.

Figure 9-1 compares courier transport and direct-connection transport.

Value-Added Networks. Point-to-point links often present a scheduling problem to trading partners. Often it is not convenient for the receiver to receive transactions when the sender chooses to send them. The solution to this problem is a value-added network that provides a "store and foreward" mailbox service. CompuServe, Telenet, and Tymnet are examples of value-added networks.

The sender connects with the value-added network and sends its EDI transactions to the recipient's mailbox, where they are stored. The sender then disconnects from the service. At some point that is convenient, the recipient can connect to the network and receive those transactions from the recipient's mailbox. With this approach, both sending and receiving parties must use the same EDI standard transactions.

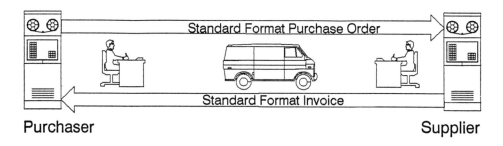

Purchaser   Supplier

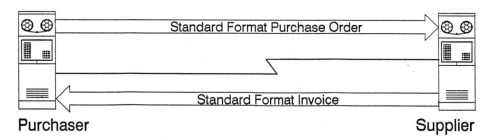

Purchaser   Supplier

Figure 9-1   *Courier transport (top) as compared to direct-connection transport.*

Third-Party Services. Another approach is to use a third-party EDI service. Third-party service providers use a network with individual mailboxes in the same manner as the value-added networks. Third-party vendors also include translation among their services. This approach is attractive when cross-industry transactions are required or when one trading partner has converted to X12 while other trading partners have not. (Figure 9-2 compares the value-added network transport process and the third-party network transport process.)

Third-party EDI service providers include

Control Data's Redinet

General Electric Information Services

IBM Information Network

McDonnell Douglas Applied Communications

Sterling Software's Ordernet

Most third-party service vendors provide software tied to their services. In an interesting move, IBM announced it's expEDIte Family of EDI products in April

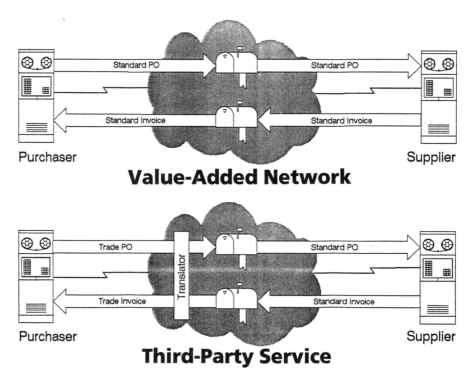

Value-Added Network

Third-Party Service

Figure 9-2 *The value-added network transport process as compared to the third-party network transport process.*

1989. The expEDIte Family includes the IBM expEDIte DataInterchange Series and the IBM expEDIte Communication Series.

The expEDIte DataInterchange Series is a set of translators that run across a wide range of IBM's product line. DataInterchange runs on a personal computer running OS/2, the System/3x and AS/400 mid-range systems, and the System/370 line of mainframes from the 9370 to the 3090. Data-Interchange converts internal documents into standard format. DataInterchange supports either the ANSI X12 or the international EDIFACT standards (discussed later in this chapter). The translators run either in interactive or batch mode and can be called from user-written programs.

The expEDIte Communication Series is a set of communication products designed to connect with the IBM Information Network. What makes this announcement interesting is the unbundling of the translator from the communications software. This allows you to choose the IBM translator without being tied into the IBM Information Network for communication services. You can then choose the appropriate transport media for your business, while using an off-the-shelf EDI translator.

BENEFITS

EDI is a productivity-enhancing tool that replaces less-efficient and error-prone human processes involved with inter-company communication. EDI provides benefits to both the buyer and the seller, as outlined below.

Buyer benefits include:

- *Lower inventory levels.*
- *Quick order acknowledgments.* If a supplier cannot provide the product desired, the buyer can quickly seek an alternate supplier.
- *Efficient invoice processing.* The amount of time spent matching invoices to POs and re-keying invoices into an accounts payable system is reduced.

Supplier benefits include:

- *Elimination of problems and delays caused by order-entry errors.* Manual order entry can result in errors in as many as 50 percent of all documents. Errors in order entry mean missed ship dates, shipment of wrong items or quantities and lower customer satisfaction.
- *Personnel reductions.* There are estimates that currently as much as 70 percent of all computer output becomes computer input. With EDI, the supplier is relieved of the process of re-keying orders and the verification of orders.
- *Inventory reductions.* While EDI is often used in just-in-time inventory approaches that place the burden of inventory on the supplier, it is possible for the supplier to achieve reduced inventory levels also. Produc-

tion schedules can be tuned more closely to customer demand to reduce finished goods inventory.

- *Improved cash flow.* Time taken out of the invoicing/payment cycle improves the cash flow of the supplier.
- *Improved customer service.*
- *Improved sales tracking.*

Cost Savings.   A common benefit to both buyer and supplier is cost savings. Input, a California based market research firm, recently published a survey of *Fortune* 1000–size businesses, universities, and public companies, entitled "The North American EDI Service." One of the results of the survey was a comparison of the cost of manually prepared documents to EDI documents. The survey showed that a manually prepared and transferred document costs about $49, while the EDI document cost about $4.70. That 10-fold savings per document is impressive, and when you think about the millions of these documents generated in some companies, you can see why there is pressure to implement EDI.

EXAMPLES OF EDI IN ACTION

Auto Loans.   A major part of the automobile manufacturer's business is the financing of the sale of its vehicles. Auto companies finance over one-third of all cars purchased in the United States. General Motors Acceptance Corporation is one of the largest financial institutions in the world. To be more responsive to their customers, auto companies have implemented electronic links to credit bureaus such as TRW.

The normal process is for the auto company to request a credit history from the credit bureau via an EDI connection. The auto company's computer system electronically receives and analyzes the credit report. Each report is scored, and then credit approval is provided without human involvement.

There is now movement toward allowing the dealers direct transaction input. This moves the personnel cost of data entry from the auto company to the dealer. This is also an advantage to dealers as it allows them to respond better to their customers. It is possible to get back quicker, if not instantaneous, response to credit authorizations. Credit authorizations are often returned while the customer is still on the sales floor. The real payoff in this example is the extra competitive advantage that is garnered by the dealer that offers immediate credit.

General Motors.   General Motors has integrated EDI and electronic funds transfers at 30 percent of it's assembly plants. Electronic shipping receipts are sent electronically from the GM plant plant to an Electronic Data Systems (EDS, a subsidiary of GM) computer center, where they are matched against electronic invoices and POs. Shipping receipts are grouped by supplier, and one payment is made. This single payment may represent dozens of different shipments to different plants. These payments are also performed electronically via electronic funds transfers.

JCPenney. Sales of Stafford suits jumped 59 percent after JCPenney linked up with its supplier, Lanier Clothes. EDI allowed JCPenney to replenish stock quickly enough to meet demand while cutting the company's overall inventory of suits by 20 percent.

Rockwell. Rockwell, a major automotive supplier, received design-change notifications directly from the automakers via EDI. Rockwell has been able to react faster to its customers' constant design changes while reducing its inventory of finished goods. Parts now bypass warehouses and go directly from production lines to the shipping docks.

Textile Industry. With EDI, the textile industry is beginning to fight back against Asian competition. While the United States textile industry is hard-pressed to compete on a cost basis, EDI is helping textile companies to provide superior service. Service is making it easier and faster to do business with a U.S. supplier.

U.S. Customs. U.S. Customs accepts electronic customs documentation, in advance of goods shipments. This reduces port delay and provides a competitive advantage for those ports of entry that support EDI.

Wal-Mart. An EDI link between Wal-Mart and one of its suppliers, Seminole Manufacturing Co., cut the delivery time of Seminole slacks by 50 percent. This resulted in a 31 percent sales increase of these slacks in the first nine months after the link was established.

MARKET OUTLOOK

The Yankee Group, a Boston-based market research group, estimates that one-third of all business transactions will be electronic by 1995. The EDI survey published by Input (mentioned earlier) found that 34 percent of *Fortune* 1000–size businesses, universities, and public companies are currently using EDI. An additional 20 percent are planning EDI implementations. Input also forecasts that EDI service market will grow to $1.9 billion by 1993. That's an annual 56 percent per year growth rate from the 1988 market size of $208

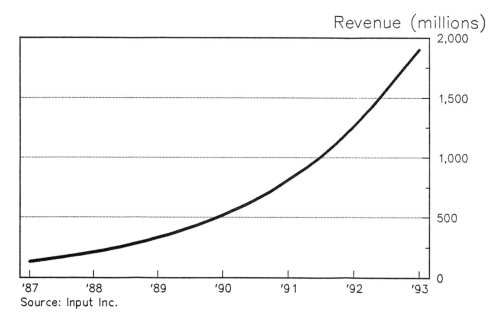

Figure 9-3 *Growth forecast for the EDI service market.*

million (see Figure 9-3). While EDI has been around for a while, it is still in its infancy as far as market potential. This opportunity has been recognized by companies such as AT&T, Telenet, ADP, CompuServe, Martin-Marietta, and Western Union, all of whom have jumped into the EDI service provider arena in the last two years.

What Is Causing EDI Growth? One of the main reasons for the explosive growth of the EDI service market is that the business environment finally contains all the pieces to make EDI possible. Clearly, standards are a major factor. By 1986, there were over 150 standardized transaction types. Standard transaction development has had a cascading affect. The EDI Purchase Order begat the Invoice. The Invoice begat the Shipping Notification. The Shipping Receipt lead to the desire to make electronic payments, which spawns another batch of electronic transactions.

The spread of computers and available software has been a factor in EDI growth. The acceptance of the personal computer has been a stimulus to EDI. It is possible to develop an EDI solution based on a personal computer with less than $1000 invested in hardware.

Another factor in EDI growth is what could be called the "domino effect" within industries. The domino effect, as it applies to EDI, occurs when large

236

companies in the center of an industry coerce their trading partners to adopt EDI. Soon, the second-tier suppliers require EDI links to the third-tier suppliers, and so on. The automobile industry is an example of an arena in which this domino effect has come into play.

There are two approaches to getting supplier compliance to EDI: incentive and force. Some companies have offered incentives for electronic linkups. Conrail, for example, offers discounts to its electronic trading partners. The automobile industry relied on force with deadlines and ultimatums. If you supplied production material to an automobile plant, lack of EDI support meant loss of business. Even within the automobile industry, there were some levels of incentive provided. One automaker chose to sell a PC-based EDI interface to the suppliers, while another gave it away. Which approach do you think garnered the most support?

What Is Inhibiting EDI Growth?　Input's current market forecast is for 56 percent annual growth of the EDI market. This 1989 forecast has been reduced from their previous predictions of 88 percent annual growth. There are several factors that are inhibiting EDI growth:

- Lack of upper-management awareness
- Companies too busy fighting today's fires
- The "not invented here" syndrome
- Application development backlog in MIS departments
- Turf battles
- Perceived lack of standards
- Electronic payments that reduce payee's "float"
- Fear of improper authorization and duplicate electronic and paper transaction
- Fear of outside links to the production environment

One of the solutions to the fear of linking outsiders to the production environment is being addressed today with the use of PCs and Minicomputers as EDI front-ends. The outside world is connected to the PC or the mini, and not to the production system. EDI will eventually overcome all of these inhibitors to acceptance because it addresses a basic business goal within every company, that is, the goal of reducing administrative overhead.

HOW TO APPROACH EDI FOR YOUR COMPANY

The first step toward EDI implementation is to form a task force with broad company representation. EDI implementation is not simply a Systems Department exercise; it affects the entire company. Select people across departmental boundaries to reduce resistance and turf battles.

Set your task force's goal of determining *when,* not *if,* to implement EDI. By setting the goal of when to implement EDI, you are acknowledging that almost every company will use EDI at some point in the future. The key emphasis should be when does it make business sense for your company.

Now clearly, if you have a large customer that is coercing you into electronic trading, you can certainly make a business case for doing it now. The threat of loss of your biggest customer can make the rest of the issues moot. But, even if no one in your industry uses EDI, the task force should examine the possibilities of strategic use of technology to take a competitive advantage.

Educate task force members on EDI and the internal operation of the business. Make sure everyone understands that the business is a system and EDI is simply another business tool that may or may not be appropriate at this time.

Consider whether it is appropriate to team up with other similar companies in your industry to share in EDI development. This might sound like a contradiction to what was written earlier about competitive advantage, but there are times when it is helpful to the entire industry to have many companies working on this issue together. The cooperation in the development of the airline industry's reservations system is an example of how cooperation in a very competitive industry has benefitied all companies in the industry. Even while you are working on an industrywide EDI project, you can still maintain a competitive advantage by building a company reputation of being a pioneer, or industry leader.

Carefully evaluate trade and industry standards. The old adage of not reinventing the wheel applies. Stick with the ANSI X12 standards as much as possible, but constantly monitor the X12 standard for changes. EDI is not a one-time project, but an evolving process.

Determine what form of transport, or third-party, services are appropriate and select software and service vendors accordingly. Service providers are often good sources of information and support that you can leverage to your advantage.

Determine the overall commitment to EDI within your organization. EDI can be implemented as a stand-alone process where a PC simply receives electronic orders and prints them on paper. The rest of the process is business as usual. EDI could also be implemented by integrating it within the overall business operation. The second approach can totally change the way you do business today, but only you (or your task force) can determine what level of integration is appropriate for your business. If the integrated approach is desired, do not underestimate the innate human factors that cause resistance to change.

If the task force determines that it is appropriate to implement EDI, make sure that the report includes plans for a pilot phase and for post-pilot expansion. A pilot phase is a period during which a select group of functions and/or customers are placed on an EDI system as a trial to shake down the process and determine if the approach is viable.

If the determination of the task force is that the timing is not appropriate for EDI, make sure that its findings include a list of conditions that must be met before EDI would be viable for the organization. This list of considerations can be reevaluated periodically and can serve as a road map for future EDI projects.

FUTURES

EDI is still in its infancy, and you can expect tremendous growth in the future. By the end of the 1990s you can expect to see EDI affecting almost every business in the United States. The amount of standard transaction will steadily increase. Electronic orders, shipments, and payments will be common. There will be increased product code standardization. The UPC code used by grocery store scanners will steadily support more and more products. Further expansion will occur in multi-industry standards, because few companies really operate in just one industry. Grocery stores, for example, sell many nonfood items.

As competition between third-party service providers increases, these service providers will become more aggressive in providing and marketing their services.

There will be increased international EDI activity. It has been estimated that between 5 percent and 7 percent of the value of goods traded internationally can be saved by EDI. Even though the United States has been involved in EDI since the 1960s, some experts believe that Europe is only 18 to 24 months behind. Several international EDI standards organizations already exist, such as the Organization of Data Exchange by Teletransmission in Europe (ODETTE). ODETTE was founded in 1984 and represents nine countries.

Also, the United Nations' Economic Commissions for Europe, Working Party on Facilitation of International Trade Procedures, meets in Geneva semi-annually to coordinate EDI standards for world trade. Over 40 major trading nations and 12 world trade organizations send representatives to this conference. The U.S. delegation is headed by a representative from the Department of Transportation. In addition, a joint team of European and U.S. standards bodies, known as the Joint Electronic Data Interchange (JEDI) project, has made significant strides in the convergence of the various EDI formats. This has led to a new standard known as EDIFACT, an acronym for *EDI For Administration, Commerce, and Transport*. EDIFACT is creating excitement in Europe and has been accepted by the International Standards Organization as the ISO 9735 standard.

A trend currently under way that will continue is the bundling of function. Expect to see third-party service providers bundle EDI services along with electronic mail, electronic funds transfers, online databases, videotex, and online news services. The electronic mail standard CCITT X.400 will play a major role in the bundling of features. The X.400 protocol will become the standard transport vehicle for EDI transactions as it already has become for text-based electronic mail.■■

Glossary

analog: Of or relating to the representation of data by continuously variable physical quantities. Voltage changes transmitted as smooth, undulating waveforms are said to be analog, as are voice patterns transmitted over normal telephone lines.

ASCII: The system defined by the American Standard Code for Information Interchange to represent the uppercase and lowercase letters, numbers, and other symbols used in the transmission of text between computers. The ASCII system uses a 7-bit binary code which assigns a number (0 to 127) to each character or symbol found in text-based information.

asynchronous communications: Start-stop communications with each piece of information delimited by specific markers. Asynchronous communications are the most common form of computer communications and are almost imperative when telephone lines are the medium of data transport.

audiotex: The computer-assisted presentation of information through digitally recorded and reproduced speech. Delivered by computer, audiotex information is accessible by and can be controlled from any touch-tone phone.

baud: A variable unit of data transmission speed, often used interchangeably (but incorrectly) with bits per second (bps). While the concept is confusing, Toby Nixon offers one of the clearest explanations I have seen. Mr. Nixon, who represents a major U.S. modem manufacturer on several international standards committees (including CCITT), describes the difference between "bits-per-second" and "baud" as speedometers in this way:

> Computers store and transfer data as "bits" in digital form (1/0). The current analog telephone system, however, is able to carry sounds, not bits. Modems convert the serial digital bit stream coming from computers into

analog waveforms (sounds) that the phone system can carry. The number of times per second that a modem changes the pattern of sound that it is putting on the phone line is known as the modem's "baud rate."

In simple modems (such as 300 baud Bell 103A modems), the sound changes for every bit from the computer. Only the frequency of the sound is changed, while the amplitude and other elements that make up the sound remain constant. In these modems, the "baud rate" and the "bit per second" rate are the same. In more advanced modems (1200 bps and above), however, the modem uses various combinations of amplitude (loudness) and phase (the portion of the sine wave transmitted during a unit of time), to transmit multiple bits for each distinct "sound" (known as a "symbol") that it makes on the phone line.

For example, a 2400 bps CCITT V.22 *bis* modem changes the sound it makes on the phone line 600 times per second (it is a "600 baud modem"), but there are sixteen possible combinations of amplitude and phase that it can transmit during each of these 1/600th-of-a-second periods. Sixteen is the number of possible combinations of four-digit binary numbers (bits), so the modem is able to transmit four bits for every baud. 4 bits/symbol * 600 symbols per second = 2400 bits per second. I suppose one could boil it down to baud being "the number of times the modem changes the sound it's making on the phone line each second" and bps could be "baud, multiplied by the number of bits that can be represented by a single sound by the modem."

BBS: Bulletin board system, a public system which can be called by computer MODEM. Most BBSs are free to all users and allow electronic messaging to other users and the ability to DOWNLOAD SOFTWARE.

bibliographic database: A DATABASE limited to only abstracted information from an article or book chapter (compare FULL-TEXT DATABASE).

binary system: A numbering system (used by computers) that uses the digits 0 and 1 in series to represent data.

bit: Abbreviation for *bi*nary digi*t*, A bit, the smallest piece of information a computer deals with, represents either an "on" or "off" situation (1 or 0). Eight bits compose a BYTE, or character.

boolean operators: Logical operators (AND, OR, and NOT) based on the algebraic theories of the English mathematician George Boole. Such operators are used by DATABASES to refine search commands.

bps: BITS per second, a measure of the speed that information is transferred across a MODEM to another computer host and back (not to be confused with BAUD rate).

byte: A computer representation of a single character; consists of 8 BITS.

CAIR: Computer-assisted information retrieval, the process of accessing and utilizing information stored on a remote computer through your own computer.

CCITT: Consultative Committee in International Telegraphy and Telephony, an international group composed of representatives from many nations that meets at four-year intervals to make recommendations for various communications modalities. CCITT produced communications PROTOCOLS X.400 and X.500.

command stacking: A timesaving capability of some systems to send more than one command at a time, rather than sending a single command and waiting for a response to the next menu.

database: A collection of information organized especially for rapid search and retrieval. In this text the term is generally applied to bibliographic or text information stored on a computer and accessible in a systematic way.

data bits: The number of BITS that can be used to make up a BYTE of information for transmission. Either 7 or 8 BITS is acceptable.

digital: Of or relating to the representation of data by numerical digits or discrete units. The electrical waveform used within the computer to transmit and receive data is digital, having sharp spikes of "on" and "off" states. Digital data is the only form of data computer chips can understand.

DOS: Disk operating system, the SOFTWARE that controls the most basic functions of a computer.

download: The information received from the host computer to the terminal accepting the data. *Download* can be either a noun (the data itself) or a verb (the process of retrieving the data).

dumb terminal: The earliest devices used to communicate with the large computer databases, consisting generally, of a display (which could be either a monitor or simply a printer) and a keyboard. Dumb terminals, connected to a mainframe either by cable or through a MODEM, have no "smart" capabilities found with the modern computers and SOFTWARE (e.g., data capture, MACROS, command files, etc.).

E-mail: Electronic mail, that is, electronic text messages that can be sent to a remote computer and stored for retrieval only by a selected addressee.

FCC: Federal Communications Commission, the agency that regulates the TELECOMMU-NICATIONS and broadcast industries.

false drops: Also *false hits*. This refers to records retrieved from a SEARCH STRATEGY that fit both the terms and the logic used but which are irrelevant to the true intent of the search.

fiber optics: The technology of guiding and projecting light (used as a communications medium) via hair-thin glass fibers. Sometimes called *lightguide* or *optical fibers,* these fibers allow light beams to be bent and reflected with low levels of loss and interference. Fiber optics greatly increase the number of simultaneous voice or data transmissions which can occur within a small diameter cable.

field: See FILE.

file, record, field: The separate and distinct parts of a database and its information. The analogy is used of a collection of cancelled checks: the entire set of checks is a file, the individual checks in the file are the records, and the date, payee, etc. on the individual checks are the fields.

firmware: A computer component that has characteristics of both HARDWARE and SOFTWARE. Firmware might be touchable, like HARDWARE, but also have an "invisible" element, like SOFTWARE. An example is a computer chip which also contains a set of instructions or a program.

format: The structure of an individual DATABASE; how the individual RECORDS are set up in a DATABASE; what FIELDS are available for searching and the contents of each FIELD. *Format* is also used to define the options available for displaying information. Most systems use short, medium, or long display formats, and the content of each format varies among systems.

framing bits: BITS used in ASYNCHRONOUS computer communications to demarcate separate BYTES of information. Typically, a start bit and a stop bit define the beginning and end, respectively, of each data BYTE.

full-text database: A DATABASE system that includes the entire text of an article, book chapter, or book (not limited to abstracted information). See BIBLIOGRAPHIC DATABASE.

handshaking: An exchange of electronic signals that occurs before a communications session between a MODEM or a fax machine and a like device. The handshake determines the proper electronic connection and the "rules" that the devices need to follow to understand each other.

hard disk: A device that has a large capacity to store information in a computer. The speed with which data is stored and retrieved from a hard disk is faster than from traditional floppy disks. Also referred to as a "fixed" drive, a hard disk cannot be taken out of a computer as floppy disks can.

hardware: Computer equipment that can be touched, seen, or handled, such as monitors, keyboards, MODEMS, etc. See SOFTWARE.

Hayes command set: A command language initially developed by the manufacturer of the Hayes MODEM allowing for control of the "smart" functions of a MODEM, including autodial, autoanswer, etc. The Hayes command set has been almost universally adopted by the MODEM industry as a standard.

hits: RECORDS of a DATABASE called up by a SEARCH STRATEGY input by the user of the database; retrieved citations; search results.

hot key: A term applied to an unusual combination of keystrokes that can be used to activate SOFTWARE that is in a RAM-RESIDENT or "terminate and stay resident" (TSR) mode. A hot key is an unusual combination of keystrokes so that you are unlikely to inadvertently call up the TSR program.

identification (ID) code: Any alpha, numeric, or combined alphanumeric code which a host system uses to identify a legitimate user.

ISDN: Integrated Services Digital Network, a proposed system of DIGITAL switching and transmission systems. Synchronized so that all DIGITAL elements speak the same "language" at the same speed, ISDN will accomodate voice, data, and video in a unified manner.

install: To prepare HARDWARE or a SOFTWARE program to run on a computer system.

kilobyte (K): An amount of computer storage equal to 1024 BYTES.

library: A collection of related DATABASES on a system, usually grouped for ease of access on a menu-driven system.

logoff: The process of entering the appropriate command(s) to exit and disconnect from a remote host computer.

logon: The process of connecting to a remote host computer, entering the appropriate password and other indentifying information, and being "admitted" to the system.

macro: A series of keystrokes assigned to a single key. Once a string of characters has been assigned to a key, you can send a long series of characters to a host system by simply pressing one key. Macros can help you considerably by speeding inputting commands to a remote computer, which is particularly important if you are a slow typist.

modem: A device used to convert the DIGITAL signals of your computer to ANALOG signals which can be carried across common phone lines and back to DIGITAL on the receiving side. *Modem* is short for *mo*dulate-*dem*odulate.

online: In direct communcation with a computer.

offline printing: The capability of some systems to print the results of a search and mail the results to you as a paper copy, as opposed to your displaying or printing the search results on your terminal.

packet: A unit of DIGITAL data with a set number of BITS, including some BITS that are destination or "address" codes. Packets of data from many sources can be interspersed in a single communications channel.

packet-switching network: A computer-directed commercial system whereby computers can connect to remote computers at rates reduced over direct long-distance costs. A packet-switching network can be thought of as a computer party line on which information from several computers going to the same remote system is packaged together and sent over common phone lines along a specific route to the receiving computer. At the destination, the information is separated and acted upon as input from individual computers. The major networks are Telenet and Tymnet.

parity bit: A primitive form of error checking for correctness of data sent and received, which functions by adding an extra BIT to each BYTE of information sent to ensure that the arithmetic total of the BITS of every BYTE is either even or odd, as agreed upon by the sending and receiving computers.

password: A unique alpha, numeric, or combined alphanumeric code used to maintain security on computer networks.

polling: The process of a central machine calling a remote unit and "asking" if the remote unit has any information to send. If there is waiting data, it can be accepted by the central machine at that time. The term is generally used to describe an option available on fax machines.

protocol: A set of rules that defines procedures for the transfer of information in a communications system.

public domain: A term usually used to describe a SOFTWARE program that is released by the author for free distribution.

RAM: Random-access *m*emory, a type of computer memory that can store information, usually temporarily, for retrieval. RAM is often SOFTWARE-controlled, and new information can be written, erased, and rewritten to RAM.

ram-resident software: A type of computer program that can be loaded in the computer's memory and can remain out of sight while you load and use another program. When you want to switch to the hidden program, even while still using the other program, you press the HOT KEY and the second program pops up for your use.

real time: The actual time during which an action occurs.

record: See FILE.

ROM: Read-only memory, a type of computer memory (usually permanent) that contains information stored during manufacture.

script file: A series of commands written to orchestrate the signing on, retrieving of information, and signing off activities for various ONLINE systems. Script files, which are usually composed on a word processor, are saved to disk and read by the communications SOFTWARE when it is connecting to a remote DATABASE.

SDI: Selective dissemination of information (synonymous with "current awareness"), a process by which a DATABASE system can automatically run a user-inputted SEARCH STRATEGY at regular (usually monthly) intervals and report the recent additions to the DATABASE on that search subject to the user. The reports are usually mailed to the user as a printout.

search strategy: Those commands and phrases and terms used to direct a DATABASE to find specific information stored in a DATABASE.

shareware: See USER-SUPPORTED SOFTWARE.

software: Computer information that is stored on disk or other media that cannot, itself, be touched or felt. The term is commonly used to allude to computer programs or data that is stored on disk. See HARDWARE.

start bit: See FRAMING BITS.

stop bit: See FRAMING BITS.

sysop: System operator, a person in charge of a BBS or other such computer-accessible system.

telecommunications: The communication of voice, data, or images over a distance.

terminal emulation: The capability of communications SOFTWARE that enables a personal computer to ''appear'' to a remote computer as a DUMB TERMINAL, necessary on some remote computer systems to allow for proper display of information on the computer screen.

transfer protocols: Standardized methods used to accomplish the transfer of complex file types (programs or heavily formatted data such as a spreadsheet) from one computer to another. Transfer protocols are far more complex than simple ASCII file capture with extensive error checking and use of 8-data BITS. Common PROTOCOLS are XMODEM and KERMIT.

truncation: The shortening of a word with a specific symbol to form a WILDCARD search term. Truncation expands the search term to encompass various suffixes and (in some cases) prefixes. Truncation can be ''left'' or ''right,'' depending on the system used.

upgrade: A new, usually improved version of a computer SOFTWARE or HARDWARE product.

user interface: The way a computer and its operator interact to transfer information from one to the other, which can include the keyboard (how the operator sends data in) and the monitor display (how the computer returns data).

user-supported software: Copyrighted, commercial SOFTWARE that is marketed by allowing the program to be freely copied and distributed to anyone and used on a trial basis without charge. If the program continues to be used, the user is required (on the honor system) to pay for (''register'') the SOFTWARE.

videotex: A developing technology of using TELECOMMUNICATIONS between computers to display, in increasingly innovative formats, news, weather, advertisements, and many kinds of other general information. This rather generic term has been applied to many system formats and has yet to be clearly defined.

wildcard: A search term formed by applying a TRUNCATION symbol, which causes the term to assume a wider range of meanings and typically expands the amount of information that will be retrieved. Sometimes, a special wildcard symbol can be applied within a word to expand its meaning; for example, ''wom*n'' on MEDIS will retrieve ''women'' and ''woman.''

word processor: A computer SOFTWARE program that is used to create, edit, and format text.

Suggested Reading

Chapter 1: General

Edwards, Paul and Sarah: *Working from Home,* Jeremy Tarcher, Los Angeles, 1987, 436 pages; $12.95.

This excellent overview of the home business boom covers a number of key points in defining which computer is right for you and how to go about using it for a variety of purposes. Don't let the title fool you. Much of the book has tips useful for any small business—home or storefront.

Chapter 2: Modems

Glossbrenner, Alfred: *The Complete Handbook of Personal Computer Communications,* St. Martin's Press, New York, 1985, 546 pages; $14.95 (paperback).

This book contains an exhaustive discussion of how modems work and how to use them to access both general information systems and specific electronic mail and information database systems.

Chapter 3: Software

Glossbrenner, Alfred: *How to Buy Software,* St. Martin's Press, New York, 1984, 644 pages; $14.95 (paperback).

This book covers what to look for in all genre of software, from word processors to databases, and offers a superb chapter on communications software. While seemingly dated by its publication year, it still has general concepts and points of comparison that make it timeless as a way to approach buying software.

Glossbrenner, Alfred: *Master Guide to Free Software,* St. Martin's Press, New York, 1989, 528 pages; $18.95 (paperback).

The absolute, authoritative, definitive guide to finding valuable public-domain and shareware programs for the MS-DOS family of computers.

Chapter 4: E-mail

Manes, Stephen: *The Complete MCI Mail Handbook,* Bantam Books, New York, 1988, 498 pages; $22.95 (paperback).

MCI Mail is one of the largest and most consistently favorably reviewed electronic mail systems available. Manes book is one reason why MCI Mail should continue to be popular.

Bowen, Charles, and David Peyton: *How to Get the Most out of CompuServe,* Bantam Books, New York, 1989; 492 pp. $21.95 (paperback).

Glossbrenner, Alfred: *Master Guide to CompuServe,* Brady Books, New York, 1988; $19.95 (paperback).

These two books put into clear perspective the vast resources available on CompuServe. Extensive coverage of EasyPlex is included.

Chapter 5: Information

Glossbrenner, Alfred: *How to Look It Up Online,* St. Martin's Press, New York, 1987, 486 pages; $14.95 (paperback).

Another classic. The definitive resource for those interested in using electronic information systems. Covers each of the major database collections and how to use them effectively.

Lambert, Steve: *Online,* Microsoft Press, Bellevue, Washington, 1985, 320 pages; $19.95 (paperback).

This book provides a good introduction to modems, electronic mail, and information access.

Chapter 7: Fax

King, E., and Daniel Fishman: *The Book Of Fax,* Ventana Press, Durham, North Carolina, 1988.

Chapter 8: The Future

Naisbitt, John: *Megatrends,* Warner Books, New York, 1984, 333 pages; $3.95 (paperback).

This insightful analysis of the direction we are headed in both our business lives and personal lives presents some interesting views of how technology and communications will become increasingly important as we move toward a more global economy.

Toffler, Alvin: *Future Shock,* Bantam Books, New York, 1981, 537 pages; $4.95 (paperback).

This classic view of our future scrutinizes the impact of technology on how we will live and work in the years ahead.

Chapter 9: Tips

Dewey, Patrick: *Essential Guide to Bulletin Board Systems,* Merkler Publishing, Westport, Connecticut, 1987, 205 pages.

A useful discussion of what BBSs are and what they look like to a user. Several example systems are discussed.

Index

Index